ONE CHORD WONDERS
Power and Meaning in Punk Rock

Dave Laing
Foreword by TV Smith

PMPRESS

One Chord Wonders: Power and Meaning in Punk Rock
© Dave Laing
This edition © 2015 by PM Press

Every effort has been made to trace the copyright owners of illustrations used in this book. If any have been inadvertently overlooked, they should contact the author and publisher

ISBN: 978-1-62963-033-5
Library of Congress Control Number: 2014908071

Cover: John Yates/Stealworks.com
Layout: Jonathan Rowland

PM Press
P.O. Box 23912
Oakland, CA 94623
www.pmpress.org

10 9 8 7 6 5 4 3 2 1

Printed in the USA by the Employee Owners of Thomson-Shore in Dexter, Michigan
www.thomsonshore.com

Contents

Foreword

What just happened? That's what I was thinking when my band the Adverts broke up at the end of 1979 after two years of being in the forefront of the UK punk scene. What was punk anyway? I had been writing songs since I was at school, I'd had various bands that went nowhere, and then suddenly it all changed. I wasn't just in a band anymore—I was in a *punk band*, part of a movement that I was helping create even as I was simultaneously swept up in it. People were suddenly interested in what my band was doing, even though we were just beginners and as musicians strictly amateur. Now—and this had been inconceivable just a year earlier—the question of how well or badly we could play didn't matter anymore, apart from to a few old-school critics who were clinging desperately to the sinking ship of pre-1977 rock. For the rest of us, the so-called professional musicians had nothing we wanted, nothing we could relate to. The doors had opened for people with ideas; the renegades and mavericks who took an alternative view of the way bands should look and sound, and what their songs could be about. Lack of conventional musical talent was a spur to try harder, not a handicap. In January 1977, within months of forming the Adverts, I found myself on stage at the Roxy club in London in the company of kids—on stage and off—who were desperate for music made by people like themselves, 'normal' people talking about 'normal' lives—not an untouchable and self-indulgent rock 'n' roll elite living a life of absurd extravagance paid for out of their audience's pockets. Many of those watching us that night went on to form bands themselves, no longer intimidated. After just a few gigs we were signed by Stiff Records and were able to put out a single, 'One Chord Wonders'. By the summer of 1977 we were in the UK top twenty with 'Gary Gilmore's Eyes' and appeared on mainstream television's *Top Of The Pops*, previously the heavily defended territory of the old guard music business, the very people who a short time earlier had scorned punk rock and actively tried to stop its progress.

So, what happened? Why now? What led up to this? What had changed? And for a movement that still has powerful resonance nearly forty years later, why did it all fall apart so quickly? These are some of the questions Dave Laing addresses with impressive rigour and objectivity in this fascinating book, and in developing his argument tells us something about not just punk rock but also the social and political landscape that brought it about, as well as giving us a razor-sharp insight into music, and the music business, in general. There are many books that describe what happened during the punk rock era. A few even dare to ask questions about it. Here at last is one that provides some answers.

TV Smith

Preface to the PM Press Edition

One Chord Wonders was originally published in 1985 and after about a decade it was out of print and very difficult to find. Over recent years, I have had many requests from scholars and fans for copies and, if only for their sake, I'm pleased that PM Press have decided to bring out this new edition. I've taken the opportunity to correct a few misprints and expand the index. Otherwise, the book is unchanged.

Thinking about republication, I considered whether to add new material but soon realised that punk has taken so many new forms and new directions since the 1970s that it would be impossible to do justice to them in a few pages. In addition, there have been numerous chronicles and analyses of that later history of punk and its derivatives. I shan't mention any here, but I will recommend a few studies that bear directly on the music and the era that One Chord Wonders attempts to illuminate.

First, Jon Savage's England's Dreaming: Sex Pistols And Punk Rock (1991), which was published several years after my own book and also places the Sex Pistols at the centre of the scene. Unlike me, Jon was an active participant and so brought a more direct perspective to the evocation of British punk. Another participant was the singer, songwriter, guitarist and scholar Helen Reddington. Her The Lost Women Of Rock Music: Female Musicians Of The Punk Era (second edition, 2012) opens up a highly important topic that is only briefly touched on in One Chord Wonders. A third book, that goes into greater depth on another aspect, covered in chapter 6, is Rip It Up And Start Again: Postpunk 1978–1984 (2005) by Simon Reynolds. I'll be thrilled if my book finds its place alongside these, and other, excellent chronicles of punk.

Acknowledgements

Although nobody else should be held accountable for the ideas put forward in this book, I have benefited greatly from the ideas and arguments of a number of people in the process of writing it. They include Phil Hardy and Mike Flood Page, with whom I collaborated in the late 1970s; Martin Jacques who allowed me to develop my ideas in the pages of *Marxism Today*; Dave Harker and Richard Middleton who are critical and constructive editors; in discussions on general and specific points, Simon Frith, Gary Herman, Deborah Philips, Jenny Taylor, Penny Valentine and Richard Woodcock; and Sally Quinn for her encouragement and friendship.

Introduction

I n the mid-1980s, punk rock is in danger of being taken for granted. Like Elvis or the Beatles, the term is used in a way which assumes we know exactly what it was and what it meant. The music which in 1976–8 caused uproar and alarm among critics, politicians, media pundits and record company executives has now become one more convenient landmark in the conventional periodization of recent British musical and cultural history. We are in a 'post-punk' world, it seems.

One aim of this book is to question the assumptions upon which punk's landmark status is based, to make it problematic and even unrecognizable. To do that means questioning the various identities that have been provided for punk rock both by close observers and participants and by critics and theorists. Punk was particularly well-served by contemporary observers, notably in the books by Caroline Coon, Julie Burchill and Tony Parsons, and Fred and Judy Vermorel, which are listed in the Bibliography. The more considered explanations are often less rewarding, though those of Dick Hebdige, Greil Marcus, Robert Christgau and Simon Frith are all of value.

In the present account, 'punk rock' is used in no special sense. Its meaning is that established through the consensus of users in the 1976–8 period, a consensus made up of the authors listed above together with musicians, journalists and other participants in published discourse. Chapter 5 deals directly with the range of nuances within this consensus, while elsewhere 'punk rock' refers to a complex of artefacts, events and institutions which flourished in the years 1976–8. The *artefacts* include the many hundreds of recordings and many dozens of 'fanzines' and other published writings, plus the items of visual style that make up the material archive of punk rock. The *events* of punk were both the live performances of the era and certain other key incidents, such as the notorious television interview involving Bill Grundy and the Sex Pistols and the series of concert cancellations and acts of censorship that occurred in the early months of 1977. The *institutional* framework of punk rock involved both the new organizations thrown up by the music (record labels, clubs and shops) and the manner in which established parts of the music industry (record companies, broadcasting stations, music press) tried to incorporate or exclude punk.

The context in which these elements emerged through an interaction of various forces (economic, aesthetic and ideological) is described in Chapter 1. That chapter's title, 'Formation', has a double sense. It means both a process—the manner in which a new music emerged by the mingling of elements old and new—and a shape: the structure of the punk rock field at its most dynamic moment, in 1977. Chapter 6 follows on by chronicling both the wider influence of British punk and also what happened to its fragments after its collapse in 1977–8, a collapse the causes of which are considered at the end of Chapter 1.

Together, these two chapters offer a sketch of punk rock's history, its rise and fall, while Chapter 8 provides a chronological outline. The sketch does not pretend to be a full historical account, something which is acutely needed. Such an account might deal in depth with the considerable range of local punk rock activity which grew up throughout Britain, providing an amount of musical productivity in many towns which had not been seen since the beat group era of 1963–6.

This book, however, is not primarily historical. The central part of the book, Chapters 2–5, deals with the issue of the *meaning* of punk rock. The key questions here are how did punk generate meanings, what were those meanings and which of them were consumed by listeners to the music and in what way. Underlying those questions is another one: how far do the answers to them justify claims that punk rock was essentially *different* to other, more conventional types of popular music?

The issue of difference emerges in Chapter 1, which uses the method of content analysis to show how far punk rock's lyric themes diverged from those of the songs in the Top 50 of the time. That method, though, is atypical of the methodology employed in the central chapters, which is broadly derived from the discipline of semiology, which approaches communication and cultural activity as products of systems of signs within which meanings are made possible through convention and through the play of difference between signifiers. (For semiology, a sign consists of a signifier—the sound or sight of the word 'punk'—and a corresponding signified—the mental image or idea evoked by the signifier.)

Semiology has a two-fold value as a means of understanding how popular music makes its meanings. Because it brings into equivalence all types of sign (written, spoken, sung, played, gestured), it offers the chance of showing how all of these combine together to produce an effect of pleasure (or displeasure) for an audience. It thus provides a way of avoiding the difficulties encountered frequently by purely musicological or purely linguistic analyses of popular songs. For each of these tends to privilege just one aspect of a song (the musical structure of chords, harmony, melody, etc. or the meaning of the lyrics) to the detriment of the rest. It is surely clear that in many instances neither of these constitutes the centre of attention for an audience. Most often in popular music, the focus is the singing voice, combined in the spotlight of live performance with the physical presence of the singer her/himself.

The second way in which semiology is especially useful lies in its contribution to understanding that dimension signalled by the word 'popular'. For popular music (including punk rock) belongs not only to the domain of the musical but also to that of popular culture. The meanings attributed to it by listeners frequently derive from associations or connections between an element of the music and something belonging to another area of popular culture. An important instance is the singing voice itself. Chapter 3 includes a discussion of the *connotations* of Johnny Rotten's voice in which reference is made to the significance of cockney accents in the culture as a whole.

'Connotation' is the term I have chosen to indicate the mechanism by which 'extra-musical fields of association' (to use a phrase of Philip Tagg's[1]) contribute to making of meaning in punk rock. In linguistic and semiological parlance, connotation is the opposite term to *denotation*, where the latter refers to a strictly limited, primary signifier of a sign. In language, this would be a 'dictionary definition', while in music it might refer simply to the place of a specific sound within a system of sounds (such as a scale or a set of chords). The level of connotation is that of the culturally-defined web of associations a word or sound has acquired. Thus, while 'red' denotatively stands for a certain colour, a band of the spectrum, its connotations include 'danger', 'passion', 'the Left'. The connotative level, too, is the level at which ideology emerges. For the ideological battle over, for instance, the real meaning of the term 'freedom' is a battle about which connotations will prevail in the popular consciousness.

Like words, purely musical elements can acquire extra-musical connotations, as Tagg has shown in his exhaustive analyses of Abba's song 'Fernando' and the theme music of the *Kojak* television series.[2] Briefly, his approach depends on locating other uses of a particular musical element (a harmony, rhythm, instrumentation or melodic fragment) noting what connotations are evoked by each use and sifting out the connotations common to all. This enables the *predominant* (but not inevitable) connotation of a certain element to be discovered, that which most listeners can be expected to find in the sound. Punk rock provides an interesting case for this kind of connotational analysis since some of its elements were previously 'unheard' by many listeners and had no earlier connotations in a musical context. For such elements, the connotations appeared through a negative process, through an awareness of those sounds of which the punk elements were the *opposite:* for punk's hoarse, rasping, chanting voices, the more melodic and sleeker vocals of the mainstream of rock; for the minimal guitar solo, the elaborate and extended one. In each case, the punk sound connoted first of all a disruption of convention and normality.

As readers of Dick Hebdige's *Subculture: The Meaning Of Style* will have realized, the current work is not the first attempt to understand punk through the medium of semiology. That book, published in 1979, was an ambitious attempt to yoke together semiological approaches with the sociological notion of 'youth subculture', just as the present work places semiology and history together. There are a number of points where *One Chord Wonders* meets up with *Subculture*, and these have been duly noted in the body of the work. But there is a fundamental difference between the two books which is exemplified by the way in which each uses the term 'punk'. In *One Chord Wonders*, with very few exceptions, the word is always short for 'punk rock', a specific musical genre. But for Hebdige, music is only one part of a stylistic ensemble called 'punk', and judging by the limited space he devotes to it, not the most important part. That role is reserved for the visual display of what I have called (in Chapter 4) the 'punk look'.

This contrast is a crucial one which I believe explains the critical attitude of *One Chord Wonders* to any notion of a punk 'subculture' separated from some other 'mainstream' youth life-style. Unlike nearly every other youth subculture (the teds, mods, skinheads, etc.), punk began as music and punks themselves began as music fans and performers. In every other case, the youth subculture adopted an already existing type of music. This musical origin of punk had far-reaching consequences, the most important of which were punk's inescapable links with the popular music industry. Punk rock began as a kind of outlawed shadow of that industry and its fate depended equally on the response to it of the industry. And while punk as a life-style developed a certain distance from the fate of punk rock, it remained dependent on the existence of a musical focus to give its own identity a stability.

The approach of classical semiology tends to isolate the production of meaning from specific contexts. Connotational analysis, for instance, can effectively provide a way of getting all possible meanings for a sign, but is not adequate to determine which meanings will 'work' for particular audiences in particular places. To undertake that part of this investigation into punk rock—its effect for listeners—I have made use of two further ideas, those of *shock-effect* and of *discourse*.

Several pages of Chapter 3 are devoted to expounding the concept of shock-effect (pp.96–102), so here I want simply to say that this concept emphasizes a psychological (and potentially psychoanalytical) dimension of the listener, as my grafting of notions of pleasure in consumption onto the idea of shock-effect indicates. Discourse, however, implies a different, though not incompatible, image of the listener: an image of someone occupying a role or position that has been pre-set for him or her by the play of the discourse itself.

'Discourse' itself has become something of a vogue (and a vague) word in recent cultural theory and criticism, and its use in the present volume may well not have escaped such vagueness. In order to try and clarify how it is used here, it seems best to begin by explaining the reason for its introduction at all. Briefly, it is that 'discourse' provides a bridge between the semiological and the historical aspects of the treatment of punk rock. In the words of a recent author, it is the place where 'language-systems and social conditions meet'.[3] Too much cultural criticism, particularly from a marxist viewpoint, has been content to privilege 'social conditions' over 'language-systems' (and their products, such as songs or films), so that the meaning or value of a song is seen to lie in how adequately it *mirrors* contemporary social reality. This general attitude was also strong among the pundits of punk rock, and was exemplified in Mark P.'s review of the first Clash album in his influential magazine *Sniffin' Glue*. The value of introducing a bridging concept such as 'discourse' is that it helps avoid the danger of reducing the signifying level of songs to a mere effect of the current class struggle or social conditions. It can emphasize that even when, for example, a song lyric takes unemployment as its subject-matter, the meaning of that utterance is dependent on its specific character as part of a musical and popular cultural structure. To that extent, the meaning for and effect on a listener is likely to be very different from that of the same words uttered at a political meeting or on a television news programme. This does not mean that somehow the musical sphere is sealed off from politics. But it does mean that the political effects of a musical utterance are first and foremost a factor within the particular politics and balance of forces *within* music, which in turn has complex relations of autonomy and dependence with other, more conventionally politicized spheres of social and economic life. This point is returned to in the concluding chapter of the book.

The starting point for the particular twist given to 'discourse' in this book is the statement of the French author Michel Foucault:

> In every society the production of discourse is at once controlled, selected, organised and redistributed by a certain number of procedures whose role is to ward off its powers and dangers, to gain mastery over its chance events, to evade its ponderous, formidable materiality.[4]

To a large extent, this book deals with the production of the discourse of punk rock through such processes as control, selection, organization and redistribution, of which the agencies were not only those hostile ones of broadcasting, news media and various state agencies. Control and selection were also events internal to the punk milieu, where both musicians and spokespersons (journalists, disc-jockeys, etc.) undertook to prescribe *le vrai punk*.

But what are the 'powers and dangers', the 'formidable materiality' of discourse, which Foucault sees as the objects of control and selection? They derive from the innate *polysemy* of all signifiers. Polysemy can be defined as 'many meaninged' and is used in semiology to point to the fact that the separate existence of signifier and signified precludes any simple one-to-one relation of meaning between them, and allows for a certain free play of the signifier. Potentially not one but several meanings can be generated. This feature has clearly been harnessed in certain discourses, notably that of humour through the pun—which depends on a signifier having two or more signifieds simultaneously. More generally, though, the need of those controlling discourses is to ensure that one particular meaning is generated and the others excluded. That meaning is referred to as the 'preferred' or 'dominant' meaning in semiology. One important way in which this is achieved is by defining the role of the listener, the audience, the receiver of the discursive message, in such a way that only the preferred meaning 'makes sense' to them. Other possible meanings are then dismissed as inessential, irrelevant or even unintelligible. Thus, the discursive procedures of mainstream popular music, faced with a political 'protest' lyric, might well set up the vocal sound as the preferred meaning, denying significance to the political message of the words.

Foucault and others using his ideas sometimes employ the term 'discursive formation' in addition to 'discourse'. Confusingly, too, these terms are often used interchangeably. In this book, though, I have attempted to distinguish between discourse-in-general, which is the process of signification as such, (as described in the above quotation from Foucault) and the specific discourses of a culture whose boundaries are marked not by linguistic but by social categories: the discourses of 'youth', 'sexuality' or 'politics' for instance. In turn, these specific discourses with their built-in assumptions, positions and exclusions are combined into discursive formations, whose shape and activity are determined by the social, political or economic interests of the institutions in which they are housed. For the purpose of *One Chord Wonders*, the most important discursive formation to be analysed is that of the mainstream of popular music which is part of what I have termed the 'leisure apparatus' of British society, which itself includes such institutions as broadcasting stations, record companies and the music press. This discussion occurs at various points in the book, but most extensively in Chapter 3.

Discursive formations are always the product of power, of the ability of those involved to enforce or negotiate definitions, exclusions and positions which reinforce their interests. One of the most significant achievements of punk rock was its ability to lay bare the operations of power in the leisure apparatus as it was thrown into confusion. The power to exclude was used frequently and crudely by broadcasting authorities and retailers who banned records and by the local State which refused access to public halls. The more subtle power of selection, re-definition and incorporation of punk rock into the mainstream discursive formation was exercised by the three record companies which signed the Sex Pistols. EMI's publicity photographs defined the band as high-spirited mischief-makers squirting beer at the camera, but the Grundy incident (described on pp.48–9) and subsequent pressure from other ruling class sources led the company to reverse its policy and cancel the group's contract.

But the working of power need not be negative. Power can deny or exclude meanings, but it also produces them. As Chapter 5 indicates, the meaning of the term 'punk' itself was the result of a range of pressures from different sources, pressures which opposed or reinforced one another in putting forward their own preferred meanings. This intimate connection of power and meaning is not peculiar to punk rock or even to popular music as a whole. But the case of punk rock, its emergence, its complex, contradictory and unstable challenge to the musical establishment and its subsequent disintegration, offers an unrivalled chance to show how power makes meaning in cultural history.

One
Formation

THE MUSIC MACHINE BEFORE PUNK

I n 1976, two-thirds of the British record market was shared between six major transnational companies. These 'majors' were vertically integrated: not only did they originate recordings by signing artists and putting them into the studio, they also manufactured discs and tapes and then distributed and promoted them to the shops. Each controlled three of the four main aspects of the record business, while EMI had a stake in the fourth—retailing—through its chain of HMV record shops.

Table 1 below shows the percentage of the British market held by recordings originated by the big six in 1976. In some cases the proportion of record sales in which a major had a financial interest was even higher, since many smaller record companies used the majors to manufacture and distribute their products. Thus it was estimated that EMI handled about one-third of all records sold in Britain during the mid-1970s.

Internationally, the picture was similar. Each of the majors had overseas branches, ranging from EMI's 28 to the handful owned by RCA and Decca, but they also had licensing arrangements which could ensure access to every market of significance in the Western and Third worlds. A survey of 19 of the most important countries for record sales by Martti Soramaki and Jukka Haarma showed that the proportion held by the five largest transnationals in 1975–6 (excluding Decca) was under one-half in only Israel and was generally over 60%, as in Britain.[1]

Table 1 The percentage of the British market held by recordings originated by the six largest transnational companies in 1976.

Firm	Country of ownership	Singles	Albums
EMI	Britain	21	22
CBS	USA	16	9
PolyGram*	W. Germany/Netherlands	13	13
WEA	USA	6	6
RCA	USA	4	5
Decca	Britain	3	7

*Includes both the Polydor and Phonogram companies which traded separately in Britain.

Source: *British Phonographic Industry (BPI) Yearbook* 1977.

The economic dominance of the major companies had its musical counterpart. Like their corporate activity, their approach to popular music was transnational. In seeking artists or sounds to promote the majors tended to prefer those most likely to attract audiences across national boundaries to those whose appeal was limited to a single linguistic or cultural community. Such transnational products would obviously have very high unit sales (over 30 million in the later (1983) case of Michael Jackson's album *Thriller*) and, because of the somewhat unusual economics of music as a commodity, profits which rose ever more steeply.

The unusual element was that the manufacturing cost of a record or tape is only a small part of the overall price—some 20% of the wholesale price paid by the retailer. And while artist and composer royalties have to be paid on every copy sold, the other principal expense for the record company is that of origination—the cost of studio recording and mixing. Therefore, once that origination cost has been recouped by a certain level of sales (which obviously varies with each recording) the proportion of the record company's income from each unit sale which is pure profit jumps dramatically. The company's gain in increasing sales from, say, 200,000 to 400,000 is then not double, but several times as much.

The classic transnational sound of the 1970s was that of the Swedish group Abba. Their recordings were actually the property of their own production company, Polar Music, but were leased to CBS for worldwide manufacture and distribution. Abba sang in English, but a particular transnational kind of English which had been established through the global hegemony of the United States in popular culture, through movies and television series as well as songs. Abba's lyrics were free from any local (i.e., Swedish or Nordic) references or themes which might have impeded their reception in Japan or Colombia, relying instead on stereotypes related to those of Hollywood or Tin Pan Alley. Musically, too, their sound was a skilful blend of pop-American styles from the previous two decades, as Philip Tagg shows in his exhaustive analysis of Abba's hit record 'Fernando'.[2]

Britain had been a major source for this transnational music ever since the Beatles had emphatically proved that it wasn't only Americans who could become global stars. By the 1970s, in fact, its importance for the majors was less as a large market for records than as a 'talent pool' from which they could fish out potential international superstars. This was the prime motive for a number of American companies opening up their own branch companies in the UK, discontinuing previous arrangements under which their records were licensed to either Decca or EMI. With a British office and local scouts, promising acts could be signed directly to the American transnational. As a result, the majority of British musicians with international status in the mid-1970s were associated with foreign-owned companies. They included David Bowie (RCA), Bay City Rollers (Arista), Fleetwood Mac and Rod Stewart (Warner Bros-WEA) and Led Zeppelin (Atlantic-WEA).

The transnational perspective, then, defined the criteria for success in popular music in the 1970s. It also had its repercussions in the process of recording itself. Since the rewards from a global hit were potentially vast, the majors were willing to invest large sums in the preparation of both artists and recordings. Most of that money was spent on and in recording studios, whose technology had become increasingly sophisticated. In particular, the exponential increase during the decade in the number of tracks, or channels of sound, into which the music to be recorded could be separated, allowed musicians and producers to manipulate the sounds to an unprecedented degree.

In the popular music sphere of 1976, the expert manipulation of that technology (preferably by a respected record producer) had become accepted as the precondition for successful and competent music. Although punk rock was soon to prove that exciting and valid recordings could be made for a fraction of the cost, the generality of musicians in 1976 identified good records with expensive ones. And since the only source of adequate finance for the studio costs of a good recording was the major or large independent label, the only path to artistic success musicians could imagine lay through convincing those labels that one's own work would prove commercially viable.

The grip which held musicians in thrall to the priorities of the major companies was doubly reinforced by the fact that there were (apparently separate) artistic reasons for taking the 'capital-intensive' road. Since the late 1960s, the 'progressive rock' genre had emphasized the primacy of recorded music over live performance, and had equated musical excellence with a meticulous (and time-consuming, hence expensive) attention to detail in, and maximum use of the technical resources of, the recording studio. The pattern had been set by the Beatles and the Beach Boys, whose 'Good Vibrations' single in 1966 reputedly took six months in four separate studios and cost £5,000 (over $10,000) to produce.

This gigantism had its effects on both the live performance and the forms of progressive rock. Live shows were increasingly expected to provide an exact recreation of the studio recordings, and therefore demanded large investments in extra musicians or various pieces of electronic equipment. In many instances, such shows ran at a loss and the record companies covered the costs, regarding them as a form of publicity for the album proper. Meanwhile, the musical forms used by the bands became larger and larger. Three-minute songs seemed unsuitable to the opulence and grandeur of the studio machinery and the musicians' ability to demonstrate virtuosity on guitar or keyboards. Song-cycles ('concept albums') abounded, and there were lengthy instrumental pieces like Mike Oldfield's massive hit, *Tubular Bells* (1973). The themes of the concept albums were also inflated, as groups like Pink Floyd, Yes or Genesis grappled in various ways with the mysteries of life.

Progressive rock, however, represented only one strand of British popular music in the mid-1970s. Performers in the genre concentrated on making albums rather than singles and many of them had first achieved prominence in the 1960s or early 1970s. Their audiences also tended to be composed of those whose sense of a musical tradition stretched back to the Beatles and the Beach Boys. Progressive rock itself had emerged in the late 1960s as various musicians tried to distance themselves from the 'unserious' pop music of the singles charts. The rock/pop schism was still apparent in 1976, with so-called 'teenybopper' music (exemplified by the Bay City Rollers) and the emerging disco dance music of artists like Chic and Tina Charles forming the main pop trends.

These two genres (progressive rock and pop) represented two poles of music in the mid-1970s, however, and between them were a range of other styles. Most notable, perhaps, were a number of survivors from the pre-schismatic era, whose work intermittently hinted at a unified approach which could straddle the pop/rock divide. They included ELO, Elton John, and Paul McCartney, whose 'Mull of Kintyre' sold over two million copies in Britain alone. Far more artistically significant, though, especially for the future personnel of punk rock, was David Bowie. His ambitious attempt to re-unify the musical elements scattered between pop and rock in a modern (rather than nostalgic) way will be considered later in this chapter.

Meanwhile, the record industry was faced with the growth of a new market, one which was stimulated by forces from outside the music companies themselves. In 1972, a Canadian company, K-Tel, had launched the first television-advertised album of recent hits. Its success drew the major record companies themselves into the same field so that by 1976 the total spent on the advertising of 'TV albums' was over £5 million. The most heavily promoted albums could expect to sell over a million copies in Britain, as EMI's *Beach Boys 20 Golden Greats* did in 1976–7.

It was assumed that the audience contacted through television were not regular record buyers, and were in a slightly older age group. Hence, they were sold 'oldies' collections by stars of the 1960s or else new albums by already established superstars. So determined was the assault on this television audience that in 1976 nine of the top 20 best-selling albums in Britain were TV-advertised re-issues.

The sales of these records were assisted by a retailing revolution in the mid-1970s—the move into record selling by the large multiple stores, Boots, Woolworth and W.H. Smith. These groups immediately began a policy of selective discounting on the best-selling albums, which maximized sales on those records already in the Top 20. The result of this was that the 'turnover' of album titles in the charts slowed down considerably, making it more difficult to succeed, especially for newer artists. In addition, those newer artists lucky enough to be signed to a major company faced the prospect of less support from the label as the advertising budget for TV albums soared. A further difficulty for those artists lay in the fact that the growing market share of the multiple stores (30% by 1976) was made at the expense of the specialist record shops. These independent retailers, whose numbers now began to diminish, would invariably stock a far wider range of titles than the multiples. They would certainly be more likely to make available records by new or unknown musicians.

By 1976 the shape of the record industry in Britain had changed sharply from that of the late 1960s. In the earlier period, rock music (not pop) had been at the centre of the record companies' strategy. The profit margin on an album was greater than that of a single and it seemed that the Beatles had proved that rock musicians were durable and could be expected to retain their popularity for some years.

In the mid-1970s, it was more difficult to locate a centre. There was no guarantee that the new teenyboppers would follow the evolution of their predecessors of the early 1960s, who graduated from screaming at the Beatles to analysing the lyrics of their later songs. On the other side, there seemed to music industry figures to be a slowing down in the emergence of new talent in rock, a process exacerbated by the pressure on funds available for investment in such talent caused by discounting and TV advertising. And was it the case, some people wondered, that the future lay not with the pop or rock sphere but with the new-style MOR (middle-of-the-road) audience revealed by the success of TV marketed albums? Over all of this hovered the awareness that in global terms the discovery of one new superstar could revolutionize the fortunes of the lucky company.

WORRIES IN THE INDUSTRY

> It is certainly time we got a super new UK thing like the Beatles.
> The music business needs a shot in the arm. We are overdue for it.
> (Wayne Bickerton, producer and small label owner, August 1976)[3]

These issues came into sharper focus when the sales returns for the latter part of 1976 were published. As Fig. 1 shows, the overall figures for the year showed a no-change position for singles and the first decline in album sales for a number of years. More immediately, the figure for the third quarter dropped by 30% compared with July–September 1975.

These statistics were set against a general recession in the British economy. Unemployment had climbed to over one million and inflation had reached a peak of 18% in 1975. In this context, there was evidence that the proportion of their disposable income that consumers were prepared to devote to recorded music was slipping. Figures from the record industry's own trade association showed that in 1974, 0.4% of all consumer spending in Britain had gone on records. By 1976 this had dropped to 0.34%, a decline of around one-seventh.[4]

The music press of the time provided other indications of unease about the state of popular music, and especially rock, in Britain. In July 1976, around the time punk rock was beginning to surface as far as the media was concerned, *Melody Maker* published a discussion about the incidence of violence in the current scene. There were references to a new mood of cynicism and aggression in the audiences for expensively-priced outdoor events like 'The Who Put The Boot In' and the Reading Rock festival, while bands such as Doctors of Madness and Heavy Metal Kids were accused of 'inciting the audience to violence'.[5] That this was precisely the comment that would soon be made about the Sex Pistols perhaps suggests a previously unnoticed continuity between punk rock and the music scene which preceded it.

Figure 1 Units—millions.

7" Records (Singles)		
46.2		1972
54.6		1973
62.7		1974
56.9		1975
56.9		1976

12" Records (Albums)		
59.3		1972
81.0		1973
89.5		1974
91.6		1975
83.8		1976

Source: *British Phonographic Industry Yearbook* 1978.

A year earlier, in one of the same paper's routine surveys of 'The Future of Rock', Peter Jenner of Blackhill Enterprises, an agency concerned principally with 'underground' and alternative music, made this comment:

> The Big Show will vanish. . . . I think the political thing is a possibility. I'm thinking of someone who's 16, who's going to start saying, 'Look, all this stuff these bands do with these huge P.A.s and lights, that's not where it's at. It's down to the people. And I'm going to get out my acoustic guitar and sing revolutionary songs in pubs, working-men's clubs and factories.'[6]

Jenner's percipience was marred only by his assumption that the reaction against the 'Big Show' would take the form of a re-run of the folk-protest of the 1960s.

His attitude was not widely shared within the record business. In May and June 1976, the Big Show had its finest hour when the vast spaces of Wembley Stadium and Earls Court were filled with fans of Bowie, David Essex, Uriah Heep, Elton John and the Rolling Stones, who were even visited backstage by Princess Margaret.

In so far as anyone was concerned seriously about the future of the record industry (and the chairmen of both Decca and EMI warned their shareholders of 'adverse trading conditions' ahead in their end-of-1976 statements), they took the view expressed above by Wayne Bickerton. The difference between the Beatles and other new stars had been that the Beatles' success had benefited not only the record company for whom they recorded, but the whole industry. It had led to an overall rise in the level of recorded music sales, and a strengthening of the position of British companies within the world music market. Ever since the break-up of the Fab Four, many people in the music industry had nursed the hope that there would be a 'Next Big Thing', the New Beatles phenomenon, to lift the British record industry to a new plateau of profitability. Talent scouts and A&R (Artist and Repertoire) managers were on the lookout for the Next Big Thing.

On the Beatles' model, the place to find such an animal was 'at the grass roots', among the clubs and pubs of the suburbs or regional cities where the heroes of the 1960s had started out. But by the mid-1970s, there seemed to be very few grass roots left to nurture such musicians. Again this was due to the dominant modes of both rock and pop in the mid-1970s rather than a physical lack of facilities. The church halls and pub rooms still existed, but young musicians could not see them as relevant places to perform, as rungs on the ladder to a success comparable to that of T. Rex, Queen or Slik. The new recording stars of the era had a polished and opulent aura that clearly owed nothing to a musical apprenticeship in the beat clubs of Hamburg or Humberside.

PUB ROCK: THE OLD THING AGAIN

There was, however, one type of location in the mid-1970s where something like 'grass roots' might be discovered. In the words of one commentator, 'On some nights, a dozen A&R men, record executives and agents would be sniffing out new talent in the same tiny bar.'[7] The object of their attention was the 'pub rock' scene, which flourished in London from 1972 onwards. Much of its early motivation was a conscious reaction against the condition of mainstream popular music in the early 1970s. Interviewed in late 1972, Barry Richardson of the pioneering pub rock band Bees Make Honey said:

> A loss of shape, increase in volume, the subsequent loss in impor-
> tance of the singing, the songs and the words. In fact, loss of swing.

All these things have happened in rock, especially English rock. We can't do that. We *do* remember enough to try and do the old thing again.

And Nick Lowe of Brinsley Schwarz spoke of a pub circuit that would be 'something like the old R&B club circuit, small places where you get some feedback and a bit of magic in the air.'[8]

To go against the grain of contemporary rock, the pub bands needed a different *aesthetic*, as well as the need to play live music. They found it in the past, or rather several pasts. There was the golden age of rhythm and blues and rock 'n' roll, which had been canonized in Charlie Gillett's widely influential history book, *The Sound Of The City*, published in 1970. And there was the period of the early 1960s in Britain, when a generation of bands followed the Beatles and the Rolling Stones out of the small clubs and into the charts. If an ideal of shape and directness in songs was inherited from the American golden age, the virtue of smallness was taken by pub bands from their folk memory of the Merseybeat and British R&B era. The size of the bar-room allowed for, even insisted upon, the intimacy between musicians and audience they believed was somehow essential for meaningful music. Pub rock's stance implied that things went wrong for bands when they became superstars and 'lost touch' with their original audiences.

Aficionados have discerned four chronological phases of pub rock[9] but virtually all the bands shared a commitment to some idea of musical 'roots', without succumbing to the purism about re-creating the past that had been such a feature of the British R&B movement. From Bees Make Honey onwards, pub rock bands mixed 'standards' from the rock 'n' roll and R&B tradition with their own compositions in the same idioms. Among other things, pub rock was a school for songwriters, as the later achievements of ex-pub alumni Ian Dury and Elvis Costello were to testify.

If pub rock had lacked that element of original material, the record industry would have taken less interest. As it was, nearly every record company signed its pub rock band during 1973–4. One group, Ace, had a Number 1 hit with 'How Long' in 1974 while Dr Feelgood briefly topped the album chart in November 1976 with *Stupidity*. But they were the exceptions. Sales of albums by most pub rock bands were modest, perhaps because most regarded the studio as a place to transcribe their live performances, an 'old-fashioned' attitude in the mid-1970s.

The arrival of the first punk bands also underlined the old-fashioned nature of some aspects of pub rock. To the lack of recording success was added a challenge from a musical style which emphasized dynamism in performance and cared nothing for roots or tradition. In so far as a shift in pub rock style had been apparent over time, it involved an increase in performance dynamism. While pioneers like Brinsley Schwarz and Ducks DeLuxe were content to stand still and let the music speak for itself, Dr Feelgood and then Eddie and the Hot Rods brought a new intensity to pub rock on stage. Although it was still based in rhythm and blues, the music was louder and faster than the American originals. Indeed, by 1975–6 Eddie and the Hot Rods were being classed by commentators like Mark P. of *Sniffin' Glue* as part of punk, not pub, rock.

At the same time, one of the newer pub bands, the 101ers, was breaking apart under the impact of punk (and specifically the Sex Pistols). Dan Kelleher went off to an agit-prop rock band The Derelicts while Joe Strummer formed The Clash. The case of Strummer suggests one musical link between pub rock and punk, among their many contrasts: in some cases there was a shared concern to return music to a basic simplicity, to which questions of tradition or stylistic authenticity were secondary.

But punk's most important debt to pub rock lay in its opening up of a *space* for both performing and recording which lay outside the constraints of the mainstream music industry. Despite the general 'roots' orientation of pub rock bands, the venues themselves were also an open space for music of various types ignored or neglected by the record industry. From his earliest days with Kilburn and the High Roads, Ian Dury found an audience there for his quirky, comic songs. In this respect, the role of the pubs was akin to that played by the folk clubs a decade earlier. In the mid-1960s, these clubs offered a place to perform for a wide variety of singers, songwriters and instrumentalists, many of whom turned out to have little if any connection with 'folk' as a musical genre. In a parallel fashion, the Nashville—one of the key venues on the pub rock circuit—gave houseroom in early 1976 to the early punk bands, the Sex Pistols, Stranglers and Damned.

More far-reaching was the pub rock approach to making records. Ironically, it was only because of the failure of the established record companies to sell records by pub bands (and the consequent withdrawal of interest by these labels) that pub rock acquired its own labels, Chiswick and Stiff. The latter was founded by two men who formerly managed pub rock bands. With £45 borrowed from Dr Feelgood, they bought studio time to cut the label's first single, by Nick Lowe. The record sold over 10,000 copies, netting Stiff a reasonable profit. Independent label economics had been born.

The first principle of that economics was its refusal to heed the imperative of the hit parade. Among the mainstream record companies, majors and independents alike, the first (and often the only) point of recording and releasing a single was to get it into the Top 20 chart. The route to this goal lay through sufficient airplay and (to a lesser degree) press coverage. To get airplay on BBC radio and the growing network of commercial radio stations necessitated (the companies thought) that particular quality of recorded sound to be got from a sophisticated studio and an expert producer, plus the services of a team of promotions staff to 'sell' the disc to radio producers and later to shopkeepers.

In choosing which records to make, two strategies were used within the record industry. The smaller companies tended to release a very limited number of discs, but to carefully construct each according to the specifications for hit-making which the particular producer believed in. This was the approach, for instance, of Mickie Most's Rak label. In the period September 1974 to August 1975, Rak had 12 Top 20 hits out of 34 releases. Promotion, manufacture and distribution were handled by EMI, which therefore shared in Rak's success.

EMI itself epitomized the second strategy, often called the 'mud against the wall' approach, after the adage that if you throw enough mud against the wall, some of it will stick. In the same period during 1974–5, the EMI label itself had just ten hits out of 145 releases, and the CBS and Epic labels together had 17 hits out of 214 singles released. While a producer like Mickie Most relied on his intuition to predict what would prove to be popular, underlying the EMI strategy was a certain fatalism that, apart from repeating the style of recent hits, the trends of the future were ultimately unpredictable. It was better therefore to use a scattergun approach, by releasing a variety of sounds in the hope that one at least would prove successful.

It was because of this immense operation which lay behind the majors' singles policy that the figure of 20,000 (sometimes 23,000) sales was frequently cited as the 'break-even' point for a single. The figure concealed the calculations involved, which relied on setting off the costs of a number of very low-selling singles (often with only a few hundred sold) against one very large hit, with sales of perhaps a quarter or half a million.

By dispensing with the need for expensive productions, promotional staff and the other overheads of chart-oriented companies, Stiff and the other small record labels which set up from 1977 onwards to release punk rock and new wave material, could work to 'break-even' figures which could be as low as 2,000 copies for a single.

The first Chiswick label release was of the pub R&B band the Count Bishops. It cost £700 to record and manufacture 2,500 copies of an EP. Within four months all had been sold through specialist record shops.

The pub and punk labels weren't the first to operate in this manner, by-passing the hit parade philosophy. There were two kinds of precedent. The first was that of the 'collectors' market'. Chiswick owner Ted Carroll was initially the owner of a record shop specializing in oldies, and saw the music of the Count Bishops and other bands as ideal material for the collectors: 'I knew there wasn't a large market for such groups, but felt sure there would be a small, but large enough, collector's market. I guessed most of my collectors would be American so I settled on a really English name, Chiswick.'

The 'collectors' market' had been served by small labels willing to release or re-release material large companies found too 'uncommercial' in the fields of jazz and blues for some years. Chiswick was new in being among the first to recognize a collectors' market in the rock field.[10] It had been preceded by Oval, a label run by rock historian Charlie Gillett. Chiswick itself was the forerunner of several key punk labels which grew out of record retailing operations. The others included Beggars Banquet, Raw, Rough Trade and Zoom.

The second precedent for the kind of record label formed to present first pub and then punk rock could also be found in other spheres of music: the phenomenon of artists producing their own discs, to be sold primarily at their own live performances. This was quite widespread in jazz and especially folk music, where the album served as a kind of 'memento' of a live performance. Part of the momentum behind Stiff came from this kind of impulse.

With the winding-down of pub rock in 1976 (due to economic pressures on the remaining bands and to the disillusion of those who had hoped to find wider success through the pub scene as well as the growing challenge of punk for both venues and audiences), manager and producer Dave Robinson was left with many hours of live tapes from the scene. Stiff was envisaged as a label which would make available these recordings almost as an epitaph for pub rock, although its strategy soon altered to one which provided a stepping-stone of one-off singles for various artists and bands without recording contracts. These included both pub veterans like Nick Lowe and early punks like The Damned.

Sensible Records of Edinburgh provided a different example of the 'memento' style label. It was formed by a local promotion man for a national record company in his spare time. Its purpose was to get local band the Rezillos into the studio to make a single of two of their best stage numbers. Some 20,000 copies were sold, netting the band and the label owner around £1,000 profit.

There was, then, both contrast and continuity between pub rock and punk. If the contrasts were primarily ideological—a music concerned with tradition versus an iconoclastic—the connections lay in the material forms of musical production. Early punk shared both the venues for live performance and the disdain for the transnational philosophy of recording which the pub rock milieu had pioneered in the British music scene of the mid-1970s.

PUNK SIMILARITY: OTHER PUNK ROCKS

At the level of musical genre, too, the nascent punk rock of 1976 was 'recognized' as both the same as and different to earlier types of rock music. The most important point of similarity which the critics and commentators saw between the new London bands like the Sex Pistols and the Stranglers and previous music was summed up in the name the new music was eventually given.

The cultural history of the word 'punk' is considered in the first part of Chapter 2, but within the rock music discourse it had been applied to a number of American artists operating at various points in the years since 1964. It would be extremely difficult, if not impossible, to unearth the first reference to these musics as 'punk', but the aim and effect of the process of identifying them as such was to establish the value of a particular strand running through American rock music. That strand, for the critics and authors involved, was seen as very much in danger of being overlooked by the dominant critical opinions of the day.

Before elaborating on this motivation for establishing 'punk rock' as a genre, it is necessary briefly to describe the music in question. This representative definition refers to the earliest records of the genre:

> Punk rock was the music of thousands of bands, mostly of high-school age, who formed in the aftermath of the Beatles and the British rock invasion . . . where these groups (e.g., the Beatles et al.) had a modicum of style, innovation, and either an innate sense of cool or a genuine innocence, the punkers took a stance of spoiled suburban snottiness. Most classic punk records shared a number of attributes, from fuzztone on their guitars to an arrogant snarl in the vocals, and lyrics usually concerned

with uncooperative girls or bothersome parents and social restrictions.[11]

Perhaps the only one of these American records to have an international impact was 'Louie Louie' by The Kingsmen, which became a beat group standard in Britain during the mid-1960s, just as the American 'punk' bands had adopted The Troggs' 'Wild Thing' as an anthem. However, hardly any of the groups had more than local success, and those that continued into the late 1960s undertook a mutation in style which led them towards the excesses of 'psychedelic' music. The interface of punk and psychedelia is well exemplified by 'I Had Too Much to Dream Last Night' by the Electric Prunes.

The next point at which a general trend in American music was identified as punk came in the early 1970s, with the emergence of a number of bands in New York, most notably the New York Dolls. In between, several isolated musicians were picked out as embodying that punk essence. These included the Velvet Underground, the MC5 and The Stooges. On the surface, these three had little in common. The Velvet Underground were associated in the mid-1960s New York with Andy Warhol and his 'pop-art' milieu. The band performed at Warhol's mixed-media show, the Exploding Plastic Inevitable. The MC5 were from Detroit and to begin with gained a reputation as rock 'n' roll revolutionaries because of their manager John Sinclair's involvement with the short-lived White Panther Party. The Stooges (whose lead singer Iggy Pop later went solo) had no such artistic or political trappings, emphasizing instead outrageous stage antics and lyrics.

The common element linking these bands backwards to the mid-1960s post-Beatles groups and forwards to the glitterati of the New York Dolls et al. was not cultural but musical. 'Punk' meant an attitude towards musical performance which emphasized directness and repetition (to use more than three chords was self-indulgence) at the expense of technical virtuosity. A critical guide to albums by these 'punk' bands published in 1980 included these characteristic descriptions: 'High energy on vinyl . . . heavy, monotonous, industrial, mechanical . . . relentless power-drill sound . . . shambolic firepower, tenement toughness, sparse musical knowhow . . . irresistible melodic drone.'[12]

If that was the punk essence and tradition as constructed before the arrival of the Sex Pistols and the other British groups of 1976, when and why was it constructed? Ellen Willis stated in an essay on the Velvet Underground that 'the word punk was not used generically until the early seventies when critics began applying it to unregenerate rock-and-rollers with an aggressively lower-class style,[13] while looking back to 1973, Greg Shaw wrote that:

> Punk rock in those days was a quaint fanzine term for a transient form of mid-60s music considered so bad (by the standards of the time) that it was a joke to the 'critics' who made their living analyzing the neuroses of Joni Mitchell.[14]

The arrival of the punk *concept*, then, occurred in about 1972–73, well after the disappearance of most of the bands to whom the term was then applied. In part, the role of the punk genre was to rehabilitate some of the lost legions of past popular music. But Shaw's comment also locates the context of the naming of punk. It occurred not in the dominant organs of rock criticism, most notably *Rolling Stone*, but in the fanzines, the small-scale, semi-underground publications of music enthusiasts. Among them were Shaw's own *Who Put The Bomp*, Mark Shipper's *Flash* (which included a 'Punk-Rock Top Ten' of early 1960s records in its June 1972 issue) and Billy Altman's *punk magazine*, whose first issue appeared in May 1973.

Greg Shaw's swipe at 'critics' and this extract from Altman's editorial made clear the polemical intention of the championing of 'punk':

> Wimps take heed! You will find this tabloid boring, offensive, possibly insulting. And that's just the way we want it. The legions are now forming and soon all of us rockers will bury you beneath your pile of James Taylor, Cat Stevens, Grateful Dead and Moody Blues records.

The construction of punk as a musical type and ideal, then, took place in America in the early 1970s as part of a reaction against the centrality of progressive rock in its various forms. In July 1976 the first issue appeared in London of *Sniffin' Glue*, a fanzine with the subtitle, '+ other Rock 'n' Roll Habits for Punks'. Part of its editorial, by Mark P. (Mark Perry, a young clerk who would become a major figure in the development of British punk rock), had distinct echoes of Greg Shaw and Billy Altman: 'We believe rock'n'roll—and especially "punk rock"—is about enjoyment and *nothing* else—leave the concepts to the likes of Yes, Mike Oldfield etc.'[15]

Sniffin' Glue went on to give its list of favoured bands. As well as those already canonized as punks by the American fanzines, it included the Mothers of Invention "66–68", and the comedian Lenny Bruce (presumably in recognition of the iconoclasm of both Frank Zappa—leader of the Mothers—and of Bruce). Included, too, are some British groups whom Perry believed to embody the punk spirit. As well as those who would later be hailed as leaders of the new British punk rock (Sex Pistols, Stranglers) there were bands from the harder, more demonstrative end of pub rock: Roogalator, Dr Feelgood and Eddie and the Hot Rods.

Perry was able at this stage to see all those British bands as part of the same thing because he was working with the purely musical definition of punk. As soon as a cultural dimension entered, however, the separation of Sex Pistols from Dr Feelgood was swift. That dimension was added by Perry himself and by other writers, notably *Melody Maker*'s Caroline Coon when she described the Sex Pistols and their audience as 'classic punk: icy-cool with a permanent sneer. The kids are arrogant, aggressive, rebellious.'[16] Despite the demurring of other journalists,[17] by July 1976 a British 'punk rock' had been identified. As well as providing the new music with a sense of a 'past' (through the implied link with American punk), the naming made it visible to a broader audience than the 'in crowd' who attended the first punk bands' early performances. It also gave those bands an identity which they couldn't refuse, even if many were less than happy to acknowledge it, since it made them part of a movement or genre instead of unique individualists.

PUNK DIFFERENCE: 'DO IT YOURSELF'

'I bet YOU don't hate US as much as WE hate YOU', Johnny Rotten told the audience at an early Sex Pistols gig. One appropriate parallel between British punk rock and the American concept of 'punk' which preceded it was hostility to the status quo in popular music. The difference lay in what followed from that hostility. While the Americans were content to publish fanzines and rehabilitate through re-release the lost punk sounds of earlier years, British punk was more thorough-going. Schematically, its hostility to the mainstream in the music scene took three major forms: the 'do it yourself' attitude which refused to rely on the institutions of the established music industry, whether record companies or music press; a challenge to the orthodoxy of 'artistic excellence' in punk's choice of musical style; and the aggressive injection of new subject-matter into the lyrics of popular songs, some of which broke existing taboos.

Punk rock's emphasis on self-reliance came through in various ways. The Sex Pistols, for instance, acquired some of their first equipment through theft including some taken from the London house of Rolling Stone Keith Richards.[18] More conventionally, punk had its own counter-institutions to those of the music business: the fanzines and the independent record labels.

The term 'fanzine' had originally been applied to magazines concerned with science fiction, and written by 'fans' rather than critics. In them, fans were able to share information and enthusiasm with each other. Punk rock was the first musical genre to spawn fanzines in any significant numbers. The occasional surveys in the orthodox music press suggested that during 1977–8 there may have been over 50 appearing in all parts of Britain. As well as initiating the trend, *Sniffin' Glue* played a pivotal role in establishing punk's self-image. If any communication implies a definition of the receiver of the message (in terms of the attitudes or codes of understanding needed to make the communication work), that implied by the fanzine is very specific. The 'fan' is defined by his or her possession of a particular knowledge of the fanzine's subject, unavailable to the uninitiated. 'We're the only mag that knows what's happening' proclaimed the cover of *Sniffin' Glue* 3 'A. Access to that knowledge is through knowing the code, understanding the allusions to (for the outsider) obscure artists and understanding the special jargon of the fan milieu.

It can also mean belonging to a group of people with a special name. Fans of the TV series *Star Trek* are 'Trekkies', and the cover of *Sniffin' Glue* 1 announced itself to be 'FOR PUNKS'. It was the first time the audience rather than the music had been defined in that way. The definition offered to punk and punks by the fanzine's editor, Mark Perry, went beyond the usual parameters of fandom. As well as expounding the variety and the solidarity of attitudes and music within punk rock, he constantly returned to the issue of drawing punk's boundaries with the world outside, and in particular exhorting punk to retain its independence from the music industry:

> I don't wanna see the Pistols, the Clash etc. turned into more AC/
> DCs and Doctors of Madness. This 'new-wave' has got to take in
> everything, including posters, record-covers, stage presentation,
> the lot! You know, they'll be coming soon, all those big companies
> out to make more money on the 'new, young bands'. Well, they can
> piss off if they're hoping to tidy up the acts for the 'great British
> public'. The Pistols will be the first to be signed and I know they'll
> stay like they are—completely independent!
> (Mark 'angry young man' P., *Sniffin' Glue* 3 1/2, September, 1976)

Although some of *Sniffin' Glue*'s vitriol was reserved for the established music press ('Certain writers in the established rags are latching onto the new bands in the same way that they change the fashion of their clothes'), it located the main threat to punk rock's independence in the 'big companies'. By describing those companies as 'out to make more money' and 'hoping to tidy up the acts' Mark Perry was echoing a common theme in commentaries on popular music. As early as 1899 Sir Hubert Parry, inaugurating the English Folksong Society, had contrasted the authenticity of folk music with the 'got-up glitter' of popular song which had been contaminated by the commercial motivation of its promoters.[19] Such a contrast became a standard theme for any number of critics of contemporary popular music throughout the century, with the content of each side of the model shifting until the 1960s when the contrast was placed *within* popular music rather than between it and some more admirable artistic product (whether folksong, jazz, blues, etc.). Thus liberal-minded commentators from outside popular music could talk of the demands of 'commercial recording' destroying the 'direct contact and mutual sparking off of enthusiasms between performers and listeners'[20] in a very similar way to that of the champions of pub-rock. By the 1970s, the so-called 'counter-culture' associated with progressive rock was employing the same structure of argument (authentic vs. commercial) while shifting the content again. A press release announcing the formation of Threshold, a label owned by members of the Moody Blues stated:

> We feel the trouble with the big record companies at the moment
> is that they are too big, and because of their structure, are more in-
> volved in the commercial aspects of the industry than the artistic.

Finally, this motif of commercialism and 'tidying up' had been given a fresh relevance in the mid-1970s by the phenomenon of 'teenybop' and of the Bay City Rollers. Even the vilified *Melody Maker* had presented what later might have seemed a punk-like view, in the introduction to its 'State Of Rock' feature in June 1975.

> If the Beatles were a musico-sociological phenomenon, the Bay
> City Rollers, today's contemporary teenage heroes in Britain, have
> been shaped by merchandising demands. . . . It may be unaccept-
> able, but at the heart of the Rock Dream is a cash register.[21]

(In the use of that one word 'may' is summed up the whole symbiotic relationship between the established music press and the established music industry. A genuinely independent journal would have said 'is', not 'may'.)

If the punk critique of the 'big companies' was something of a commonplace by 1976, its second main mode of 'do it yourself' after the fanzines had also been tried before: the organization of alternatives to the large record companies. During the later 1960s, the rise of progressive rock and associated counter-cultural ideologies had brought with them a series of new record labels. Some were simply the 'hippie' faces of the big companies (EMI's Harvest or Phonogram's Vertigo), but others were independently owned. Chrysalis was founded by two managers of bands, Island represented an expansion of a previously specialist reggae label, Virgin came from a chain of cut-price record stores, while Apple, Swansong and Threshold were all owned by rock stars. Apart from some degree of adherence to a 'small is beautiful' idea of record companies, all these labels were formed and financed by people with established places in the music business, as retailers, performers or managers. By 1976, too, the artist-owned labels had ceased to show any initiative in the policy-making sphere, while from the punk vantage point, Virgin, Island and Chrysalis shared many of the values of the transnational major companies.

The new record companies of the punk era were clearly distinguished from those earlier independents by their numbers, their size and their geographical location. A catalogue of small labels published by *ZigZag* magazine in 1978 listed 120 companies with a repertoire of punk material, mostly with just a handful of titles and nearly all based outside London. The metropolitan monopoly of the record industry had been seriously challenged for the first time by the likes of Anonymous Records of Macclesfield, Duff Records of Bangor, Good Vibrations of Belfast and Vole Records of Wolverhampton.

Many of these labels were a vinyl equivalent to the fanzines which multiplied in the wake of *Sniffin' Glue*. The 'small label economics' pioneered by Stiff and Chiswick had proved that to start a record company only a few hundred pounds and not a vast bank loan was needed. The sleeve of Scritti Politti's first single even itemized the costs of producing 2,500 copies of that very record:

Recording (14 hours) incl. master tape	£ 98.00
Mastering (making the 'master disc')	40.00
Pressing	396.36
Labels	8.00
	542.36

Just as the fanzines demystified the process of producing and publishing the written word, so the early punk labels demonstrated the simplicity with which anyone could become a recording artist.

Scritti Politti themselves had been inspired to make their record by the example of the Desperate Bicycles, who had included the following note on the sleeve of their second single on their own Refill label:

> The Desperate Bicycles were formed in March 1977 specifically for the purpose of recording and releasing a single on their own label . . . 'No more time for spectating' they sing and who knows? They may be right. They'd really like to know why you haven't made your single yet. 'It was easy, it was cheap, go and do it.' . . . now it's your turn.

'Xerox music's here at last' was another of the Desperate Bicycles' slogans and it was a useful term to describe an important stratum of punk recording involving hundreds of groups in dozens of small local studios throughout Britain. At earlier stages of the British record industry such bands would have first recorded to make a demonstration tape to send to an established label in the hope of being signed. Most weren't and so never released a record.

Many of the 'Xerox' record labels were very short-lived. But punk rock also had another layer of record companies whose forms of ownership and style of operation showed some similarities to small companies in earlier phases of rock music history. Step Forward Records, which featured Mark Perry's group Alternative TV, was one of a group of companies run by Miles Copeland, a mainstream rock group manager, later to handle The Police. Others, like Factory of Manchester and Fast Product of Edinburgh, were headed by the punk equivalent to the 'record men' identified by Charlie Gillett as key figures in the historically progressive role played by American independent labels in rock and R&B since the 1950s. Those figures—people like Ahmet Ertegun of Atlantic and Sam Phillips of Sun—combined artistic perception with business flair. Punk's cultural entrepreneurs included graphic artist Bob Last of Fast and television journalist Tony Wilson, a co-founder of Factory.

For labels like Factory and Fast Product, the distribution of records became a key issue. 'Xerox' records could be delivered to local shops by hand and perhaps sold by mail order as well. But as soon as a company's or band's ambitions stretched to wanting to make a national impact it entailed arrangements with distributors, whose fee would cut the profit margin to the group themselves. At this stage, punk rock labels could choose to find some form of *modus vivendi* with the music industry's distribution arm, or to set up or find their own independent system of national distribution.

Some companies placed themselves in the same relationship to the majors as the 1960s independents. Both Stiff and Chiswick signed an agreement with EMI whereby the major would manufacture and distribute the records. Beggars Banquet in 1978 made a similar deal with WEA, which included facilities for promotion by the major with the exception of those records thought to be 'uncommercial'. In the cases of both Stiff and Beggars Banquet (with Gary Numan), this arrangement brought them into the orbit of the Top 20, where both had hit singles.

But others among the punk labels preferred the alternative of distribution without the aid of the majors. Two pre-punk distributors of various 'specialized' minority-interest records, Pinnacle and Spartan, added a number of punk labels to their roster, providing them with access to a national audience. There was also a new distribution network organized from within punk rock, centred on London's Rough Trade shop and label. It had acted as an informal resource centre for bands wishing to make 'Xerox' records, providing advice and information as well as a retail outlet. And, to start with, Rough Trade would buy at least some copies of virtually all punk or new wave records to sell. Eventually, it evolved a link-up with other shops or local distributors around Britain which became known as 'The Cartel', making a further chain of distribution independent of the major record companies.

Even in this situation, however, punk rock labels were not finally out of the shadow of the majors. With their ability to find far greater cash advances, and to provide large publicity budgets, some major companies were able to sign up artists whose first recorded work had appeared on punk rock independent labels. Good Vibrations of Belfast found that four of their first six artists had been snapped up in this way, while both Small Wonder and Step Forward took the view that the process was inevitable, given their inability to compete in the rock market place with the large advances available to major companies. 'We, the indies, are like Freddie Laker', said Miles Copeland.

> We're quick moving, we're the future, the future that the record in-
> dustry will follow. The big companies will always do the marketing
> and manufacturing, but we are the creative side. I found the Squeeze
> and now they're with Polydor. I found the Cortinas, took them on
> for management and put them with CBS. We're a small label. We
> can't compete with a big company once a group starts happening.

Copeland's analogy with cut-price airline operator Freddie Laker (whose operations were to go bust in 1980) was more gestural than precise. For Laker had challenged the majors of his industry in every department, while Copeland's view of the small record labels was that they could excel in only one area—the strategically important one of origination, the discovery and presentation of new musical ideas. The Laker position, in fact could more properly have been compared to that of Rough Trade, an independent which sought to control its destiny in the marketing and distribution of recorded music as well as in origination. The ideological motivations involved, however, were poles apart. Laker was an aggressive capitalist entrepreneur, later to be knighted by Margaret Thatcher's government. Rough Trade's business ideals owed most, perhaps, to the atmosphere of the head shops and underground magazines of the hippie era, together with some input from the growing 1970s interest in Britain in producers' co-operatives as a form of economic organization.

But how far did the stated ideology of operation of the new small labels (whether Copeland's entrepreneurship or Rough Trade's rejection of big business methods) coincide with the actual economic logic of their performance? And how far did they change the relation of the musicians to and their control over both the production (origination) of their recorded work and its distribution and consumption?

The customary position of musicians in the production process of the record industry is an unusual one for an industry of the mass production of commodities. The classic role of sellers of labour-power in order to turn out goods for sale is taken by the workers in the record-pressing plants. Musicians are involved at the stage which in other industries would be called *design*: the preparation of a prototype from which mass production can begin. The prototype in the record industry is the 'master tape', the product of work in the recording studio.

Some of those involved in the studio process are in fact wage-labourers. Session musicians and sound engineers receive a single payment relative to the time spent in the studio. But the musicians and (increasingly) the producer whose names will appear as 'authors' of the recorded work have a different relation to the finished product. The image of an author is relevant here, since the position of musician and producer is similar to that of an author of a published printed work who receives not wages for his or her labour but a *royalty*, a payment based solely on the number of copies sold of the work.

This, of course, is also the basis on which the income of the book publisher or record company is dependent. Their economic motivation is to maximize the audience for the work in question, a process which many analysts of the cultural industries have shown to have its implications for forms of origination themselves: the drive for standardization and repetition of previously 'successful' (best-selling) works being among the most important.

The fact that musicians' income is based on the same principle as that of the record company seems at first sight to confer some special status on the performer, an assumption encouraged, for instance, by the publicity photographs published in music trade papers showing contract-signing ceremonies which seem to place transnational executives and teenage guitarists as partners in some great enterprise. (Similar photographs aren't often published when shop-floor workers sign their contracts of employment.) And in a few cases this equality may be a fact. The signing of an established superstar to a contract with a royalty of 20% (as Paul McCartney is reputed to receive from EMI) can result in the artist making as much money from his or her records as the company.

But generally, the royalty system involves the acceptance by the musician of the priorities of the record company in two ways. Artistically, it entails the acceptance of the centrality of the values of the market in the definition of artistic success. Decisions in the recording studio are guided by the issue of whether this sound 'will sell', as well as whether it is musically appropriate. It is therefore easier for record companies to get artists to internalize the values of the market place: the equation of what is good with what is 'commercial' is brought closer. In strict economic terms, the acceptance of the royalty system ensures that the artist shares the risks taken by the record company in marketing his or her work, although in practice many artists are cushioned by the receipt of a non-returnable advance against royalties. The risks derive from the company's relative lack of control over the market. It is clear that there is a definite demand for recorded music, but what is less clear is which *particular* recorded music.

In the terminology of political economy, this peculiarity of cultural commodities has been linked by Nicholas Garnham to 'the nature of its use-values' (i.e., its value to the consumer, the reason why he or she takes pleasure in it). Garnham goes on:

> These have proved difficult if not impossible to pin down in any precise terms and demand for them appears to be similarly volatile. . . . Thus the Cultural Industries, if they are to establish a stable market, are forced to create a relationship with an audience or public to whom they offer not a simple cultural good, but a cultural repertoire across which risks can be spread.[22]

That offering of a 'cultural repertoire' has already been discussed in relation to EMI's policy of issuing singles. What is being established here is the standard record company practice of associating the artist with its own risk-taking. Generally, this involves the artist acquiescing in 'risks' and decisions over which he or she has little or no control.

These can range from any aspect of origination—the choice of material to record, the choice of record producer, the amount of time spent in the studio and the choice of which recorded tracks will be actually released—to marketing and distribution issues. The latter include the promotional budget (advertising and pressure for airplay), presentation (album sleeve design) and pressing costs (how many copies will be manufactured and distributed).

It can broadly be said that in the sphere of the mainstream record industry dominated by the transnational companies, very few artists have any control over marketing and distribution, while nearly all have some control over what happens in the studio. This contrast may, however, be more apparent than real. It may be in the interests of the record company to allow the artist a certain power of decision-making in the recording process partly because in most cases the values of the market are already present 'internally' as a form of discipline, but also because the 'volatility' of audience demand makes it prudent to allow for the emergence of something partially unplanned and novel, which may prove to be popular.

One important economic reason for small record companies offering musicians greater control over their work than the larger ones has already been mentioned. 'Small label economics' involves very little fixed costs in terms of administration and investment. At the height of the punk era, it was generally the case that any record released by an independent label could be sure of selling at least 2,000 copies and thus probably covering its costs. But while this provided a situation in which the barriers to artistic control by the artists themselves were far smaller, it did not automatically guarantee that control. The degree of control varied from case to case, depending on other variables, one of which was clearly the structure of ownership of the small label. Where ownership was vested in the musicians themselves (as with the Desperate Bicycles' Refill Records) such control was virtually inbuilt, while in instances where a label was owned by entrepreneurs to whom bands had a 'royalty' relationship, who held artistic control was a result of negotiation. It depended, for instance, on how far the entrepreneur saw himself as merely a marketing force, or whether his role extended back into the recording studio.

But more crucial in considering the *difference* between punk rock independents and the mainstream companies was the lesser importance of the values of the market for the new independents. Clearly, they were obliged to show some surplus in order to continue operations, but the hold of the drive to maximize audiences and sales was far less strong. Here, the distinction between those who controlled their own distribution and those who relied on mainstream systems was a vital one. To feed original material into the latter, as Miles Copeland saw the new independents inevitably doing, was to surrender it to the definitions of the 'cultural repertoire', the hit parade and the hard sell. To rely instead on one of the several systems of independent distribution was to evade to some degree the insistence of market values and forces and increasingly to offer different definitions of music and different positions and roles for the listener. (Garnham notes that 'some analysts would claim that cultural goods are pure positional goods, their use-value stemming from their function as markers of social and individual difference.') Here, that would mean that punk rock's difference stemmed from how it was distributed and marketed—as 'independent' music—as well as from its intrinsic musical features. It is to some of those musical features that I now turn.

PUNK DIFFERENCE: ONE CHORD WONDERS

'Here's a chord' said *Sniffin' Glue*, 'Now go and form a band.' 'You can't play', the Sex Pistols were told at one of their first performances. 'So what?' replied one of the band.[23] Punk rock had an ability to pick up, amplify and wear with pride the negative comments made about it. Musically, those comments were summed up by The Adverts when they recorded a song called 'One Chord Wonders'.

By denouncing it as 'not music', punk's critics had been joining a lengthy tradition. Each major innovation in popular music during the twentieth century had been subjected to very similar insults. In 1956, the eminent British orchestral conductor Malcolm Sargent had greeted Bill Haley's music with the comment that 'Rock 'n' Roll has been played in the jungle for centuries'.[24] A generation earlier, his counterparts gave this kind of welcome to jazz in America: . . . a raucous and inarticulate shouting of hoarse-throated instruments, with each player trying to outdo his fellows, in fantastic cacophony'.[25]

Apart from its publicity value, the 'not music' description of a new musical form encourages the view that it is also *revolutionary*, having been created *ex nihilo*, rather than formed out of the available existing musical material. But, while the *project* of punk rock, its musical matrix, was new, various styles of the 1970s provided the musical elements it needed to carry out that project.

A relevant starting point is the musical apprenticeship of the first punk rock bands. Like any other young musicians, their first performances contained a fairly high proportion of other people's songs, and clear debts to others' styles. In 1975, for instance, London SS was a rehearsal band containing future members of Clash, the Damned and Generation X. They tried to combine the music of the New York Dolls, MC5 and The Stooges, all bands of the 1970s which adapted and extended the initial punk rock style of the 1960s. Another source, for the early Sex Pistols, was the music of the Small Faces and The Who, British teenage rock of a decade earlier. With the addition of Alice Cooper, the singer whose record Johnny Rotten was miming to when he was asked to join the Sex Pistols, these artists comprise a compact and consistent background. The sound was heavily rhythmic and richly chorded, guitar based with assertive vocals presented (except for the Small Faces' Steve Marriott) with a white rock intonation, generally eschewing the mannerisms of soul singing.

As sound, this was not very far away from parts of the mainstream of the 1970s. Despite the popularity of teenybop and progressive rock, a number of British performers had been successful with music of this type. As far back as 1970, John Lennon, in a punk-like gesture, had presented his Plastic Ono Band in 'Instant Karma', using a stripped-down sound. Many of the performers classed as 'glitter' or 'glam-rock' held to musical values comparable to those of The Who or The Stooges. Slade, T. Rex, Sweet, the Sensational Alex Harvey Band and Gary Glitter all had hit records whose sound re-emphasized rhythm and guitar rock.

While presenting a similar musical emphasis, the early punk rock groups brought an extremism of attitude to the matter of guitar and rhythm rock. An important model for the British instrumental approach was the New York punk band The Ramones, whose first LP was released in Britain in 1976. Even more than the New York Dolls (whose glittery and glam-rock appearance linked them to other musical trends), The Ramones were hailed by the American fanzine champions of punk as the purest incarnation of the spirit of that music. In Britain, the first issue of *Sniffin' Glue* hailed them as standard bearers for 'what 1976 punk rock is all about'. And even the band themselves began to accept this portentous role, as this quotation from one of the band, Tommy Erdelyi, shows:

> We took the rock sound into a psychotic world and narrowed it
> down into a straight line of energy. In an era of progressive rock,

with its complexities and counterpoints, we had a perspective of non-musicality and intelligence that took over from musicianship.[26]

But the special importance of Alice Cooper and the other early influences on the musicians who became the first wave of punk rock performers lay in the sense of outrage which pervaded their stage appearance and behaviour, and in the consequent oppositional position they occupied in relation to the musical establishment. The same could not be said of Slade or T. Rex. The most significant figures here were Alice Cooper and the New York Dolls.

The Alice Cooper style of outrage involved the extensive use of theatrical props. A boa constrictor, a sword to disembowel a dummy, a strait-jacket and so on. Describing a London performance by Cooper in 1971, one reviewer wrote: 'by taking things about as far as they could go short of killing someone on stage, [Alice] confronted us with ourselves and it wasn't nice looking in that particular mirror'.[27] Paul Cook of the Sex Pistols recalled seeing the Dolls on the television programme, *Old Grey Whistle Test*, generally regarded as a stronghold of progressive rock: 'They were really funny. And they just didn't give a shit, you know. And Bob Harris at the end of it went: "tut, tut, tut, mock rock" or something. Just cast it off in two words. I thought it was great though.'[28] As a description, that would fit some of the Sex Pistols' own later performances. In fact, there was a direct link between the New York Dolls and the Sex Pistols, in the shape of Malcolm McLaren. During the group's tour of Britain in 1974, McLaren, proprietor of the Let It Rock clothes shop for teds (which he would soon rename Sex) was also impressed. The Dolls, with their high heels, lipstick and post-Jagger androgyny, were the leaders among a string of New York bands hailed as the 'new punk' by American critics. The names of the others give a sense of their determination to outrage: Teenage Lust, The Harlots of 42nd Street, Street Punk, Kiss, Luger.

The fact that both sex and pistols were already there may not have escaped McLaren's attention when he went to New York in 1975, having taken over the management of The Dolls. He replaced their 'trash transvestite' image with one derived from Westernized images of the Chinese Cultural Revolution—singer David Johansen came on stage waving the Little Red Book—but the group split up soon afterwards. Returning to Britain, McLaren organized the formation of the Sex Pistols towards the end of 1975.

While McLaren's experience with the New York Dolls can be seen as the catalyst for the emergence of British punk rock, there was one British musician whose example proved to be all-pervasive in the ways in which punk itself developed. As early as 1972, David Bowie's music had been described in this way:

> a conscious attempt to throw together some of the most diverse components of pop-rock connecting a thoroughly punky aggressiveness, urgency and non-seriousness with a view of the world that's simultaneously personal, apocalyptic and radical.[29]

Bowie's work tried to go beyond the division between frivolous pop and serious rock characteristic of the music industry of the 1970s. His ambition was to recapture in some way that unity represented by the Beatles in the mid-1960s. Then, the unity seemed to appear spontaneously. In the 1970s, Bowie needed a deliberate strategy of reconstruction involving the explicit discussion of such issues as the nature of the stardom and the society in which he was embroiled. The key locus was his 1972 album, *The Rise And Fall Of Ziggy Stardust*. This was a concept album (a rock notion) executed in three minute songs (a pop form). On it, Bowie set out to tell the story of a type of superstar. The intention, on record and in live performance, was strictly dramatic: though dressed as Ziggy Stardust and singing his songs as well as those of the album's narrator, Bowie intended to *signify* Ziggy, not become him.

There are modes of drama where such signifying is made visible to the audience. Roland Barthes has written of Bunraku, the Japanese marionette theatre, where not only the puppets, but the puppeteers and the sound-makers who provide voices and music are on stage and on view.[30] This is clearly a theatrical work. Even when the voice says 'I', it is telling us of the feelings of a 'she' or 'he'. Contrast this with the extreme of an autobiographical work, where the 'I' of the speaker and of the character coincide. In contrast to musical theatre, much popular singing is heard within the space of the autobiographical: the skill of a singer or songwriter is judged by how far the audience is convinced of the authenticity of the emotion portrayed; the singer must be felt to *really* feel it in their own life. Hence, the ambiguity of Bowie's portrayal of Ziggy allowed the slide into the autobiographical for much of his audience. For them, he *was* Ziggy.

Issues of artifice and autobiography were also to play their part in punk rock. Because Mark Perry and other partisans claimed punk songs to possess a 'realism' lacking in other music, it became important to show that performers like The Clash or The Stranglers were reflecting their own experience. On the other side, the complex status of 'Johnny Rotten' and his relationship to John Lydon the songwriter and performer is usefully illuminated by the Bowie/Ziggy example. It seems to have been the case that this relationship oscillated between one of identification (where there was no disjunction between Rotten's 'We hate you' to the audience and Lydon's general artistic strategy) and one of signification (e.g., the persona of 'anarchist/ antichrist' in 'Anarchy In The UK' or the fractured protagonist of 'Holidays In The Sun' discussed on p.84, where the singer acts out a role rather than 'being himself'). Sometimes the confusion between artifice and autobiography could be dangerous. Lydon/Rotten's symbolic violence on stage led directly to real violence being perpetrated on him in June 1977.

More directly, David Bowie's use of artifice influenced the formation of punk rock through his version of the visual excess and outrage he shared with the New York Dolls and Alice Cooper. Like them, he deliberately opposed the 'natural' denim look of rock with a series of determinedly 'made up' images. In 1971 he was described as 'the pop star with the poison green eyelids and hair like an orange lavatory brush' by one hostile journalist.[31] The different images of the early 1970s revolved around notions or ambiguous connotations of transvestism and bisexuality. The basis principle of production of these images was *camp*, in Susan Sontag's definition: 'the essence of Camp is its love of the unnatural: of artifice and exaggeration.'[32]

The point, then, for Bowie, was again to play with the distinction between first and third person. The artifice and exaggeration rendered ambiguous any simple recognition of Bowie as *in reality* a transvestite or bi-sexual. Through the artifice he was signalling that he was first of all *dressing as* such a person. Sontag's definition of Camp reinforces the point by arguing that Camp sensibility has a semi-permanent relation to the androgynous, to the blurring of the signs of gender difference. Among male punk performers such blurring was rare, while it was emphasized occasionally by Siouxsie Sue (of Siouxsie and the Banshees) in some of her early stage ensembles. Instead, punk visual style, like its attitude towards song lyrics, seemed more concerned to de-sexualize. Performers either set out to make themselves appear distinctly unattractive in conventional terms, or they used 'artifice and exaggeration' in attempts to mock the fetishistic garments of established sexuality: this was the intended function of bondage trousers, fishnet tights, etc., which is fully considered in Chapter 4.

David Bowie affected punk rock in two other ways. First, as a kind of musical patron, he sponsored the work of the key American figures Iggy Pop (of The Stooges) and Lou Reed (formerly of the Velvet Underground) by producing albums of their work in 1972–3 which brought them to the attention of a wide audience, including the future personnel of British punk rock. Secondly, Bowie provided an example of a *vocal accent* that had not been imported from America. This was an essential element for that strand in punk rock that leant towards the autobiographical rather than the dramatized: 'We sing in English, not mimicking some America rock singer's accent. That's just pretending to be something you ain't', said Joe Strummer of The Clash.[33]

Prior to punk rock, British accents in British rock music had been in a small minority, and had acquired specific connotations. During the 1960s there had been a light, comic voice, usually with a cockney accent, to be found on records like 'Right, Said Fred' by the comedy actor Bernard Cribbins and 'Strawberry Fair' by Anthony Newley, better known for his starring role in the British musical, *Stop The World—I Want To Get Off*. The early David Bowie adopted a light tenor similar to Newley's which was not so much comic as whimsically sensitive in its connotations. A less deliberately Anglicized, but still non-American, singing voice could be found on certain records of the 1970s, notably by Slade (in, for instance, 'Mama Weer All Crazee Now') and by John Lennon ('Give Peace A Chance'). These had a new, raw, raucous quality analogous to the shouts of street gangs, football crowds and political marchers. From these sources came the various non-American voices of punk: Ian Dury's transformation of the recitative of comics like Cribbins, Rotten's addition of the exaggerated techniques of melodrama through such devices as long drawn-out syllables and Joe Strummer's own raucous street cries. The new connotations acquired by these voices are discussed in Chapter 3.

In sum, the punk rock approach to its inherited musical material involved two contrasting principles of organization. The first had its links with the orientation in song-making and performance towards 'autobiography' and is suggested in this statement by Johnny Ramone: 'We're playing pure rock 'n' roll with no blues or folk or any of that stuff in it.'[34] This purity, with its refusal of the *purism* of the folk or blues fan, was the other side of the coin of the accusations of incompetence, of the 'one chord wonders' insult. It stressed the need for directness of self-expression unhindered by the sophisticated considerations of musical traditions which had been central to pub rock, or by the complexities of progressive music. It was to be transparent music, through which the singer's feelings and experience could shine directly. As such, it was the proper sort of music to accompany an 'autobiographical' message.

Also, within punk rock, were the principles of artifice, exaggeration and outrage. Here the unnecessary complexities of existing music were to be challenged not by a purer, simpler sound but by a frontal assault. The sounds were to be distorted, dirtied and destroyed, so that their meanings were mangled. At its strongest, this principle of musical organization challenged the very characteristics that punk's other pole had sought to emphasize—simplicity, directness, authenticity. Here, the very basis of the making of meaning through music could be brought into question. The special quality of the Sex Pistols was to combine both music poles of punk in their brief recording career.

PUNK DIFFERENCE: SUBJECT MATTER

Whatever its other differences with the musical mainstream, pub rock shared its lyric concerns. The subject-matter of the songs in the pub rock repertoire belonged to the well-established themes of love, dance, hard luck and so on. But it was here that one of the clearest breaks between punk rock and its contemporaries (including pub rock) soon became apparent. A large proportion of punk rock songs were about different things.

Table 2 compares the subject-matter of the lyrics on the debut albums of the first five punk groups to achieve prominence in 1976–7, with the Top 50 best-selling singles in Britain in 1976. The five punk albums were The Damned: *Damned Damned Damned*; The Clash: *The Clash*; The Stranglers: *IV Rattus Norvegicus*; the Sex Pistols: *Never Mind The Bollocks, Here's The Sex Pistols*; and The Vibrators: *Pure Mania*. A full list of the titles of the songs on the albums and of the Top 50 can be found in Appendix 1.

Table 2 The subject matter of the lyrics of five punk groups.

	Punk	Top 50
Romantic and sexual relationships	21% (13)	60% (31)
Sexuality	15% (9)	—
First person feelings	25% (16)	3% (2)
Social and political comment	25% (16)	4% (2)
Music and dancing	7% (4)	18% (10)
Second and third person	7% (4)	3% (2)
Novelty	—	8% (4)
Instrumental	—	4% (2)

Figures in brackets denote the actual number of songs in that category.

Source for Top 50: *Star File* 1977.

Table 2 measures only one dimension of recordings, and not necessarily the most important. The methodology involved—that of content analysis—is equally a limited one. It relies, for instance, on abstracting from the totality of organized sound simply a theme of the lyric. In later chapters, I shall be dealing in greater depth with the linguistic, vocal and musical dimensions of punk records. Nevertheless, content analysis can clearly reveal a divergence between punk songs and those which typified the mainstream in 1976. The categories chosen are particularly valuable in this respect since they correspond to those into which the music industry itself has traditionally sorted songs. 'Ballads,' 'dance' and 'novelties' were the three main recognized types in the pre-rock era, and Table 2 suggests that, at this level at least, the popular mainstream may have changed less than the concept of a 'rock 'n' roll revolution' might imply. Taking 'romantic and sexual relationships' to approximate to the subject matter of the ballad and adding the songs in the 'music and dancing' and 'novelty' categories gives a total of 86% of the Top 50 corresponding to the industry's established modes. The equivalent figure for punk is 28%.

What, then, were the categories of subject-matter in which punk exceeded the mainstream? Table 2 shows a distinction between 'romance' and 'sexuality'. In the first category, the vocalist is concerned with those 'affairs of the heart' that make up the conventional discourse of romantic love. Usually the beloved, would-be beloved or ex-beloved is addressed directly: 'You Broke My Heart' (Vibrators) and 'Don't Go Breaking My Heart' (Elton John and Kiki Dee).

A lyric of 'sexuality' is one where the specifically sexual is given precedence over the sentimental, if indeed that appears. It is characteristically a lyric of lust, obsession or disgust. Often, the vocalist is a commentator on sexual behaviour of some kind. The Clash's 'Janie Jones' describes a white-collar worker's obsession with a figure at the centre of a 1970s prostitution and corruption scandal, while 'Peaches' by The Stranglers is the confession of a seaside voyeur and ogler of women. Another Stranglers' lyric, 'London Lady', belongs on the borderline between the 'romantic' and 'sexuality' categories, since the vocalist describes his 'lady' in a highly objectified and hostile manner.

The 'first person feelings' lyric occurs when the *main* focus of attention is the singer's own emotions or situation. If others are referred to, they are primarily there as objects off whom his or her feelings bounce. 'New Rose' by The Damned, for instance, foregrounds the singer's elation rather than the 'her' with whom that feeling is associated. That song, in fact, is among only two of the 16 punk lyrics in this category which present what could be termed 'positive' feelings. The flavour of the remainder can be suggested by some titles: 'No Feelings' and 'Pretty Vacant' (Sex Pistols), 'Born To Kill' (Damned), 'What's My Name' (Clash) and 'Ugly' (Stranglers). In contrast, the Top 50 has very little that fits here. Part of Abba's 'Fernando' is concerned with the narrator's feelings of loss and nostalgia, while Paul McCartney's 'Let 'Em In' deals with the singer's warmth towards family and friends.

There have been, however, areas of popular song in which these lyrics of 'first person feelings' were as prominent as they were in punk rock. Bed-sitter singer—songwriters went in for much emotional self-examination, from Paul Simon's 'I Am A Rock' onwards, and then there were the lyrics of 'states of consciousness' to be found in the late 1960s. These presentations of emotional states unfocused by another person were an important component of what was described as 'psychedelic' music. 'Within You Without You' by the Beatles and Donovan's 'Sunshine Superman' were well-known examples.

The egotism of punk rock emphasized different feelings, though. While psychedelia usually presented well-being as the solitary emotion, and the singer-songwriters went in for angst or self-pity, punk egotists were frustrated, angry, or apathetic. In the case of The Clash and, to a lesser extent the Sex Pistols, those feelings were found in other songs, but as a minor theme, subordinated to commentaries on aspects of the social and political system. Against this quarter of all punk lyrics, the Top 50 provided only Rod Stewart's 'The Killing Of Georgie' (about the murder of a gay friend) and Brian Ferry's patrician reading of the R&B call to action 'Let's Stick Together'.

The overwhelming number (ten out of 16) of 'social and political comment' lyrics came from the first Clash album. The topics and targets of these and the other songs in this category included royalty, the USA, dead-end jobs, the police, watching television, record companies ('EMI' by the Sex Pistols), sexual hypocrisy, war, anarchy and riots. Though similar issues had entered mainstream song lyrics before, they had been infrequent and, as the 'protest song' of the 1960s, in a different manner. Those lyrics of Bob Dylan, Tom Paxton and others had been more precisely songs of persuasion, since most were sung at an audience whose minds the singer wanted to change: 'How many roads must a man walk down/Before you call him a man?' sang Bob Dylan to a listener he called 'my friend'. Other Dylan songs approached the task of persuasion more obliquely, turning on its head the ideology of the war-makers in lyrics like 'With God On Our Side'. And there was a third type, less common in Dylan's protest lyrics, that of the outright denunciation. The finger-pointing 'Masters Of War' is a supreme example. That ranting tone (compared to the irony of 'With

God On Our Side' and the plaintiveness of 'Blowin' In The Wind') was adopted by Barry McGuire for what was stylistically a punky protest hit, 'Eve Of Destruction'; it re-appeared in Britain on *Third World War*, a 1971 heavy rock album by an eponymous group whose lyrics dealt with MI5 (the British Secret Service), the music business, the life of a local skinhead, communism, 'Working Class Man' and 'Ascension Day' which cried 'Power to the people when we rise'.

Third World War made a small media impact—this was soon after John Lennon's 'Working Class Hero' and 'Power To The People'—and its concern to denounce and literally to protest, rather than persuade, made it an isolated precursor of The Clash's 1976 ranting style of lyric. *Third World War*, though, offered a notion of political rhetoric that took social class as its reference point—it was a kind of marxist heavy metal. The lyrics of punk social and political comment, in their turn, contributed much to the claims which have been made for a radical political purpose in punk during the 1976–8 period. These claims were usually based on one of two arguments: that which saw punk lyrics *reflecting* the political events or beliefs of the time, and that which saw in them a political *analysis* fitting in with the far-leftist political groups of the period.

The first issue to establish is that while there was a significant increase in both unemployment and inflation during the 1975–7 period—the jobless total dropped briefly in 1978–9—adverse comment on the parlous nature of Britain was not confined to the young or the Left. The whole of public discourse in Britain was subject in the mid-1970s to periodic outbursts of 'crisis' or 'doom' rhetoric. It was this topic to which the progressive rock group Supertramp referred in the title of their 1975 album, *Crisis?—What Crisis?*

The principal event which acted as a trigger for the crisis rhetoric was the national miners' strike of 1974. Following the same union's successful strike in 1972 (which had been the first national dispute in the industry since the General Strike of 1926), the Conservative Government of Edward Heath called an election claiming that the union had usurped the government's right to govern. In the wake of Heath's narrow defeat by Harold Wilson's Labour Party, media speculation in the summer of 1974 concentrated on the threat to democracy from 'hyperinflation' and on possible moves by the military.

In particular, publicity was given to retired soldiers like General Sir Walter Walker and Colonel David Stirling who tried to set up 'citizen armies to cope with the immediate crisis following a general strike or near general strike.'[35] Although such proposals were roundly dismissed by the pundits, the issue had been firmly placed on the agenda of media discussion. *The Times*, for instance, had former Government minister Lord Chalfont asking, 'Could Britain Be Heading For A Military Takeover?', while Charles Douglas Home, a senior journalist and future editor of the paper, opined that the Army could be brought in to 'protect the community from the more violent consequences of hyper-inflation—food riots, looting and major demonstrations'. Further comment came from Peter Jay, Economics Editor of *The Times* and a future British Ambassador to Washington ('the last chance for British democracy before extinction') and from the newspaper's editorial column itself: 'The probability is that we shall not be able to maintain our present system in its present form because it does not appear to have any good answer to inflation.'

That type of overblown rhetoric coincided in the mid-1970s with a number of political incidents which led those setting the tone of media commentary to conclude that a new violence had arrived in Britain. This period saw a series of bomb attacks by the IRA on targets in England, including the explosion at a Birmingham pub which killed 21 people in 1974. It also saw a revival of fascist organizations in the form of the National Front and the death of Kevin Gately, a student taking part in an anti-fascist demonstration. And it saw the heavy policing of the Notting Hill Carnival in 1976—an event organized by London's West Indian population—which ended in street battles between black youths and the police. This incident directly inspired The Clash's 'White Riot' which expressed admiration for the insurgent spirit of the blacks and said 'We [the white youth] wanna riot of our own'.

The apocalyptic tone of that lyric and the other songs of social and political comment in punk, then, were very much part of a more general tone of public discourse. This point is usefully made in Dick Hebdige's *Subculture: The Meaning Of Style* which notes that even a style apparently as alien to established society as punk must include:

> Some of the *preferred* meanings and interpretations, those favoured by and transmitted through the authorised channels of mass communication . . . the punks appropriated the rhetoric of crisis which had filled the airwaves and editorials during the period and translated it into tangible (and visible) terms.[36]

Punk lyrics dealing with the theme of work and unemployment bore out Hebdige's observation. 'Right To Work' by Chelsea was one of the best known of the early punk songs. Its title echoed the slogan of a left-wing campaign against the rising jobless totals of the mid-1970s. But though the song is a protest about 'standing around just waiting for a career', its diagnosis of the *cause* of unemployment was impeccably right-wing: the lyric blames the power of the trade unions.

'Career Opportunities' from The Clash's first album did not, like 'Right To Work', adopt the 'preferred interpretations' of right-wing ideology, but neither did it adopt the Left's alternative which called for the creation of full employment to fulfil the 'right to work'. It emphasized instead a general critique of the work-ethic and of the powerlessness of those in the most menial occupations. In so far as an ideology can be extrapolated from the lyric of 'Career Opportunities' it resembles those of anarchist positions which rejected the whole concept of 'wage-slavery' and of Situationism, a set of ideas against which several of the 'back room' figures of punk rock (including Malcolm McLaren and Tony Wilson) had brushed in the 1960s (see p.173 for a fuller discussion of the Situationist influence in punk rock).

The degree of divergence between the way punk lyrics dealt with the unemployment issue and that of the organized left can be seen by comparing them with those of The Derelicts, a band which included Dan Kelleher, a former colleague of Joe Strummer's. This was linked closely with the politics of claimants' unions (which fought for the rights of people on welfare benefits) and of squatting (the movement to put homeless people into empty houses). The agit-prop songs of The Derelicts, such as 'Three Little Magistrates Sitting In A Row' with its nursery rhyme echoes, were designed to satirize figures of authority and raise the spirits of those struggling against the system. The lyrics of The Clash had no such specific strategy: as Hebdige indicates, their strength lay in the tangible images they conjured up, not in some flawless ideological argument.

If punk rock's concern with political and social topics took its cue from general ideological trends, its achievement was nevertheless to introduce such themes into songs, something which the mainstream of popular music had successfully resisted for a decade. The final subject-matter category which needs some explanation is one where the difference between punk and the Top 50 of 1976 is less marked: that of 'second or third person'. In these lyrics, the topic is a person other than the vocalist, and not a lover. Usually in punk rock, these lyrics are finger-pointing exercises. 'Liar' and 'Problem' by the Sex Pistols are examples of these, with the latter's approach very similar to that of Bob Dylan's 'Ballad Of A Thin Man' ('Something is happening and you don't know what it is, do you, Mr Jones?').

Punk offers no examples of the Top 50 categories 'instrumentals' and 'novelties'. In lacking any tunes without words, it followed the general trend of beat group music from the Beatles to the Bay City Rollers. Novelties are comedy songs (The Wurzels' parodies in 1976 of 'Una Paloma Blanca' and of Melanie's 'Brand New Key') and those involving current fashions ('Convoy' by C.W. McCall, using the argot of citizens band radio, and 'Jeans On' by David Dundas, an adaptation of an advertising jingle). Again like other popular song genres, punk included comedy as an acknowledged exception, in the contrasting forms of Ivor Biggun's puerile bawdy and John Cooper Clarke's surreal wit.

Both punk rock's supporters and detractors in 1976–7 emphasized the ways in which it was alien to the contemporary musical mainstream: its 'do-it-yourself' stance, its lack of musical sophistication and its concern with different and taboo lyric subject-matter. And the eagerness of both sides to see punk as 'new' for their own reasons, clouded how far it represented a re-working of motifs familiar from rock music history: the battle of the entrepreneur against the corporation, for example, or the narcissism of some lyrics and the social protest of others. A number of A&R personnel from the established record companies in particular, began seriously to wonder whether punk might not turn out to be a 'Next Big Thing' to revive the fortunes of the music business.

NOT THE NEXT BIG THING

During 1977 and the early part of 1978, those A&R men took out their cheque books and signed punk groups to recording contracts. The principal signings included the following:

> **A&M:** Sex Pistols
> **Anchor:** Adverts
> **CBS:** Clash, Vibrators
> **Chrysalis:** Generation X, Blondie, Stiff Little Fingers
> **EMI/Harvest:** The Saints, Tom Robinson Band, Sex Pistols, Wire, X-Ray Spex
> **Ensign (distributed by Phonogram):** Boomtown Rats
> **Polydor:** Jam, Jolt, Sham 69, Siouxsie and the Banshees
> **Sire (distributed by WEA):** Rezillos, Undertones
> **United Artists:** Stranglers, Buzzcocks, 999
> **Track:** Johnny Thunders
> **Virgin:** Penetration, Sex Pistols, XTC, X-Ray Spex

Perhaps the fact that even here the 1970s companies (Chrysalis, Virgin) were more active than the multinationals indicates that before the end of 1977 it was clear to the record industry that punk would not become any kind of Big Thing. There had not been 'the predicted domination by the punks and their associates' wrote one relieved commentator.[37]

To understand how far punk rock fell short of the kind of 'colonization' of the musical mainstream achieved in 1963–4 by the Beatles and the groups which followed in their wake, it is useful to look at the Top 30 singles charts. For, while these are not an infallible guide to actual sales figures, they indicate which artists and musical genres are in the spotlight of the music industry's institutions, and which are likely to influence future developments in the recording studios as the record companies seize on them as blueprints for success.

The album charts are also of relevance here (and in 1977 just three of the Top 50 were of punk origin), but by 1977 the rigid separation between singles and albums—paralleling that between teenybop and progressive rock artists and audiences—had begun to disappear. There were now probably a majority of recording artists who aimed to succeed in both spheres. In Table 3 the figures for 1963 and 1964 refer to beat groups and R&B artists, while those for 1977 and 1978 are of punk bands. In each case, there is some problem in deciding which performers should be included but, as a guide, the earlier figures exclude certain solo artists (Cilia Black and Sandie Shaw, for instance) while the punk totals leave out Nick Lowe, Elvis Costello, Squeeze and Ian Dury. A full list of the 1977–8 hits included here is given in Appendix 2.

Table 3

	1963	1977	1964	1978
Number of singles in Top 30 from the new genre	25	13	63	25
Number of artists	11	7	31	15

A second aspect of any Next Big Thing was its ability to increase the overall record market. It was felt that the success of any new stars would attract many people whose previous interest in music had been minimal, and would also 'capture' a new teenage generation for music as the Beatles and Rolling Stones had. In that earlier period, the numbers of records sold rose by 11% between 1962 and 1963 and by 19% the following year. But for the two years from 1976–1978, the corresponding figures were only 3.5% and 6.6%. Not only that, these rises were actually smaller than in the earlier years of the 1970s. The average annual increase in the 1970–6 period had been around 10%.

Punk rock, then, had failed to emulate the kind of commercial success of that earlier Next Big Thing, and consequently its stylistic impact on the musical mainstream was a limited one. The factors contributing to the fate of punk rock in the 1977–8 period can be divided into external and internal ones. Externally there was competition from another candidate for Next Big Thing, the disco music genre, there was a 'split' in the music industry's attitude towards punk, with some parts of it (notably radio stations) intent on excluding it, and there was a more general social and state harassment involving exceptional media hostility and many acts of censorship and banning. Two internal features of punk rock as it emerged, which are pertinent to its eventual outcome, were the stress on exclusivity already noted in Sniffin' Glue's editorializing and what can be called the 'negative unity' which characterized its very existence as a compact musical genre. What happened to punk rock in the period in which it was publicly recognized as such a genre was the result of the complex interaction and pressure of these various factors.

Disco records made particular headway in the singles market in 1977–8, notably with the rise of Boney M and then the Saturday Night Fever phenomenon. In particular, 1978 was a year in which four of the eight highest ever selling singles were released by Boney M and Travolta/Newton-John. (Christmas 1977 had been the release date of the actual best-seller, Wings' 'Mull Of Kintyre'.) These unusually large sales for individual records coupled with the low overall growth of the market would leave little economic space for the other new music, punk (this is assuming that a certain conservatism of buying habits prevailed in other music areas, e.g., TV albums, progressive rock). Additionally, disco music provided one ingredient lacking in punk (even if it was all that it did provide!): dance music. Popular music history, particularly since the 1950s, suggests that any music capable of re-organizing the mainstream (as rock 'n' roll and the beat music of the 1960s did) must contain a dance element. No ballad genre, including that of Bob Dylan and the singer—songwriters, has achieved a comparable impact. And though punks did have their own dance (the pogo) this was sufficiently deviant in conventional terms as to be seen as 'not dancing' just as punk sounds were frequently dismissed as 'not music'.

Disco, too, was 'radio music', while punk emphatically wasn't. Radio play has a crucial role in the popular music machine, in the economy of hit-making. Broadcasting is one of the main 'gatekeeping' institutions within popular music. As a sociological term, a 'gatekeeper' is a figure who interprets a product for its intended audience, acting as an intermediary between producer and consumer. From the standpoint of the producer, the smoothest functioning of gatekeeping is when that intermediary shares the aims and values of the producer: the encouragement of consumption. This pure symbiosis between gatekeeper and producer is reached only perhaps in fashion and motor car journalism, where there is no disjunction between the interests of the two. In popular music, such a symbiosis is less common. The music press varies in its own goals and aims, with 'artistic' critical criteria as important as the 'consumer guide' approach. With radio, the gap between programmers and record companies is more systematic in origin. Music radio wants to attract audiences not as consumers (or potential consumers) of records, but as either a market for advertisers (commercial radio) or as a largest possible number at a certain time of the day (BBC radio). Thus, the criteria for 'good music'—in radio, what will hold the right type or number of listeners—may well diverge from that of the record companies.

A keynote phrase for radio programming was 'easy listening': the music must not disrupt the presumed 'majority mood' among those tuned in, a mood of relaxation or distraction. Since one of punk rock's avowed aims was disruption, it was virtually inevitable that it never found any place in the playlists for the mainstream daytime programming. It was relegated to the various 'specialist' rock programmes in the evenings or at weekends.

That distancing of radio from punk rock was reinforced by the 'moral panic'[38] surrounding the music, its exponents and their audiences following the Bill Grundy incident of December 1976. Along with the Sex Pistols' God Save The Queen' record, this was the most effective piece of provocation of the punk era.

Previous rock performers had gained a generic reputation for various types of immoral behaviour through an accretion of petty misdemeanours (drug arrests, urinating against petrol station walls, etc.), but these had always occurred 'off-screen'. The brilliance of the Grundy affair was that it was a live television event, at 'family viewing' time. It took place on Thames Television's news magazine show *Today*, of which Grundy, a middle-aged 'down to earth' former newspaper journalist, was one of the comperes. After a clip of the Sex Pistols in performance had been shown, Grundy began to interview the band by referring to their contract with EMI:

> **Grundy:** I am told you have received £40,000 from a record company. Doesn't that seem to be slightly opposed to an anti-materialistic way of life.
> **Glen Matlock:** No. The more the merrier.
> **Grundy:** Really?

Glen Matlock: Yeah Yeah.

Grundy: Tell me more then.

Steve Jones: Fucking spent it, didn't we.

Grundy: I don't know. Have you?

Glen Matlock: Down the boozer.

Grundy: Really? Good Lord. Now I want to know one thing. Are you serious or are you just trying to make me laugh?

Glen Matlock: Mmmmmm.

Grundy: Beethoven, Mozart, Bach and Brahms have all died . . .

Glen Matlock: They're all heroes of ours, ain't they?

Grundy: Really? What were you saying sir?

Johnny Rotten: Oh yes. They really turn us on.

Grundy: Well, what if they turn other people on?

Johnny Rotten: (whispered) That's just their tough shit.

Grundy: It's what?

Johnny Rotten: Nothing—a rude word. Next question.

Grundy: No no. What was the rude word?

Johnny Rotten: Shit.

Grundy: Was it really? Good heavens you frighten me to death. What about you girls behind. Are you married or are you just enjoying yourself?

Siouxsie Sue: I've always wanted to meet you.

Grundy: Did you really? We'll meet afterwards, shall we?

Steve Jones: You dirty sod, you dirty old man.

Grundy: Keep going chief, keep going. You've got another five seconds, say something outrageous.

Steve Jones: You dirty bastard.

Grundy: Go on, again.

Steve Jones: You dirty fucker!

Grundy: What a clever boy!

Steve Jones: You fucking rotter!

Grundy: (to camera) Well, that's it for tonight. I'll be seeing you soon, I hope I'm not seeing YOU again.[39]

The interview lasted all of one minute, 40 seconds but during it Bill Grundy both managed to sketch in the popular stereotype of punk and to expose himself as envious, patronizing and vulgar. The envy was clear in his first jibe which accused the Pistols of hypocrisy in taking EMI's money, in the mistaken belief that punks shared the 'anti-materialism' of the hippies. This was followed by a forlorn attempt to cow the group by wielding the authority of classical music, by the grotesque sexism of his remarks to 'you girls behind' and his final 'triumph' in goading the band to live up to the punk stereotype through swearing.

The massive media uproar and the cancellation of concerts which followed this incident can only be understood in terms of the peculiar myth of 'family viewing' which colours the organization of British television. Its origins in the BBC monopoly had led to a first law of programming which assumed a single, national audience at any one time. This then became directed by the fact that TV consumption was private and domestic (rather than the public position of a cinema or concert hall audience) into a definition of that audience as a 'family' one. There was an assumption, long since dissipated in other media, that this watching family was fundamentally culturally homogeneous and that the 'box in the corner' should conform to the supposed norms of decency and banality which defined the discourse of the family circle. To then have a broadcast set-to like the Grundy-Pistols row could be felt as equivalent to a direct invasion of one's home by the stereotyped juvenile delinquent of the era mouthing obscenities (and at 'tea-time'—another ritual of 'family life'). Such was the sense of a violation of domesticity, that in one home the Grundy incident caused an actual explosion when a patriarch kicked in the screen of his TV set: 'I don't want this sort of muck coming into my home at teatime.'[40] (And even the 'muck' itself had a certain style: 'Fucking rotter' mingled street-corner adjective with mockingly aristocratic noun.)

The notoriety earned by the Sex Pistols and by punk rock as a result of the Grundy incident continued into 1977. Its repercussions eventually caused EMI to cancel the group's contract after the company (with memories of the various incidents surrounding the Rolling Stones a decade earlier) had at first tried to ride out the storm. But this was part of a contradictory response to punk on the part of the music industry as a whole. With the important exception of the Sex Pistols, no bands were 'sacked' by mainstream record companies (and the Pistols themselves were eventually taken on board by Virgin Records). But some of the records released and promoted by those companies suffered from censorship by broadcasting stations and sporadic refusals to stock them by chain stores infected by fits of morality. A number of concerts were also cancelled by theatre owners (principally local councils) on grounds of either predicted 'crowd violence' or general 'immorality'. Although this undoubtedly had some effect in isolating punk from the musical mainstream, it is worth recalling that the arrival of rock 'n' roll in Britain was marked by strong hostility too. A dozen towns banned the Bill Haley film, *Rock Around The Clock*, and the official chorus of bishops, MPs and other types of musicians denounced rock 'n' roll. But rock survived as a musical force. If punk didn't (or only as a minor genre), were the causes within itself?

To answer that, it's worth returning to the contradiction between the record companies' response and that of the other institutions involved in popular music. That contradiction can be reformulated to state that while 'private' consumption of punk was encouraged by the release and promotion of records, its 'public' space was severely restricted through lack of airplay and through lack of large halls to play in. This had two effects. First, some musicians were encouraged to dissociate themselves from 'punk' and re-classify their work as 'new wave', thereby hoping to evade the stigma and hoping to get airplay and live performance spaces. Secondly, the contrast between punk's private accessibility and its public invisibility strengthened what earlier were called the 'exclusivist' tendencies within it.

In considering those tendencies it is important to distinguish the tendency towards independence in punk rock from that towards separation from the mainstream. The distinction is that while 'independence' (expressed mainly in terms of production and distribution of records) may be concerned to reach the same people as are reached by the musical mainstream, but by a different route, 'separation' is concerned with consolidating a special community of punks, to whom punk rock will have special meanings.

Quite often, though, these two aspects of punk rock exclusivity were to be found together. The early issues of *Sniffin' Glue*, for instance, both championed its list of musicians whose work was against the mainstream in its assertion of the true values of rock 'n' roll, and began to address its audience as 'punks', separating them from 'footballs', 'discos' and 'ageing hippies'. In order to align oneself with *Sniffin' Glue*'s list (as, later, with independent records) it was necessary only to be a certain kind of *listener* (one who could make the link between Frank Zappa and the Ramones). But the other kind of identification ('punk' not 'disco') implied allegiance to an overall style or even subculture within which music would eventually become only one sort of badge to indicate belonging.

The high point of this punk exclusivity in its stronger, 'independent' sense was undoubtedly the 'God Save The Queen' episode. Released by Virgin in June 1977, at the height of the national hysteria over the celebration of the Queen's Jubilee, this

Sex Pistols' single, an anti-national anthem, was promptly denied any airplay by all broadcasting stations in Britain. It was also banned by the main chain-stores selling records throughout the country, while several publications refused to print an advertisement showing a picture of Elizabeth II with her eyes masked out by the song title and her mouth covered by the group's name.

The effect of this repression was to drive the record 'underground', so that it could be obtained only in certain smaller shops and could be heard only in private homes. But that process was also massively advertised in the establishment media. The press frothed over the 'treasonable' nature of the song's lyrics, while the very institutions that had refused to recognize 'God Save The Queen' by playing or selling it were forced to re-admit it when its sales figures won it a place in their best-seller lists. One chain-store 'listed' the disc by leaving the space next to Number 2 in its chart list blank, thereby causing even more interest in the Sex Pistols' record.

This 'inaudible' yet widely heard record sold an estimated 250,000 copies which, thanks to the censorship and boycott, were listened to in an unusually attentive way. That, too, had been unintentionally prescribed by the music industry's institutions. By defining 'God Save The Queen's' difference from the norm as total, they virtually instructed anyone with access to it that its effects on them would be totally different from the leisure pleasure provided by the context of daytime radio or *Top Of The Pops*. And, of course, most of the 250,000 purchasers of the disc were not 'punks', nor did buying it confer that status on them. But the role offered to the listener to 'God Save The Queen' was set apart from both the established music industry and the official royalist celebrations. It was an independent and oppositional role.

That oppositional role was crucial to the maintaining of an identity for punk rock through a 'negative unity', the last of the five main factors which influenced what happened to the music in 1977–8. Earlier emergent genres in British popular music had been unified by a key stylistic factor—the commitment to the sound and repertoire of Chicago blues for R&B or by that plus a geographical one—the case of Merseybeat. Although each of these played a small part in the way punk rock came to be regarded as an homogeneous genre, the most important element in the process was the common sense of *exclusion* from (and rejection of) mainstream music and its industry felt during 1975–6 by a variety of musicians. They shared the same oppositional stance towards the music business, and as long as all remained outside it and unwanted by it, the considerable differences of musical approach between the various punk groups went generally unnoticed.

But that negative unity could only be retained as long as the boundary between punk rock and the mainstream remained clearly defined. As soon as some industry figures began to consider punk to have potential in the Next Big Thing area with the consequent signing of bands, the outsider status of punk began to crumble, as did its character as a genre. For success in the singles and album charts for The Stranglers and The Clash led not to them being identified by disc-jockeys and journalists as the part of punk rock which had 'made it', but led to their re-classification as variants of mainstream rock, albeit 'radical' or extreme ones. The point about the underlying musical heterogeneity of punk rock which made its unity always provisional is clinched when that re-classification is compared to what happened to other punk hit-makers. Neither the Sex Pistols or Poly Styrene's X-Ray Spex, for instance, were easily assimilable to the norms of the musical mainstream. Arguably, too much of their musical material was designed to be dissonant with those norms. This was undoubtedly part of the reason why neither band survived the crumbling of punk rock, a process which occurred simultaneously with the music's greatest commercial successes in 1977–8.

Punk's negative unity is even more clearly apparent when it is considered alongside those features which provided the wide range of reggae music in the 1970s with a more organic form of unity. Reggae in fact exercised a strong fascination for many punk musicians, and some incorporated reggae elements into their music. The Clash recorded Junior Murvin's reggae hit 'Police And Thieves' on their first album, while Generation X put a 'Wild Dub' on the B side of their 'Wild Youth' single (a dub is an instrumental version of a song), The Slits used British reggae producer Dennis Bovell, and Mark Perry's Alternative TV used reggae rhythms. The Police, whose origins were in the punk milieu of Step Forward Records, went on to develop a best-selling synthesis of rock and reggae.

But an equal number of punk bands preferred simply to admire reggae rather than play it. The reason, perhaps, was that reggae offered the ideal of a music that seemed spontaneously to embody a culture and a politics. It had roots in an oppressed social group whose religio-political beliefs (Rastafarianism) provided a powerful and poetic means of expression. As such, reggae had achieved for young blacks what some punk ideologues wanted to claim their music was doing for the 'dispossessed' among young whites. But the effortless ability of much reggae to achieve that integration of politics, poetry, rhythm and cultural identity illuminated the very different position of punk rock and the 'punks'. Punk's intense mixture of autobiography and artifice, of the avant-garde and the social realist, of independence and separatism ensured that whatever it was it couldn't become a white equivalent to reggae. Instead, that unstable mixture began to separate out as soon as sections of the music industry began warily to embrace elements of punk rock. What occurred afterwards is told in Chapter 6. Before that, the language, the sounds and the look of punk rock will be considered in detail.

Two
Naming

Meaning in popular music has various sources: sounds, words, pictures, gestures. Names—of genres, individual musicians, bands, record labels and fanzines—play an important but often overlooked part in the process of production of meaning for the audience. Whether a name is familiar or new, it can set up expectations of the music which is to come, through what the name positively connotes but also through what it appears to exclude. One starting point in the search for the differences between punk rock and other musics is therefore the range and pattern of names within it, beginning with the term 'punk' itself. The preceding chapter considered the denotation of punk rock—the musical elements which the phrase came to stand for, to denote. Here, the focus is on the connotations of that and other names: those associations which have become attached to the word through its various conventional uses in social situations over time.

The *Shorter Oxford English Dictionary* offers six definitions of 'punk' and 'punky'. The earliest recorded usage of the term was as 'a prostitute, strumpet, harlot' (1596). This origin in the denigration of women came full circle 380 years later when the editor of the premier punk rock fanzine, *Sniffin' Glue*, wrote that 'Punks are not girls, if it comes to the crunch we'll have no option but to fight back.'[1]

Later shifts in the word's use brought it to mean a rotten piece of wood, a smouldering substance for lighting fireworks, Chinese incense, and at the turn of the twentieth century in the United States, anything or anyone worthless, 'specifically a homosexual' (1917). In his *Underground Dictionary*, Eugene F. Landy gave three senses of 'punk': 'a weak person, a homosexual, one who retaliates in an underhand manner'.

It was, then, in American English that 'punk' survived into modern times. The only British usage to be found was a 'folk' one, in a children's Hallowe'en custom in Somerset. There Punkie Night was celebrated with artistically carved, glowing lanterns made from mangel-wurzels—'punkies'.[2] In America, 'punk' had an equally specific use in the dialect of some very low status groups, and a gradually growing general sense in the mainstream language. In his *Hard Travellin'*, Kenneth Allsop wrote that a punk is 'a catamite or young male "wife" of a sodomite' in hobo terminology.[3] Writing to *Melody Maker* in 1976, Val Wilmer mentioned the same meaning as current among the black prison population. The misogynist edge to the word was retained even as it was transferred to an all-male milieu. Youthfulness was the common characteristic of that use of the word and of certain workplace forms, like the 'whistle punk' of Canadian logging, a boy with a low grade job. And youthfulness was retained as 'punk' transferred from these specialized and marginalized discourses to the American linguistic mainstream as a 'slang' term. In the detective and gangster literature of the 1930s and 1940s—the world of Dashiell Hammett and Raymond Chandler—youthful gunmen were sometimes derisively referred to as 'punks'.

The shift from the discourse of 'deviant' sexuality to that of generalized insult was parallel with the history of the word 'bugger' in British English. And just as 'bugger' could be softened by an element of affection in its derisive use, so 'punk' came to take on more neutral emotional connotations. Hence, it became one of the words available to describe the new breed of young actors of the 1950s like James Dean and Marlon Brando. The often remarked connection between those figures and rock 'n' roll, in the person of Elvis Presley, opened the way for 'punk' eventually to become part of the terminology of popular music stylistics.

STAGE NAMES

The important thing about the naming of bands and of individual singers and musicians is that it offers the chance of choosing a name and through it an identity. It can overcome the purely contingent relationship between a person and their name in everyday life. The name deliberately chosen can then take on a *motivated* relation to the person or group to which it refers, reflecting or pointing to their significant characteristics. In some cultures, of course, this is a general feature of giving names: the popular notion of the source of North American Indian names is one example. In Western Christian cultures, this privilege is reserved for only a certain group of people: those whose job is to entertain professionally and in many instances to provide an ideal image of some kind. It is important that their name contributes to this image, rather than detract from it.

The change from Harry Webb to 'Cliff Richard' is a relevant instance. 'Cliff' was one of a group of terse monosyllables (Vince, Chuck) which had an air of modernity in the 1950s, and a hint of pace in life-style. But the addition of a second name that worked both as forename and surname crucially produced the connotation of a boy without a last name, the essence of youthfulness, a person who could never be a 'Mister'. Alternatively, the name had its alibi as a 'real' name (unlike Rotten or Vicious), offering its bearer as an epitome of perfect ordinariness, the quality of a certain kind of stardom ('the boy next door'). This kind of naming, in fact, is an example of what Roland Barthes calls 'myth'.[4] The name, with all its connotations of 'youth', its Peter Pan associations, presents itself merely as natural and innocent, as *denotation*. In so doing, it can suggest that 'Cliff Richard's' qualities (youth, honesty, charm) are equally natural, rather than the product of a process of cultural (show business) construction, of which the *choice* of name is a crucial part.

Such a mechanism is less likely to be found in the naming of groups or bands, since these have no 'everyday' equivalent. There has, nevertheless, been a tendency to present groups as 'families', to trade on an association between musical and domestic harmony (a secularized version of 'the family that prays together, stays together'?). Of course, from the Carter Family of the 1920s and the Andrews Sisters and Mills Brothers of the 1940s to the Osmonds, Jacksons and Bee Gees (Brothers Gibb), many vocal groups were in reality related. But this does not invalidate the point that, just like unrelated groups (the Brothers Four or the Springfields) they chose to present themselves in a way which foregrounded the family. Punk rock, not unexpectedly, was almost bereft of such family names. The only instance was that of The Ramones whose assumption of a common surname (Tommy Ramone, Joey Ramone, etc.) was done in such a way that its character as an assumed name was made abundantly clear.

Another 'naturalistic' formula for group names in popular music involves the use of a leader's name plus followers. In rock music in Britain, this approach was especially evident in the late 1950s and early 1960s. Peter Jay and the Jaywalkers, Brian Poole and the Tremeloes, Gerry and the Pacemakers and Faron's Flamingoes were examples, with the last two also taking on the connotation of 'youthfulness' through their absence of surname. The Peter Jay example and, more famously, Bill Haley and the Comets, introduce another aspect of group names, the pun and play on words (here the similarity of 'Haley' to the 'Halley' of the comet is being used). Later punning names included the Fourmost and the Beatles. Among punk groups in Britain, puns for names were in a small minority among the lesser-known bands such as XTC (= ecstasy), Art Attax and the Crutch Plates. Among individual group members, though, such touches were more common, their clearly artificial origin standing out in contrast to the 'mythic' approach of the Cliff Richard type of name. Some instances were Poly Styrene, Rev Volting and Max Voltage.

Among the mass of group names without any naturalistic pretensions, the most important trends were those which in some way recommended the quality or the success of the band. The name had connotations either of musicality or of opulence, or both. The 1920s dance band, the Savoy Orpheans, combined a reference to a smart hotel with the name of a famous musician from Greek mythology. Among later vocal groups, particularly black American ones of the 1940s and 1950s, the connotations of musical quality were achieved by incorporating songbirds or musical instruments into names: Dixie Hummingbirds, Orioles, Robins, Harptones. Connotations of opulence and success came from contemporary status symbols: Jewels, El Dorados, Satins, Cadillacs.

The rock groups of the 1960s carried the latter approach forward with names like the Pacemakers, Paramounts, Magicians, Cruisers and Premiers. The musical references in group names had now shifted, though.

Increasingly they came from specific songs or artists typifying those who had inspired the group itself: Mojo Men, Rolling Stones, Pretty Things, Yardbirds (the nickname of jazz star Charlie Parker) and Hollies.

At this stage, though, two more genres of group names were added. There were those whose reference points were to other parts of popular culture, notably films. These included the Searchers, Mindbenders and Strangeloves. Finally, there was a 'zany' and non-sense category of names, owing much to the Beatles' choice of a punning name, and then to its copying by the men behind the Monkees. American punk veering towards psychedelia offered the Electric Prunes, Chocolate Watch Band and 13th Floor Elevators. The West Coast upsurge with the impetus of the drug/hippie culture's secret argot contributed Grateful Dead, Jefferson Airplane and others. And there was Velvet Underground.

The structure of that name and a number of others worked at the level of grammar (as an adjectival phrase or compound noun) but not at the level of meaning. So far as the domain of connotation was concerned—the range of socially sanctioned, meaningful associations of a phrase—'Velvet Underground' meant nothing. Each word in the phrase came from outside the paradigm of words which could 'meaningfully' connect with the other. Thus, words which might be linked to 'velvet' would come into the categories of objects made of that material (curtains, cushion), or, metaphorically, other objects capable of being touched or seen (skin, sky). The particularly abstract quality of 'Underground' excludes it from this paradigm, making the phrase 'Velvet Underground' meaningless in a conventional sense. This meaninglessness then effectively becomes the significance of the term itself in a rock music context: it is signalled that this name, and through analogy this band, is against the established order of meaning, is in some way avant-garde. Of course, the negation of orthodox meaning remained heroic for only a brief moment, not least because this form of naming—adjectival phrase—became commonplace among psychedelic or underground bands: Pink Floyd, Electric Prunes, Jefferson Airplane. The style of naming became associated with a style of music, just as anything prefixed by 'Blues-' had been a few years earlier.

Not the least interesting thing about the Sex Pistols is that their name was one of the very few British punk rock names to take this form previously associated with 1960s 'hippies' (another is the Desperate Bicycles). A paradigm of nouns qualified by 'Sex' in conventional discourses would include mostly 'abstract' actions: Change, Act, Offence, Dream, Talk, Therapy. The lesser number of objects in the paradigm would be Shop, Film, Book, Aid. Similarly, the paradigm of adjectives to 'fit' Pistols' would exclude 'Sex'. It would contain words denoting the physical type (Water, Duelling, Silver) or the quality (Deadly, Accurate, Unreliable). There remained, however, the grammatical 'fit': the name 'worked' as a compound noun.

There are two significant points to be made about 'Sex Pistols' as a name. The second, shared with 'Velvet Underground', is that there is a level at which it can begin to acquire meaning, a place where the two areas of connotation belonging to the separate words can be made to 'overlap' and interact. This issue will be considered after a discussion of the first point, which concerns the fact that this particular group name was speaking the 'unsayable' in popular music. It is quite likely that 'prunes' or 'underground' had not appeared in group names or indeed in songs prior to the psychedelic era; but the case of 'sex' is fundamentally different. Although the word had not previously been spoken, its referent had been almost incessant—but under other names: 'making love', 'passion', 'one night with you', 'halfway to paradise', 'rock me baby' etc., etc.

Even after this lifting of the taboo on the word, and Adam and the Ants' later song called 'S.E.X.', the BBC and several leading chains of record stores in Britain were refusing to display the adjective in the title of Marvin Gaye's 'Sexual Healing'. Previously, though, there had been a number of songs employing with impunity the word 'sexy': Hot Chocolate's 'You Sexy Thing' and Rod Stewart's 'Do Ya Think I'm Sexy' for instance. Of course, this usage, in general discourse, has taken on a diffuse sense, becoming almost a synonym for glamorous. Indeed, 'sex' itself, in the 15 years or so before the coining of the Sex Pistols' name, had become almost commonplace in the general discourse of British society. As early as 1963, a 'responsible' pamphlet had been published under the title 'Towards A Quaker View Of Sex', in which the three-letter word finally replaced such terms as 'married love'.

So, although this was a first usage in the rock music discourse, it is arguable that it was hardly a markedly radical achievement. Perhaps because of the attitude of protecting the morals of the nation's youth adopted by some institutions associated with the music industry (notably the British radio stations), rock was lagging far behind an explicit use of language already evident in many sectors of culture and society. Indeed the *name* of the Sex Pistols was responsible for very little adverse comment compared to that excited by their sound and their behaviour when they came to the notice of the general media beyond the confines of the popular music scene.

To understand the significance of the use of 'Pistols' in this group name, it is helpful to apply a commutation test. This is a technique of linguistics borrowed by Roland Barthes in his book about the semiology of fashion, *Système De La Mode*, in order to discover where the crucial meanings of a text, whether fashion photograph or caption, lay.[5] It involves the substitution of one term in the text by another taken from the same paradigm of terms, most often a synonym. In the present case, 'Gun' might be taken instead of 'Pistols'. Although both share the general meaning of firearm, there are a number of differences in connotation. 'Pistols' has a somewhat archaic sense, redolent of such male hero stereotypes as highwaymen or cowboys. Phonetically, too, the word contains loud echoes of other words. It contains 'pissed' (slang for drunk) and that word's root 'piss' (urine). More distant is its rhyme with 'bristols': in London (cockney) rhyming slang, this is a term for breasts, where 'titty' rhymes with 'Bristol City'. Unlike the more prosaic 'gun', then 'Pistols' has contact with the areas of violence, sexuality and excretion, all taboo topics as far as the mainstream media discourse of Britain, exemplified by broadcasting in particular, was concerned.

It is time now to discuss the 'overlap' which may be made symbolically between the two words 'Sex Pistols', so that they yield up some kind of collaborative meaning. This occurs as the use of the word 'Sex' foregrounds the *phallic symbolism* of the pistol's shape. There are precedents which make this a likely leap for many readers of the name. Within rock itself, the Beatles' 'Happiness Is A Warm Gun' (from the *White Album*) offered itself as an ambiguous love song, where penile ejaculation was set up in relation to a gunshot. More politely, the jargon of popular sex education used 'trigger happy' as a euphemism for premature ejaculation. Finally, this interpretation of the group name was given some visual support by the design of a T-shirt worn by Sid Vicious in an early Virgin Records publicity photograph (see p.133). Drawn in the style of certain American gay male pornographers, it showed two partly dressed cowboys whose penises hung in a position which mimed that of holstered pistols.

In this dimension, then, the lifting of the taboo on the unsayable in rock discourse ended in a new way of saying something quite old: a celebration of male sexuality as essentially aggressive and phallocentric. The phallic motif, incidentally, is echoed elsewhere in punk names: the Buzzcocks, Hot Rods, Throbbing Gristle, Skrewdriver and the consciously ludicrous (but still affirmative) Ed Banger and Ivor Biggun.

The multiple meanings of the Sex Pistols' name are rare among punk rock bands: transparency of meaning is far more common. Exceptions to that rule are The Jam (traffic, musical = informal session, even comestible), and the Vibrators, though the double-reference here (to vibration as an effect of sound and to sex-aids) is weaker. Given the punk context, the taboo-breaking aspect of 'Vibrators' would have take precedence over the other, which has some relation to the tradition of musical references in group names.

The names of the other early British punk bands emphasize just one region of meaning in their connotations. In an inversion of that earlier practice of group naming which signified success or status, the Damned and the Stranglers highlighted the socially undesirable, sinners and lawbreakers respectively. Both, too, were *excessive*. To say 'Damned' rather than 'Condemned' was to invoke an extra layer of the supernatural and in a media context to invoke the 1969 film by Visconti which caused a ripple of excitement or censure for its lurid presentation of Nazi decadence. 'Stranglers' goes further than 'Killers' would, in its specifying of a particular method of assault. It also invokes a well-known film, the dramatization of the real-life career of the *Boston Strangler*. The Clash picked another aspect of transgression of the social norm, with its connotations of violent, often politically inflected conflict. 'Clashes' in the discourse of news media were what happened between police and demonstrators or guerillas and government forces.

The number of punk bands which followed any of the previously constructed genres of naming were very few. The category of success or status might account for the Cortinas (a prized car?) or the Suburban Studs (sexual prowess, or a pun, referring also to a key feature of punk dress?). But the case of the Rich Kids, a band formed by Glen Matlock, originally a Sex Pistol, raised the issue of whether punk rock could itself contain names which appeared to transgress punk's own sense of its difference from other popular music. As the examples already discussed suggest, punk names, like those of the earlier psychedelic/underground groups, aimed to signal some kind of overturning of established meanings and hierarchies of values. Instead of the Chosen Few, punk had The Damned. Punk's names of success and status were chosen from those which had precisely the opposite connotations in conventional discourse. Thus to be called 'Rich Kids' and to be punk implied the operation of a kind of irony, a quality rare in punk rock, in which the inversion of values was itself inverted. If the irony was missed, however 'Rich Kids' could be seen as conformist and therefore no longer punk.

Punk names with musical connotations contain a few which follow the tradition of referring to admired work: Blitzkrieg Bop (a Ramones number), Stiff Little Fingers (a Vibrators tune), and Boomtown Rats (which Rats leader Bob Geldof took from Woody Guthrie). The latter group, though, are generally considered to have never been more than on the borderline of punk rock, and the few other names with musical associations have elements of the pattern of inversion already noted. The Drones are a clear example, while Siouxsie and the Banshees is more ambitious. While conventional parlance would read a phrase like 'wailing like a banshee' as a negative comment, the banshee in Celtic mythology was a supernatural being associated with death. This sense of power is therefore present in the name, which also contains in 'Siouxsie', a shift from the conventional 'Susie'—object of male desire in so many songs ('Wake Up Little Susie', 'Susie Baby')—to the connotations of the red Indians, particularly as mediated by Hollywood.

Some punk names, too, referred outwards to other areas of popular culture. There are not specific film titles, but generic names: Horror Comics and Skin Flicks follow the inversion principle, The Adverts was enigmatic, while TV Personalities was whimsical and Alternative TV suggested the oppositional strategy that the band adopted in its music. Other cultural reference points were comic and other books (Ricky & The Last Days of Earth, Arthur Comix, Generation X), show business jargon (Big In Japan, the short-lived Liverpool band which made the first British punk disc) and the Tiller Girls. This high-kicking chorus line were television regulars in the 1950s and early 1960s. Their name inspired the Tiller Boys, a recording project by Pete Shelley of the Buzzcocks. It is also virtually the only British punk name with any element of gender ambivalence or role-playing: the nearest to a name like the New York Dolls.

Referring to the wider political and media sphere were names like Spitfire Boys, Joy Division and London SS, with their Second World War associations. While the

Spitfire had been a fighter plane used by the British, the other names reflected (and played on) the continuing fascination with Nazism in British culture. Joy Division took its name from concentration camp prostitutes while the S.S. had been the Nazi storm-troopers. 'London S.S.'—the name of an early rehearsal band containing future members of Clash and The Damned—was also punning, since many welfare claimants (including unemployed musicians) referred to officials of the Social Security system as the S.S. because of their hostile attitude.

More contemporary in their references were the precursor of Joy Division, named Warsaw or Warsaw Pakt, and the Californian punk group the Dead Kennedys. This name represented a slightly different shock tactic from the early British bands: a name held to be virtually sacred in conventional public discourse was hijacked into the 'frivolous' world of music. The association of death gave the move a stronger effect than say, the black American singer of the 1980s who adopted the name 'Prince Charles'.

The vast bulk of punk band names, however, came from the simpler process of inversion. Consistent with punk's own roots in 'rotten' and 'worthless', groups looked for qualities, objects and activities that established media discourse (the Bill Grundy milieu) could be relied on to find despicable or disgusting. These qualities, objects and activities were adopted as names.

Sexual references followed the Sex Pistols in asserting male orientated definitions: Penetration, Gonads, Crutch Plates, Suburban Studs, Johnny & the Self Abusers, Ivor Biggun, Skrewdriver, Raped. Snatch and The Slits were two all-women groups, with names referring to female sexuality, with the latter intended to have a 'counter-phallic' impact. The difficulty with this strategy is that the concept of 'phallocentrism' suggests that its power derives not so much from the male genital as such, but from its primary *symbolic* role; through phallic references (e.g., Sex Pistols) rather than penile ones (e.g., Ivor Biggun). A comparable female symbol (or counter-symbol) is therefore not necessarily achieved by a form of 'inversion' such as the naming of the female genital in some way. Certainly, the use of 'Banshees' seems more effective in providing an assertive female symbol at the level of naming.

Death and violence was another taboo region raided by punk for names. Some of the names were Cyanide, Death, Electric Chairs, Tormentors, Violent, Vermin, Slaughter & the Dogs. This aspect became absolutely central to the strand of punk that led to 'Oi' music and the 'real punk' of the 1980s, discussed in Chapter 6. In this milieu can be found Ultra-Violent, Infa-Riot, Riot Squad, Destructors, I'm Dead and State of Emergency.

A further category of 'inferior beings' engaged the attention of a number of punk bands in search of a name. There were animals (Ants, Gorillas, Dogs, Rats), 'primitives' (Cannibals, Tribesmen) and a variety of social outcasts (Celia & the Mutations, Lurkers, Maniacs, Brats, Mutants, Users, Banned, Unwanted and, curiously, Outpatients). More abstract were Nothing, the Negatives and the Outsiders, while peculiarly specific were a group of names hoping to evoke physical disgust. These included Varicose Veins, Stinky Toys (a French band) and B.O. Smellie & the Honking Bacterias. With that last name, the boundary has been crossed into the small area of punk wit, inhabited by intentionally comic names like Ivor Biggun and Ed Banger and the Nosebleeds. Also trying to combine the physical, the humorous and the obscene were the Snivelling Shits.

These categories cannot be exhaustive. A minority of punk group names didn't follow the principle of inversion but showed identity with a place (Bethnal, Chelsea) or appeared to project positive or neutral connotations (Boys, Angelic Upstarts, Models, Zones, Valves, Wire). Finally, the most complex after the Sex Pistols was perhaps Sham 69, the 'second generation' punk band led by Jimmy Pursey. The *origin* of the name is well-documented: the remnant of a slogan which originally read 'Hersham 69' painted on a wall in that small town near London. It was apparently written in 1969 by a local gang or even soccer fans. Adopted as a group name, 'Sham 69' seemed initially to mainly work as another 'meaning-less' phrase, like Pink Floyd or Velvet Underground. Attached to Pursey's reputation, his commitment to 'the street' and his emphasized proletarian distrust of anything to do with the 'hippies' which had flourished in the late 1960s, the foregrounded meaning could equally be a reference to the false ideals of a past which punk rock energetically rejected.

INSTITUTIONAL NAMES

The pattern of naming among punk record labels followed that of the bands: the principle of inverting whatever was prestigious in the cultural mainstream was followed, as well as that of entering taboo areas. The latter was primarily sexual and overwhelmingly phallic. Big Cock Records was followed by Flaccid, Limp and led by Stiff, a multifaceted name. As well as its sexual content, it referred in American slang to a 'corpse' (and in the entertainment world, an unsuccessful product—a bit of self-deprecating British humour, this) as well as its slightly ludicrous connotation when coupled with 'Records'—conjuring up an image of a solid platter in contrast to the flexible vinyl of modern discs.

Early punk rock labels had their quota of anti-prestigious names: Albatross, Alien, Boring, Bust, Disaster, Hell, Parole, Rabid and Rip-Off. These, however, were balanced by those whose titles claimed something more positive, either in the terms of the cultural mainstream (Dead Good, Fast Product, City, Zoom, Good Vibrations) or in the newly established hierarchy of the punk milieu itself (Small Wonder, Garage, Pogo, Refill, Raw). Elsewhere, were those containing place names (Chiswick, Deptford Fun City) or the names of the record shops which owned them (Beggars Banquet, Bonaparte).

A small but interesting group of label names appeared to have been chosen to emphasize (or demystify?) the commercial process in which they were engaged. Industrial Records (home of Throbbing Gristle) came into this category along with two of the most important punk rock record companies, Factory and Rough Trade. Each of the latter, however, had further connotations. 'Factory' had been the name given by Andy Warhol to his New York headquarters, while 'Rough Trade' in male gay parlance referred to a certain type of pick-up or prostitute.

Among punk rock fanzines, that strand which emphasized aspects of punk culture itself in the choice of name was particularly marked. Early examples (from 1977–8) included *Garageland*, *Ripped & Torn* and *London's Burning*. The inversion principle had of course been initiated by *Sniffin' Glue* and was widely followed by such journals as *Teesside Smells*, a characterization of the north-east England heavy industrial area from which it sprang.

INDIVIDUAL NAMES

As the Cliff Richard example shows, many adopted stage names are finally 'naturalized': they no longer draw attention to their invented nature. The United States, especially, has a long history of performers of Jewish, Italian or German origin acquiring Anglo-Saxon names for their show business career. Dino Crocetti became Dean Martin, Antonio Benedetto was Tony Bennett and Norma Egstrom became Peggy Lee. Like their British equivalents such as Cliff Richard or Tom Jones (né Thomas J. Woodward), they adopted streamlined 'ordinary' names, often possessing positive connotations. 'Tom Jones' was the eighteenth century fictional hero, as well as being a common twentieth century personal name.

Britain had another trend though, dating from the rock 'n' roll era of the late 1950s. An impresario called Larry Parnes decided to give his stable of singers emblematic names, those of abstract feelings or qualities. He came up with Marty Wilde,

Billy Fury, Johnny Gentle, Georgie Fame, Adam Faith (Ringo Starr, with added cowboy connotation, was a later version of this process). With the possible exception of 'Fame', all these could be found as (albeit unusual) ordinary names, which allowed for them to become 'domesticated' fairly quickly. Like 'Cliff Richard', 'Adam Faith' worked as a *myth*. The dual-character of the word 'Faith' allowed the connotations of the abstract noun to attach themselves to a mildly talented singer.

In 1972, former singer Paul Raven re-emerged as Gary Glitter, followed a year later by Alvin Stardust (former stage name Shane Fenton, original name Bernard Jewry). These names clearly could not be easily 'domesticated'. They announced themselves as artifice, even in their show business referents. 'Glitter' could not easily be seen as a character trait of the singer as 'real person' (unlike Faith or Fury). It was more like a description of his *persona*, his adopted pose in his work.

Enter Johnny Rotten, Sid Vicious, Rat Scabies, Joe Strummer, Ari Up, Poly Styrene et al. As chosen names, these were clearly ranged on the side of explicitly artificial (in the manner of Glitter and Stardust). But for devotees of punk rock, they were intended to work in the manner of Faith or Fury, to convey to a follower that 'Rotten' represented a certain guarantee of the essence of that particular individual. There is at first sight a paradox here: faced with previous stage-name modes of the 'domesticated' which attaches special attributes to the individual and the 'artificial' which indicates how he does his job (as a singer) but nothing about his 'real character', Rotten and Vicious choose to do both. They wish to assume clearly marked 'artificial' names, but to have these as guarantors of a particular temperament as individuals.

The solution to the paradox is that punk name-taking at this level operates through a different mechanism. It is one similar to that of the *convert* to a belief who signals this conversion by changing not only their name, but the whole type or style of name. Thus, Cassius Clay became a Black Muslim and took a Muslim-style name instead of a Christian style: Muhammad Ali. The new name was the guarantee of the genuine nature of the person it signified.

The major 'artificial' names in punk rock have this function. Rotten, Vicious, Poly Styrene (a pun, but one which meshed with her lyric obsession with consumerism), Ari Up, Siouxsie, Rat Scabies, Billy Idol, Jello Biafra (of the Dead Kennedys) and Beki Bondage. Other names seem more close to the Gary Glitter mode, where they were part of the stage make-up: Adam Ant, Captain Sensible, Johnny Moped, Lawrie Driver, Luke Warm, Mad Muppet, Eddie Zipps, Gale Warning and Jimmy Giro. Some had clearly humorous, punning origin while others—Zipps and Giro—referred to elements of the punk rock culture as it established itself. The giro—welfare cheque—was, of course, quite crucial for many others besides punks.

Although only a few punk musicians took these artificial names, a considerable number identified themselves only by first names or nicknames. This was particularly true of the emphatically working-class bands of the 'Oi' era whose personnel included Mensi, Mond and Hoxton Tom. By 1983, the magazine *Punk Lives!* was referring to nearly everyone by a single name: thus a group called The Varukers are introduced to readers as Antony, George, Brick and Brains. This procedure is one which adopts as the public form, the form of naming used within the group itself. It abolishes the distance still retained elsewhere in popular music discourse between the 'record sleeve' name (John Lennon, Paul McCartney) and the name used by fans or colleagues (John and Paul). The effect is to draw fans closer in towards the musicians, binding them together within 'punk'; and to signal this space to outsiders as occupied by a unified 'cult' group, through the oddness of the naming *process* more than the specific names themselves.

For the production of meaning in punk, it is the various processes or strategies of naming which are more crucial than the connotations of an individual name, even Sex Pistols. The reason lies in the very logic of all naming. The fact of naming immediately begins to render the name itself, as a sign, transparent and uni-accentual. Its momentum is to become unambiguously an index of the person, group or object themselves, without interference from external associations. Denotation all but crowds out connotation. This is why the taboo-breaking aspect of the name 'Sex Pistols' had only a short life for anyone who heard or read it. Soon it became read only (or primarily) as a sign for four particular musicians; any shock value it retained derived not from the connotations of its constituent parts and their joining together, but from the output and the reported antics of the musicians themselves. As a *name* Sex Pistols finally resonates no more or less than Beatles.

There would nevertheless have been some continuing resonance for those who identified themselves with punk rock. The fact of hearing radio or television announcers or even rock critics pronouncing 'Rotten' and 'Vicious' in the same manner they used for 'Presley' and 'Lennon' would provide some satisfaction for devotees of punk, and a sense that such an event represented in some way a subversion or humiliation of the mainstream discourse of disc-jockey and journalist.

But of making names there is no end. Punk rock established certain possibilities of naming never fully explored before (the 'underground' era had produced only the Fugs of New York and London's Social Deviants in the way of 'antisocial' titles).

Advantage of those possibilities was taken by musicians in the 1980s, after the disappearance of punk rock as a genre. Individual names like Sting of The Police, The Edge and Bono of U2, group names like Spandau Ballet and Prefab Sprout, are examples.

Finally, the process of 'naturalization' of names is necessarily uneven. There will still be those yet to hear the phrase 'Sex Pistols', and there will still be incidents like the one described by *Punk Lives!* journalist 'Dr Syn': 'I once went to interview a band called Riff Raff. "Are you riff raff?" I asked a group of yobbos at Acton Town station. "YOU WHAT??!!" they sort of "enquired".'

Three
Listening

Artistic and commercial reasons combined to support the commonplace that popular music was primarily a recorded music. For both progressive rock bands and teenybop groups the studio was the creative source, while records themselves yielded greater financial rewards than live performances. The latter were places in which to reproduce the recorded sound.

Punk reversed this order of priority. Nearly all the bands established an identity and reputation through the live show. That, of course, is a first stage for most popular musicians (though increasingly in pop the studio came before even the formation of the band—in the case of the Love Affair, a group was created to perform a hit originally recorded by session players). But most musicians approached their transition to recording artists as a move into another mode. For punk rock, it seemed vital to maintain a fidelity to the live context within the recorded one.

This did not, however, mean that punk was an important site for the 'live' album, a recording made at a performance before an audience. The live side of Sham 69's *Tell Us The Truth* album was exceptional in this respect. It meant, rather, that techniques of recording and of arrangement were adopted which were intended to signify the 'live' commitment of the disc. The studio manipulations had the principal aim of convincing the listener that no trickery of editing, double-tracking and so on had 'interfered' with the self-expression of the musicians. The instrumentation on the records was exactly that of the bands in performance, and the 'positioning' of the instruments and voices 'mimed' that of the group on stage. The sound was 'set back' from the listener, with the voice either buried among the other sounds, or placed only a short way in front of them. The contrast is with the mix on records by 'intimate' vocalists, where the singing combines softness with volume in an 'unreal' way. When punk voices are loud it is because the singer is shouting, not because of production technology. This guarantee of the values of the 'live' act is one function too of the many instances where a punk record begins with a non-sung vocal line. The practice goes back to the Beatles (and no doubt beyond), whose first album began with a counting-in of the band: 'One Two Three Four'. Punk is replete with similar effects, Rotten's 'Right now' and his chuckle on 'Anarchy', Poly Styrene's spoken introduction to 'Oh Bondage Up Yours!', The Adverts' whispering of the title as 'Gary Gilmore's Eyes' starts.

Voices

Recordings can be thought of as spaces in which the various sounds are placed in relation to each other. Conventionally, a recording will foreground one particular element, the others arranged behind or around it as supports. Typically in popular music recordings what is foregrounded is the voice. This point can perhaps be supported negatively in that the listener notices (often with a sense of frustration) when the voice 'disappears' into what significantly is called the 'backing'. The frustration comes from a problem of comprehension (not being able to decipher the words) but also from the withdrawal of the opportunity of identification with 'the voice which typically, if not in every case, provides the level of the song which engages our desire most directly'.[1]

The amplified voice can be seen to provide a comparable object for identification to that of the screen image of the film hero or heroine. In addition, the *musicality* of the process is crucial to this sense of perfection and coherence: singing can make a voice extraordinary in a way that everyday speech cannot (though heightened, dramatic speech can—an important point for punk).

Punk voices, to start with, seem to want to refuse the perfection of the 'amplified voice'. In many instances the homogeneity of the singing voice is replaced by a mixture of speech, recitative, chanting or wordless cries and mutterings. Popular music has a small tradition of the monologue, spoken words set against a musical background. It divides into the comic and the portentous, although in most cases (Les Crane's 'Desiderata' or Wink Martindale's 'Deck Of Cards') the latter can easily collapse into the former. Philip Tagg has pointed out that recitatives (used here as a generic term for vocalizations that are between ordinary speech and singing) are among those forms 'where the verbal narrative seems often to be more important than the musical discourse'.[2] This would certainly seem to be the case with many punk records which employ recitative with serious intent, though with very different voices from the lugubrious Crane and Martindale. Virtually all the Sex Pistols tracks (with Rotten on lead vocal) and those of Mark Perry's Alternative TV are examples. The implicit logic would seem to involve the conviction that by excluding the musicality of singing, the possible contamination of the lyric message by the aesthetic pleasures offered by melody, harmony, pitch and so on, is avoided. Also avoided is any association with the prettiness of the mainstream song, in its forms as well as its contents: as has already been shown, punk has few love songs.

Yet, any hope for the pure message, vocals as reflector of meaning, is doomed. Deprived of the conventional beauties of singing as a place for identification, for distraction, the listener may shift to some other aspect of the voice. What is at stake here is that element which Roland Barthes variously calls the 'third meaning' or the geno-song'. The latter is contrasted with the 'pheno-song' which 'describes everything in the performance which is in the service of communication, representation, expression . . .'. The geno-song, by contrast is

> The volume of the singing and speaking voice, the space where significations germinate from within language and in its very materiality. . . . It is that apex (or depth) of production where the melody really works at the language—not at what it says, but the voluptuousness of its sound-signifiers, of its letters.[3]

This is not a distinction between form and content or signifier and signified,[4] with special emphasis being given to form. Barthes is concerned only with the role of singing-forms—are they subordinated to the message or content, there to underline it (as is the case in most of the Stranglers' work), or are there places where elements of form 'exceed' the message, providing a different focus for the listener? Johnny Rotten's vocal style offers some examples. In 'God Save The Queen', the word 'moron' comes out as 'mo-rrrr-on-er', with an exaggerated rolled 'r' in the middle and the addition of the extra 'er' syllable at the end. As pheno-song, two readings are possible. This presentation of the word both gives added emphasis within the narrative to the description of the Queen as a 'moron', and also connotes a relish on the part of the singer in making the comparison. So the sound 'in the service of representation' informs the listener of the most important part of the lyric message and provides information about the 'character' of the singer (and in doing so links up with the extra-musical discourse on the Sex Pistols, Bill Grundy, etc.).

But, as with the famous visual 'illusions' such as the 'duck/rabbit', by refocusing, the listener can hear Rotten's 'moron' as geno-song, as pleasure in the 'voluptuousness of . . . sound-signifiers'. For there is a sense in which the emphasis on the word is gratuitous within the lyric of 'God Save The Queen'. In the next line, for instance, the word 'H-Bomb', which semantically carries greater impact in general discourse, receives no such special emphasis. Additionally, the specific forms of emphasis have connotations in the popular music field which are very distant from the punk protest of the lyric of 'God Save The Queen'. The rolled 'r' is a feature of 'Tartanry' singing, the heavily Scottish style associated with Harry Lauder and Andy Stewart (in the latter's 'Scottish Soldier' for instance). The 'er' effect is part of an equally archaic singing style which Richard Hoggart, writing in 1957, called the 'big dipper':

> Each emotional phrase is pulled out and stretched; it is the verbal equivalent of rock-making, where the sweet and sticky mass is pulled to surprising lengths and pounded. . . . The most immediately recognisable characteristic is the 'er' extension to emotionally important work, which I take to be the result partly of the need to draw every ounce of sentiment from the swing of the rhythm, and partly of the wish to underline the pattern of emotional statement.[5]

Physiologically, the 'er' embellishment coincides with the places where the singer needs to draw breath. The 'expert' singer will inhale inaudibly, while the less professional may utter a gulp or gasp, coming out as an 'er'. But, as Hoggart's last phrase indicates, this effect is part of the pheno-song in the 'big dipper' style, it 'underlines the pattern of the emotional statement'. Johnny Rotten's use of the effect in a context far removed from the sentimentality of the 'big dipper' can be heard as either shifting it into the area of geno-song, so it no longer functions expressively, or as overturning the connotations which the effect has within the big dipper's pheno-song, as satirizing or ridiculing them.

This satirical effect is then the third possible interpretation of the 'er' at the level of pheno-song, while geno-song offers two possible ways of understanding the effect: the overstated intake of breath or a play with the potential of a consonant when the final syllable of 'moron' can be heard as an attempt to stretch out the 'n' sound.

It is thus possible (if difficult) to find pleasure in this celebrated punk rock song without the necessity of agreeing with its message. This is something which is conventionally the case with mainstream popular song—the listener can take pleasure from a vocal representation of suffering without sharing the emotion. But it is clearly an outcome that 'protest' type songs would try to exclude. If someone who rejects the message can still like the song, a gap has opened which was unintended.

There are especial difficulties here for the songs of subcultures.[6] While the sub-culture (or more precisely its interpreters) may pride itself on its ability to subvert dominant or established meanings, a listener to a manifestly punk song may be able to miss the point, and avoid reacting either as a punk initiate or as a shocked adher-ent of dominant social values. The latter should, in principle, recoil from 'Dead Cities' by The Exploited, a 'formalist punk' record (see Chapter 6). Yet, such is the frenetic pace of the piece, that the enunciation of the title can easily be heard as a kind of 'scat' singing, as 'Deh See', and enjoyed as a form of abstract (wordless) vocalizing. The point of this example is that the potential play of the signifiers will always challenge the idea of a 'pure' oppositional or subcultural music. To minimize this challenge, a subculture intent on preserving itself and its meaning must organize the context of reception (through audience dress and response) to ensure that the subcultural meaning predominates. The only place for this is the live concert; once the music is on radio or record, other meanings, inflected by other ways of listening (usually structured by the priorities of the musical mainstream) may come to the fore.

A further aspect of the recorded voice is what can be called the *vocal stance*. In his study of Abba's 'Fernando', Philip Tagg describes how the singer's mouth is 'placed nearer the listener's ear by means of mike positioning and volume level in relation to accompaniment at the final mix-down. This reflects the actual/imagined distance be-tween two persons (transmitter and receiver) in an intimate/confidential dialogue'.[7] This private and confidential stance is in contrast to a public and declamatory one, which reflects a greater distance between the voice singing and the ears listening. As Tagg indicates, both imply a communicative function for the voice and belong very much to the pheno-song aspect of music.

Indeed, the confidential and declamatory emphases tend to be aligned with specific genres of music, different lyric subject-matter and contrasting 'modes of address' in the lyric. This last term will be elaborated later in this chapter, but the genres most closely associated in popular song with the confidential vocal stance are the lyric ballad deriv-ing from the 'standard' songwriting of Irving Berlin through to Lennon and McCartney and some blues styles. The declamatory mode, by contrast, is generally rooted in main-stream soul music, the 'shouting' style of R&B singing which in turn influenced early rock 'n' roll through Bill Haley, Little Richard and Jerry Lee Lewis and a white narrative ballad style deriving via Bob Dylan from Woody Guthrie and the Carter Family.

While the descriptions 'confidential' and 'declamatory' are meant to indicate tendencies in singing, rather than hard and fast categories, it is useful to note that of the Top 50 best-selling singles of 1976—whose lyric subject-matter was analysed in Chapter 1—nearly half were clearly confidential in tendency. These included 'If You Leave Me Now' by Chicago and Dr Hook's 'A Little Bit More'. More declamatory in their stance were such records as 'Jungle Rock' by Hank Mizell and The Wurzels' 'Combine Harvester'. In general, there is a connection between the preponderance of love songs and the confidential vocal stance, while lyrics on novelty or song-and-dance themes are delivered in a predominantly declamatory manner.

Within punk rock, the confidential stance was very rare. The Buzzcocks' Peter Shelley was one of the few who presented lyrics in a manner approaching that of the mainstream balladeers. Within the declamatory mode as employed by punk, elements of the soul style were equally scarce: Poly Styrene of X-Ray Spex uses falsetto whoops on 'Oh Bondage Up Yours!', while among the few bands to adopt American vocal accents were the Vibrators, The Damned (on the first album) and the Boomtown Rats, where the debt to Mick Jagger's rock-American intonation was very noticeable.

Simon Frith expresses the general view of the innovation in punk accents by describing how Johnny Rotten 'developed an explicitly working-class voice by using proletarian accents, drawing on football supporter chants . . .'.[8] But the argument that punk imported extra-musical elements into the popular music discourse tends to underplay the previous applications of similar accents in rock music. Mention has already been made of the role of a modified 'stage cockney' by Anthony Newley and a young David Bowie in the 1960s—an accent alluded to in The Clash's 'Safe European Home' which includes the line, 'Wouldn't it be luverly'—a quotation from the hit musical My Fair Lady.

That accent influenced punk rock through some of the Vibrators' singing, but several punk bands offered a flatter London accent shorn of the aesthetic 'quaintness' which stage cockney had acquired. Prime examples were the querulous and whinging tone of Mark P. (notably on 'My Love Lies Limp' and 'How Much Longer') and the ultra-morose Malcolm Owen of The Ruts in whose singing the word 'feel' came out as 'feeyuwuh'. But if the intention in using such voices (and the far fewer non-cockney ones, like Fay Fife's Scottish accent) on record was to signify the 'ordinary', the language of the streets, the result was paradoxical. For, in the context of popular music, the mundane and everyday was actually the mainstream American or 'non-accented' (sometimes called 'mid-Atlantic') accent associated in 1976 with singers like Abba or

Queen's Freddie Mercury. What was ordinary in the streets became extraordinary on record and on radio.

Here is one point, then, where the 'realism' claimed by *Sniffin' Glue* for punk rock is connected with the exotic and unnatural element in the music emphasized by other commentators. Voices which could be strongly identified with 'real' accents acquired a colourful resonance. The more neutral connotations which were perhaps more suited to naturalistic lyrics—the transparent voice—belonged to vocals such as Joe Strummer's, where the standard mainstream rock voice was not so much replaced as *shifted*. 'White Riot' had the same phrasing as the breathless singing of The Ramones, but without the pronunciation of key sounds which fully identify The Ramones as American. In the syllable 'White', for example, the American tendency to stretch the vowel towards an 'ah' sound (which is also characteristic of rock singing in general) was resisted by The Clash, who retain the short 'ite' sound. And the final 't' was clipped off by the British voice, while most American rock pronunciation would keep it, in whole or in part.

Strummer's vocals share with virtually all punk rock singing a lack of variety. There are no moves within songs from high to low, soft to loud, or from one accent to another. One thing which gives the Johnny Rotten voice a special place within punk rock is its unusual practice of changing direction within a song, a verse or even a line. By 'direction', I refer to a vocal strategy, a general approach to the choice of vocal effects. In punk rock, the basic distinction at this level is between 'straight' and 'embellished' singing. Early Clash records exemplify the straight style, where the project is to subordinate the vocal method to the lyric message—a mode appropriate to Barthes's pheno-song. Now, 'Anarchy In The UK' by the Sex Pistols sets off in this mode, a staccato delivery of words with one syllable assigned strictly to one beat. But something happens to deflect that single-mindedness at the end of the second line: 'I am the Anti-Christ/I am an Anarchist.' The final syllable comes out not as 'kissed' but to rhyme with 'Christ'. The embellishment shifts the attention away from the message to the rhyme-scheme and could momentarily set up an ambivalent signal about the 'sincerity' of the whole enterprise. Can anyone who changes the pronunciation of such a key political word be wholly intent on conveying the message of the lyric? This relish for the signifier emerges in other ways that have already been mentioned (the rolled 'r' etc.), and works in tension with the punk ideal of 'straight' singing in the work of Johnny Rotten. As I have already suggested, such a tension can never be fully eliminated from any vocal performance, but it seems more central to the Sex Pistols' music than to most other punk bands of 1976–8.

An important precursor of the punk vocal was the chorus singing on several hit records of the early 1970s. John Lennon's Plastic Ono Band recordings of 1969–71 ('Give Peace A Chance' etc.) had deliberately introduced a chorus line which mingled the singalong' approach of nursery rhymes or pub songs with the kind of community singing or chanting to be found at political demonstrations. The singing of the choruses was deliberately loose on the records, to give the impression of audience participation rather than simply a musician's product. With the hits of Slade (17 between 1971 and 1976), a fusion of the singalong and the chants of football supporters took place in the choruses. This form was taken up again in the male choruses behind the lead vocals of Gary Glitter, whose run of British hits began in 1972. Finally, the 1970s also saw a number of topical novelty hits sung by members of various successful soccer teams, including Arsenal, Liverpool and Leeds as well as Tottenham Hotspur's Cockerel Chorus singing 'Nice One Cyril'. As singalongs, these were more than conservative than Slade or Glitter, being closer to the pub than the football terrace.

Punk rock, then, had these vocal resources to draw on, as well as those of another recently successful singer with a sound which stood apart from the majority of 1970s hitmakers. The American singer Alice Cooper had a voice without polish which cracked and bellowed on several British hits like 'Elected' and 'School's Out'. With Cooper as one model of successful rule-breaking, much punk singing promoted to the lead vocal the approach and the accent of the raucous British chorus singing. Punk also allied to these vocals different lyric themes and a considerably faster tempo than that accompanying the dirge-like chants of Lennon or even the rock romps of Slade.

MUSIC

The tempo of punk rock was one of its musical resources most commented on in reviews or eulogies which managed to regard punk as both 'going further' and 'returning' musically. Tom Carson (writing about The Ramones) is characteristic: 'they had defined the music in its purest terms: a return to the basics which was both deliberately primitive and revisionist . . . a musical and lyrical bluntness of approach'.[9]

What were the features of punk music Carson had in mind by describing it first as 'primitive' and undertaking a 'return to the basics'? In the context of the progressive rock music of the mid-1970s, the main aspects involved were a strict guitar and drums instrumental line-up (with a few exceptions, notably The Stranglers and

X-Ray Spex), the alleged musical incompetence of punk bands and the consequent lack of importance of virtuosity in instrumental solos.

Punk itself eschewed the growing use of electronic instruments to be found in progressive rock, whether synthesizers or the various adaptations of the electric guitar exemplified by the playing of Jimi Hendrix. It was not, however, strictly the case that punk's reliance on the guitar was an actual return to the roots, at least of rock 'n' roll. To begin with, the rock music of the 1950s had involved a range of lead instruments: saxophones (Bill Haley), piano (Jerry Lee Lewis) as well as guitar. In addition, the guitar techniques deployed by punk players of the 1970s were far more akin to certain guitarists of the 1960s than to Scotty Moore, Buddy Holly or James Burton. Its 'basics' were broadly those of the earlier punk music played by The Kinks, the MC5 and the New York Dolls, as well as other bands like The Who. Unlike the relatively 'clear' tone of the 1950s players, punk guitar was replete with effects based on distortion or feedback. Their use of those elements suggests that the 'incompetence' of punk musicians was more rhetorical than actual. There are a few records where the band's ambition so far exceeds their ability that the result is not a tension between the two but a dislocation. The almost total lack of any rhythmic continuity on The Mekons' 'Never Been In A Riot' ensures the collapse of the song's intended message. Instead it tells listeners that literally anyone can make a record, perhaps more effectively than the lyric exhortations of the Desperate Bicycles, a band who triumphantly prove that limited musical means could be deployed to the limit (but not beyond it) to great effect.

Even at the level of the materiality of the sounds themselves the issue of skill and competence in punk rock remains ideologically charged. In an essay on the New York Dolls, which contains virtually the only attempt at musical analysis of punk style, Robert Christgau remarks that 'they refused to pay their dues'.[10] That last phrase had a particular resonance in the rock music discourse of the 1970s. As applied approvingly to musicians it implied that these people had gone through a long and necessary period of acquiring experience and know-how as performers: that to be a rock musician was to be a certain type of skilled worker who had learned 'on the job'.

That model of self-improvement could then be pitted against the 'instant' nature of many teenybop artists, apparently with little performing experience and apparently manipulated by a producer or a manager. There was no issue in teenybop of 'paying dues', and nor was there in punk rock. In fact, quite a number of the early punk musicians had a lot of previous experience as professional musicians, notably members of the Damned, Stranglers and Clash. But this background did not count to their advantage in the punk milieu.

If progressive rock saw itself as skilled labour of an artistic type (comparable to a potter or an illustrator), punk saw itself as self-expression where skill or virtuosity carried with it a suspicion of glibness. Too much concern with the forms of musical expression could lessen the impact of the substance of the thing expressed. This sort of attitude helped to fix the role of the instrumental solo in recorded punk rock, which was very similar to that of both 1950s rock 'n' roll and of 1960s beat music. In progressive rock, soloists had often acquired as much significance as vocalists and occupied as much space and time. They frequently introduced new musical ideas into a number. The contrasting approach, which punk shared, gave the solo the more limited role of reiterating some aspect of the piece already stated. This could be either a riff or chord sequence which moved from the background to the foreground during the instrumental break, a set piece sequence of single notes emphasizing the tempo of the piece or (typically on slower tunes or ballads) an 'atmospheric' solo underlining the emotional tone of the singing.

A classic example of the riff and chord solo comes on The Damned's 'New Rose', while 'Anarchy In The UK' and 'White Riot' contain single note sequences in structures which stretch back to Chuck Berry and Scotty Moore in 1950s rock 'n' roll. There is a noticeable lack of the atmospheric solo in punk rock, however, which reflects punk's lack of concern with melody. The highlighting of the melody line in rock ballads like the Beatles' 'Something' allows the solo to enhance the mood simply by an 'emphatic' repetition of the melody. One possible punk example of an 'atmospheric' solo is Laura Logic's saxophone break on 'Oh Bondage Up Yours!' where the celebratory connotations of the rhythm & blues/soul way of playing (in the work of King Curtis and Junior Walker, for instance) can be heard to echo the defiance in Poly Styrene's declamatory vocal stance.

More crucial to punk's sense of difference from other musics is its attitude to rhythm. It is here that the apparent paradox of a music both more 'primitive' and 'revisionist' finds its most appropriate application. Perhaps the most characteristic rhythmic feature of music containing Afro-American elements is syncopation. Indeed, one of Bill Haley's accounts of the formation of his own rock 'n' roll style presents it as the key factor:

> I felt that if I could take, say, a Dixieland tune and drop the first and third beats and accentuate the second and fourth, and add a beat the listeners could clap to as well as dance this would be what they were after.[11]

Syncopated rhythms of this kind accentuate the 'off beat' and in doing so draw the listener into the music to 'supply' the 'missing' first and third beats either mentally or physically, through hand-clapping, nodding or dancing. The presence of a recognizable syncopation in the music is a precondition for all dancing in the rock-based popular music sphere. The main reason for the 'undanceability' of much punk rock (and for its adoption of the 'pogo' as a suitable dance form) is that, to quote Christgau, it tends to 'submerge' syncopation in its rhythmic patterns.

'Holidays In The Sun' by the Sex Pistols begins with the sound of marching feet, a regular, repetitive, definitely unsyncopated sound. This is followed by the drums falling into the same rhythm. This rhythmic monad (1–1–1–1), as opposed to rock's conventional dyad (1–2–1–2, where the accent is on the second beat) is a state of entropy (or perfection) to which much punk seems constantly aiming.

In effect, many punk recordings contain elements of both the monad and the dyad, either distributed in time (in different parts of the song) or in space (in different parts of the rhythm section). The distribution through time has a place in earlier rock music, where the repetition of the single beat in, say, 'Bits And Pieces' by the Dave Clark Five sets up a tension which is released by a shift into syncopated rhythm. But while the non-syncopated occupies only a small amount of the Dave Clark record, in a punk piece like Alternative TV's 'You Bastard' it is on a par with the emphatically syncopated passages.

More frequently, though, the monad/dyad contrast is distributed among the rhythm instruments, often with the bass and guitar laying a non-syncopated line over the muted syncopation of the drums. Here, Jerry Nolan of the New York Dolls, as described by Christgau, is the archetype of punk drummers: 'although drawn to the backbeat, he submerged it. . . . The effects and rhythm changes were there when needed . . . but for the most part held in check'.[12] Even earlier, Christgau also notes, Maureen Tucker of the Velvet Underground had experimented with the elimination of the backbeat: on 'Waiting For My Man', for instance. And much of Ringo Starr's drumming had seemed unsympathetic to syncopation.

The key to what Christgau calls punk's 'forced rhythm' lay in the bass playing. It is here that the monadic rhythm is anchored in a continuous and regular series of single notes which contradict the syncopation of the drumming (one source was John Entwistle's bass line on 'My Generation'). Arthur Kane of the New York Dolls and Sid Vicious were perhaps the 'purest' of punk bass players in that they went furthest in the repetition of notes of the same pitch for as long as possible. Others, such as

Clash's Paul Simonon, evolved bass runs or riffs which could shift the rhythmic balance towards the syncopated.

That balance was also affected by the orientation of the lead or rhythm guitar and the tempo of the piece. 'Buzzsaw drone' (Christgau) was the typical punk guitar sound. The 'buzzsaw' tone was achieved by combining rhythm chords of the type pioneered by Pete Townshend of The Who with a tone derived from distortion or feedback. The 'drone', which provided the continuous 'wall of sound' effect, came from the way the riffed chords bled into each other rather than staying separate as in the chopped rhythm chords of 1960s beat group rock. Combined with the monadic bass line, this guitar sound provided a feeling of unbroken rhythmic flow, as the patternings of bar or stanza divisions receded into the background.

That effect of unbroken flow was enhanced by the breakneck eight to the bar rhythm of much punk rock, a feature deriving primarily from the influence of The Ramones on British musicians. Speed, in itself, does not create the impression of 'instant blur' (Christgau). Jerry Lee Lewis's 'Whole Lotta Shakin' Goin' On', after all, was taken at a very fast tempo, but because stanza divisions were clearly signalled it lacks the 'formless' impact of much punk rock.

The fast tempo combined with the anti-syncopation tendency of many punk songs supported the connotation of urgency of utterance which declamatory vocals and their lyrics evoked. For if the pace of a song no longer functions as an impetus to dance it then becomes a sign that the singer needs to get across the message as quickly as possible.

One final point on punk music concerns the balance between monadic and dyadic rhythms. In many recordings, this balance is such that a listener can hear either rhythm as primary. Someone looking for and used to conventional syncopation can align themselves with the drumming, for instance, while a listener concerned to identify with punk's transgressive role in relation to mainstream rock can hear the non-syncopating bass line as foreground, and an incitement to pogo.

WORDS

Song as communication involves a sender and a receiver, one who addresses and one who is addressed. This process always occurs at two levels. There is an 'external' level where the performer (live or on record) addresses the audience (in the concert hall or beside the record-player or radio). There is also an 'internal' communication taking place within the lyric of the song, between the protagonist of the lyric and its addressee.

On his album *Good Old Boys*, Randy Newman has a song called 'Mr President (Have Pity On The Working Man)'. Externally, this is a communication between Randy Newman the performer and any potential listener to his album. Internally, the lyric's protagonist is a Southern working man and the addressee is the President of the United States. Thus, the lyric itself clearly signals the difference between the two sets of senders and two sets of addressees. Newman is like an actor playing the part of the 'working man', and indeed an actor of the Brechtian school who is required to make a distance between her or himself and the character, rather than fusing with it.

Most popular songs, however, do not have so unambiguous a gap between the external and internal levels of communication. Those two levels are distinguished in linguistic theory by the terms 'énonciation' and 'énoncé'. They distinguish the two aspects of any utterance: the act of uttering (énonciation) which corresponds to the external level or the performance of a song, and the thing uttered (énoncé) which corresponds to the internal level of the statement made by the song lyric.

In most songs, the protagonist of the énoncé, the lyric statement, is identified only by the pronoun 'I', rather than some other feature such as name or occupation. This makes possible the identification by the listener of this subject of the énoncé with the subject of the énonciation—the actual singer delivering the lyric in concert or on record: such was the case of David Bowie and Ziggy Stardust, discussed on p.36. The likelihood of identification is increased by the ideology of sincerity of performance which permeates attitudes towards much popular singing. This ideology judges vocal performance not by how skilfully a singer can *signify* or present an emotion, such as the frustration of Randy Newman's redneck, but by the listener's idea of how far a singer 'really feels' what is being communicated. This position is intensified as virtually all rock performers write their own material: the assumption being analogous with that of lyric poets—what you write must be what you really feel or think; anything else is bogus or contrived. Explosive moments occur only when the sincerity of a composer of a 'protest' or other song on a broadly political topic is challenged. The issue of 'belief', the accusation of 'bandwagon jumping' arises almost automatically, while it almost never occurs in relation to a love lyric. No performer or composer is made to answer whether they 'really' feel the depth of love or pain attributed to the protagonist of their lyric.

This last point is not quite true, however, if love lyrics are extended to include their obverse, a lyric of hate or degradation addressed to a past or current sexual partner. During the 1960s, a controversy developed over Rolling Stones' songs such as 'Play With Fire', 'Under My Thumb' and 'Out Of Time', which in varying degrees expressed the hatred of a male lyric protagonist for a woman, who was sometimes also the addressee of the lyric.[13] The issue concerned how far the 'I' of the words was identified with the charisma and power of the performer, Mick Jagger. Since the lyrics contained no Newmanesque ironic distancing or internal contradictions, the only ways a listener could avoid assenting to the identification of the lyric protagonist with the performer were by heavily foregrounding the énonciation (so much that the énoncé, the statement itself, was made 'inaudible'), or by what can now be seen as acts of special pleading by critics or commentators.[14]

To hear the énonciation (the performance) separately from the (énoncé) (the lyric), and to respond in contradictory fashion, with attraction towards the former and repulsion from the latter, was something discussed in some feminist writing on the Rolling Stones and on rock in general.[15] Since the Jagger voice had acquired a generic connotation of affirmation of youth revolt, its affirmative tone on 'Out Of Time' could be heard primarily as meaning that, rather than, or as well as, underlining the triumphal misogyny of the lyric.

A similar controversy arose in punk in relation to The Stranglers, whose output of lyrics with grossly sexist protagonists far surpassed that of the Stones. One difference, however, was that The Stranglers were far more diffuse at the level of énonciation. While the Jagger vocal had established itself as a stable and focal element in any recording, The Stranglers not only employed more than one lead vocalist, but also a variety of accents (mock-cockney, Dylanesque and mid-Atlantic) and 'treated' as well as 'natural' sound. (By treated is meant such effects as phasing or echo which change the sound of the voice.)

The vocal variations in Stranglers' recordings were determined by the dramatic demands of the lyric. And énonciation was subordinated to énoncé not in the manner of Randy Newman—to 'place' the lyric protagonist—but to make more overwhelming the message of that protagonist. The Stranglers are the most *literal* of punk vocalists. Their recordings most nearly approach the quality of pure pheno-song, where vocal techniques and embellishments are placed at the service of communicating the lyric message. The result is a popular music equivalent of what Barthes called 'the bourgeois art of song', which 'always want to treat its consumers as naive customers for whom it must chew up the work and over-indicate the intention, less they be insufficiently gripped'.[16] Even at its most unappetizing, the Stranglers' work is always predigested.

The 'ideology of sincerity' also works to cement énonciation and énoncé for the Stranglers. The invocation of that ideology in relation to punk extended to the 'secondary circulation' of the genre—those texts (reviews, interviews, reports) which were about punk, rather than of it. Especially within interviews, the stated beliefs of musicians, and their congruence with the perceived messages of their lyrics, became routine topics. While the necessity for songs to be seen to be autobiographical was not so crucial for the Stranglers as for, say, Sham 69, their published statements on sexual attitudes made clear their own agreement with the positions presented in their lyrics.

Not every song lyric has a first person as its central figure. Some take the form of a narrative where the main figure or figures are in the third person—he, she, they. This type of lyric is common in the folk ballad tradition, where the énoncé also includes an implicit or explicit first person, the storyteller:

> It was of an honest labourer as I've heard people say
> He goes out in the morning and he works hard all the day
> And he's got seven children and most of them are small
> He has nothing but hard labour to maintain them all.[17]

Here the 'I' of the énoncé is no longer the protagonist of the events described there, but a narrator whose position is isomorphic with that of the performer in such a way that the two become virtually indistinguishable. In both énoncé and énonciation, the 'I' is a storyteller and 'you' (the addressees of the communication) are an audience. This is in direct contrast to most lyrics sung in the first person, where the subject of the énoncé is superimposed over that of the énonciation, the 'lover' or 'protester', for instance, over the performer. In a lyric whose 'I' is a narrator and whose protagonist exists in the third person (as 'he' or 'she'), the opposite superimposition occurs: the performer over the storyteller. What each case has in common, though, is that the subject him or herself is a unified one, recognizable as an individual or group of individuals, in whom énoncé and énonciation are reconciled. The characteristics of that individual which allow the recognition to occur can come either from the details of the lyric, from the structural position of the subject of the énoncé (e.g., as narrator) or even from the pre-given features of the performer him or herself.

The unified subject, spanning and uniting both aspects of the utterance (énonciation and énoncé) provides a place for the listener's identification with the amplified voice. But the pull to identification is especially strong because of the homogeneity of the communication, the fully coherent non-contradictory nature of the subject-in-song. This process is common to the majority of performances in every genre of popular song, including punk rock. But what happens if the process of unification of the subject of the utterance does not occur, if no parallel exists between the two 'I's'?

'Holidays In The Sun' by the Sex Pistols contains a lyric with no unified point of origin. The first stanza runs:

> I don't want a holiday in the sun
> I wanna go to the new Belsen
> I wanna see some history
> Cos now I gotta reasonable economy.

An attempt to hear this as the statement of an individual subject could interpret the first three lines as a discussion of a choice of holidays or other journeys, with 'new Belsen' remaining mysterious. The fourth line, however, makes this 'naturalistic' interpretation less tenable. States, not individuals, have 'reasonable economies'. If this is an individual, his idiolect is being signified as exceptionally eccentric. 'Idiolect' is Barthes's term for the 'plurality and co-existence of lexicons [discourses—DL] in one and the same person, the number and identity of these lexicons forming in some sort a person's idiolect.'[18]

But there is an alternative response to the lyrics of this first verse, one based on recognizing links between words and their connotations across rather than within the linear narrative. That is, words are connected by their membership of the same discourse in the world of communication beyond this particular song. Thus, the presence of 'Belsen' and 'history' suggests Nazism and the Second World War, while the addition of 'reasonable economy' sets up faint echoes of terms like the 'German economic miracle' (a media cliché of the 1960s and beyond to describe the rebuilding of West German prosperity). In this perspective, the lyric becomes something like a collage put together from the discourse of newspaper, advertising, pulp fiction, sensationalized history.

Further verses and the chorus offer more material to support this response: 'Berlin Wall', 'Communist Call', 'World War Three' all make an appearance. To hear the lyric as the product of a unified psychological subject it becomes increasingly necessary to regard the lyric's 'disconnected' narrative form as itself a symptom of a state of psychological disturbance. Verse 3 begins: 'Claustrophobia, too much paranoia/ There's too many closets, when will we fall....'

The final vocal passage of the record, delivered in a recitative manner, provides a third dimension to the mode of the énoncé:

> I can go over the Wall

This third rate B movie stuff
Cheap dialogue, cheap essential scenery
I'm gonna go over the Berlin Wall
Before they come under the Berlin Wall
I don't understand this bit at all (three times)
Please don't be waiting for me.

While line 1 can be read as part of a skeletal narrative scenario, as a sign of emotional intensity or as an example of Cold War obsessions with the Berlin Wall (including an ironic reversal of the conventional wisdom that people from East Berlin are those determined to climb the Wall), the next lines introduce a new point of reference. What is the 'third rate B movie stuff'?—is this the (barely) unified psychological individual commenting on his own paranoia? Is it the producer of the 'collage' pronouncing on his raw material? Or is it a 'performer', a 'Johnny Rotten' making a comment about the words he has to sing, a comment which is returned to in the penultimate line: 'I don't understand this bit at all'?

There is no 'correct' way to hear this lyric. Where it differs from the bulk of lyrics is that the 'I' of the énoncé is not forced to be unitary. A phrase like 'reasonable economy' can thus float towards the complex of meanings suggested by the other political reference points dotted throughout the lyric. While Johnny Rotten's voice, the énonciation, still offers the pleasure of identification with a unified position, a different kind of pleasure—that which enjoys the transgression of the codes through which conventional meanings are constructed—is available for listeners to the lyric.[19]

Punk rock offers two other types of 'mismatch' between the subjects of the énonciation and the énoncé: those where the subject of the latter is presented as contradictory, and those where it shifts within the song in an unsignalled way. The classic example of the first type is 'Oh Bondage Up Yours!' by X-Ray Spex. The verse presents a 'masochistic' subject:

Bind me, tie me, chain me to the wall
I wanna be a slave to you all

While the chorus following immediately indicates a rebellious subject:

Oh Bondage! Up yours!
Oh Bondage! No more!

Unable to grasp the sense of this contradiction and obsessed with the first verse, the censors of BBC radio refused to broadcast the record. But the lyric worked rather like a classic narrative, with the first sections posing a major enigma—how can these two utterances be reconciled? The next verse offered the solution:

> Chain store, chain smoke, I consume you all
> Chain gang, chain mail, I don't think at all

In this perspective, the first verse became a metaphor for the voluntary servitude of consumers in a 'consumerist' society of chain stores and chain smoking. The chorus became a rallying cry of a consumer who refused to conform.

In a sense, 'Oh Bondage' is the lyric as drama (with two speakers) while 'Holidays In The Sun' can be heard as lyric as collage (many speakers) and the vast majority of lyrics are monologues or poems (one speaker). Siouxsie and the Banshees' song 'Mittagerzen (Metal)' is another example of the dramatic énoncé, where the 'speaking' subject shifts within the lyric. Here are the chorus and final verse:

> Metal is tough, metal will sheen
> Metal won't rust when oiled and cleaned
> Metal is tough, metal will sheen
> Metal will rule in my masterscheme

> It's ruling our lives, there is no hope
> Thought I'd drop a line, the weather here is fine
> But day and night it blares
> Commanding through loudspeakers.

The song's origin is a 1930s anti-Fascist montage by John Heartfield, which sardonically depicts a German family eating metal in a Germany where all is sacrificed to re-armament. The first person of the song's chorus is the voice of fascism or totalitarianism in general—part of the lyric's aim is to draw modern parallels with the role of television as 'conditioning'. The subject who communicates the verse, in contrast, is a victim of the metallic masterscheme. The lyrics themselves, like those of 'Holidays In The Sun', link hints of prison or concentration camps ('commanding through loudspeakers') with references to holiday-making ('weather here is fine'—a clichéd postcard message).

Despite those examples of non-unified subjects, there is little difference between most punk rock lyrics and the generality of popular songs in the position of the subject of the énoncé. But the situation of the addressee shows some contrasts. Table 4 compares the addressees of the 1976 Top 50 songs with those of the lyrics of songs on the 'first five' punk albums.

Table 4 A comparison of the addressees of the 1976 Top 50 songs and the lyrics of songs on the 'first five' punk albums.

	Punk	Top 50
2nd person singular: lover etc.	31% (21)	54% (27)
2nd person singular: other	21% (13)	4% (2)
2nd person plural: general	39% (26)	32% (16)
2nd person plural: specific	9% (6)	6% (3)

Two Top 50 records (4%) were instrumentals.

While the overall proportion of lyrics aimed at individual addressees is broadly similar, there is a clear contrast in the types of individual addressed. Nearly all Top 50 songs addressed to a single person are to an actual, former or potential romantic or sexual partner, but only just over half of the punk lyrics in this category are so addressed. Punk introduces a high proportion of lyrics addressed to individuals other than 'lovers'. The two Top 50 lyrics in this category are addressed to an old friend (Abba's 'Fernando') and a dancer (Tina Charles's 'Dance Little Lady Dance'). The punk addresses include a male friend (The Vibrators' 'She's Bringing You Down'), but are mostly aimed at male enemies.

There had been a sub-genre of American black street culture which filtered into the urban blues music, called the 'dozens'. This involved a competition to see who could invent the most imaginative and most outrageous insult to the other person involved.[20] Apart from a few of Bob Dylan's and the Rolling Stones's lyrics of the 1960s, very few white performers had worked on lyrics of the 'put-down'. Until punk that is, and especially until the Sex Pistols.

Four of the dozen songs on their first album are addressed to individuals as hymns of hate. 'New York' deals with an American, '17' is aimed at a 29-year-old who can't accept that the singer is 'a lazy sod', while 'Liar' and 'Problem' are directed to individuals who are just that. As befitted the notions of directness and authenticity surrounding punk, the targets of these songs were supposed in punk rock and journalistic circles to be actual people (just as Bob Dylan's 'Mr Jones' had been said to be inspired by the critic Ralph J. Gleason). Of the other punk bands, The Damned take aim at a journalist in 'Stab Yor Back' ('You dirty hack'), and The Vibrators pour scorn on a dead person in 'Stiff Little Fingers': 'If it wasn't for your stiff little fingers, nobody'd know you were dead.'

Elsewhere in punk rock lyrics, some individual addressees are defined in terms of their occupation, or place in the social system. But these 'agit-rock' songs—like Clash's 'Tommy Gun' (to a soldier) and Angelic Upstarts' 'Youth Leader' ('You're the one with the double face')—are rare in punk rock. More frequent are songs whose addressees are in the second person plural, and correspond to 'Them' in the common ideological couplet of 'Us against Them'. These lyrics are included in the category '2nd person plural: specific' in Table 4. The 'general' category refers to those lyrics where the form of the communication is either that of a narrative dealing with a third person (e.g., 'Janie Jones' by The Clash) or a soliloquy, where the first person presents his or her feelings without directing them to any specific listener(s).

Although they form a small proportion of the lyrics, it is significant that the 'plural specific' addresses occur more often among punk songs than among the Top 50. Elsewhere in punk rock, in fact, they are even more prominent. It is equally important to note that the plural addressees in the three Top 50 songs are connected with love ('Young Hearts Run Free') and with music ('Play That Funky Music' and 'Don't Take Away The Music'). That is, they remain defined within the standard topics of popular entertainment. The paucity of collective and specific addressees in mainstream lyrics is explained by the predominance there of love themes, which are only exceptionally addressed to a group of people ('Lovers Of The World Unite' for instance) rather than to one.

Outside the standard areas of lovers, dancers, musicians, what kind of identity can the collective addressees of a lyric be given? Within the stream of music deriving from rock 'n' roll, the overwhelming tendency has been to maintain a parallel between the receiver of the énonciation (the audience of the performer) and the receiver of the énoncé (the addressee in the lyric). The pattern is similar to that already found at the originating end of the musical communication, where the two 'I's' are so often brought together.

In this way, the addressees of the popular song are kept as numerous as possible (by not defining the nature of the listeners, they are not divided), just as in most '2nd person singular' songs, the addressee becomes as unique and as vaguely defined as possible. This clearly locks into the economic imperatives of the popular music institution—the drive for the widest possible appeal of a song would be hindered if its addressees were 'limited' to a specific type of person.

Nevertheless, some song lyrics do specify a type of addressee, usually defined in terms of gender or age. Tammy Wynette's 'Stand By Your Man' is a homily to women only, while Slade's 'Cum On Feel The Noize' is addressed to 'all you girls and boys'. Like lovers and dancers, however, these are roles (heterosexual female partners; 'Young Ones') already established as individual addressees within popular song, and the issues of identification for listeners outside these gender and age groups are to some degree similar (and will be discussed later in this chapter).

More pertinent are the even fewer instances of addressees whose definition is from outside the standard set of roles and themes in song lyrics. The folk tradition provides examples of lyrics addressed to occupational groups ('Come All Ye Bold Miners'), but work is a theme rigorously excluded from popular song[21] (Work is the Curse of the Dancing Classes?). 'Back Home', a Number 1 record in 1970 by the England World Cup Football Team, is a solitary example of addressees defined by nationality. Perhaps the place where these non-standard addressees appear most, however, is in the 'protest' mode. Lyrics with these concerns which have direct addressees (as opposed to general second person plural 'narrative' lyrics), fall into three categories. A small number are addressed to 'us', those already believing in the cause ('We Shall Overcome'). There are then those denouncing the people responsible for the social evil; 'You masters of war' sang Bob Dylan. Finally, there are a greater number whose object is persuasion, and whose addressees are more general, and might be defined in opinion poll terms as 'don't knows'. As was pointed out on p.41, Dylan's addressee in 'Blowin' In The Wind' is 'my friend', while John Lennon sings 'I hope someday that you will join us' in 'Imagine'.

While I have at several points suggested certain similarities between punk rock songs and those of the protest mode, it is here that the two diverge most sharply. While punk has its lyrics of denunciation and those addressed to 'us', there are no lyrics aimed at a friendly but non-committal listener. Politics as persuasion has no place in punk rock.

Here is a selection of lyrics addressed to the second person plural, and denouncing those addressees:

I hate the Civil Service rules/I won't open letter bombs for you.
(Clash: 'Career Opportunities')

You sit up there deciding my future
What the fuck do you think you are . . .
. . . If you like peace and flowers, I'm going to carry knives and
chains.

(Slits: 'Number One Enemy')

Your future dream is a shopping scheme

(Sex Pistols: 'Anarchy In The UK')

We're the people you don't wanna know
We come from places you don't wanna go.

(Sham 69: 'Angels With Dirty Faces')

Although only one of these comes near to giving the denouncees a name—the 'Civil Service' context suggests the State or the Government—each has a slightly different definition of the enemy according to punk rock. Together, these examples indicate the spectrum of that enemy. The Slits lyric firstly refers to a 'you' who rules and has power over the subordinate group represented by the singer. It could therefore include a range of enemies from the various functionaries of the State to the older parental generation. The second extract from 'Number One Enemy' suggests that the range definitely extends beyond the traditionally defined ruling class of The Clash's lyric: here those espousing and promoting 'hippie' ideals are part of the denouncees. 'Anarchy In The UK' introduces a further aspect. Earlier in the song, the protagonist of the lyric has declared his ambition to 'destroy passers-by', an inspired naming which underlines the clichéd nature of the word and the abject character of the social role to which it refers; a 'passer-by' as a person who avoids involvement in a situation—there is a Biblical root in the story of the Good Samaritan. The 'passer-by' idea is perhaps picked up again in the line quoted above: the kind of 'average person' or 'straight' who would be a passer-by would also be limited to the conventional notion of future improvement in their life being defined as a new shopping centre. To these notions of the enemy as the ruling class, hippies, older people and those adhering to conventional behaviour, Sham 69 adds a notion of class difference based on status and life-style rather than (or as well as) on political power. The geographical dimension ('places you don't wanna go') refers to the districts or estates inhabited by the 'inner city' stratum of the working class with which Sham 69 and many of the bands who came after them were identified.

That identification was explicitly made in the lyrics of Sham 69. 'Angels With Dirty Faces' has a chorus which includes the line, 'Kids like me and you', while the strongest example of a lyric where the addressee is directly identified with the peer-group of the protagonist is 'If The Kids Are United'. It is important to establish here that this kind of direct identification of the protagonist with a wider group, including the addressees of the lyric, is almost totally absent from the songs of the earliest punk rock bands, the 'first five'. Unlike Sham 69, the Sex Pistols, Stranglers and Clash rarely concern themselves with establishing the positive existence of a movement to which they belong. Negativity and individuality dominate the lyrics, although the 'friendly' use of the second person is sometimes to be found there. In 'Career Opportunities', Clash use the lines 'Every job they offer you/Is to keep you out of the dock', while 'Anarchy In The UK' has 'Not many ways to get what you want'.

This use of 'you', of course is at one level an alternate version of the first person singular—it equals 'I', just as the word 'one' does when used in more formal or bourgeois discourses. But it also serves to link the addressee with the protagonist, inviting the former to identify with the viewpoint of the latter. In 'linking' the two, it stands between the separation of a lyric which uses 'I' in a similar context, and the total identification expounded by lyrics like those of Sham 69.

It is clear from the lines quoted above that a number of punk lyrics have modes of address that seem to shift from one addressee to another, just as we have seen that some have no constant subject of the énoncé (e.g., 'Holidays In The Sun'). Thus, 'you' in 'Career Opportunities' changes from the Civil Service enemy to the linking of 'you' in 'Every job they offer you'. This shifting is also found in 'Hong Kong Garden', Siouxsie and the Banshees' first hit single from 1979. There, 'you' at some points refers to the Chinese (the title refers to a restaurant) and at others to the Westerners, as customers or tourists.

The vast majority of popular song lyrics have a single, stable point which is addressed, and a stable point from which the lyric is delivered. In standard love songs, of course, these positions are well established before the lyric is written: one lover to his or her partner. In protest songs deriving from folk traditions, such as those of Bob Dylan, a series of positions for addressees are marked out: they can be co-believers, those whom the singer wants to persuade, or those whom the singer is denouncing as the enemy. What happens in many punk lyrics is that two of these addressees appear in the same lyric, while in Dylan there is only one in any song.

There is a precedent for the punk approach in some soul music lyrics of the 1960s. Nina Simone's 'Mississippi Goddam' and 'I'm Talkin''Bout Freedom', recorded by Syl Johnson, are examples where both fellow blacks and the white power structure are addressed in the same song.[22] Perhaps in each case (civil rights soul and punk rock) this shifting in the lyric connotes the urgency of the message to be transmitted, which the listener is intended to realize overrides the need to observe formal consistency in the construction of the lyric. As we have seen this 'inconsistency' is a feature of other aspects of punk rock, notably Rotten's singing style.

WORDS: INTERTEXTUALITY

Chapter 1 offered a content analysis of lyric themes in punk rock and 1976 Top 50 songs. A similar exercise based on the frequency of appearance of certain words in the titles of those songs also points up a strong contrast. The titles of the Top 50 songs reveal the predictable cluster of words around 'Love', which itself appears seven times, including thrice in one song title. This cluster includes 'heart', 'kisses', 'breaking', 'angel', 'cry'. Another, perhaps less expected, linguistic area which is well represented is that of music and dancing themselves. 'Dance' occurs four times and 'music' three; with 'rock', 'songs', 'rhapsody' and 'funky' this group of words turns up in the titles of ten out of the Top 50 and in the body of the lyrics of at least two others (Abba's 'Fernando' and 'Under The Moon Of Love' by Showaddywaddy).

Among the first five punk rock albums, the song titles of The Vibrators yield three appearances of 'heart' and two of 'baby'. None of the other bands have lyric titles including words in this 'love' area, while the only ones remotely near the music and dance field is 'Garageland' by The Clash ('garage band' being a term for 1960s punk groups) and 'Fan Club' by The Damned. Remaining at the level of the vocabulary of titles, the most outstanding clusters of words in the punk rock songs are those around violence ('kill', 'stab', 'burning', 'whips', 'hate and war', 'riot', 'wrecked') and in references to actual places and people. 'London' appears three times, along with 'Toulouse', 'USA', 'New York', 'Janie Jones', 'The Queen' and 'EMI'. Compared to this the Top 50 titles have just 'Mississippi' and 'Zaire'.

Attention to individual words as an indicator of difference in song lyrics can, however, be misleading, since the centre of meaning of the word is dependent on its context. That context is both that of the immediate statement of which it is a part, and the larger discourses (of a song and a genre) of which the statement in its turn forms a part. For example, 'killing' can be found in the mainstream romantic discourse, most notably in 'Killing Me Softly With His Song', where the word clearly has a metaphorical sense. 'Burning' is another word which is similarly used to convey an excess of feeling ('Burning Love'). The Damned's title 'Born To Kill', however, reinstates the literal meaning of the word, while Clash's 'London's Burning' ('with boredom') involves a metaphorical connection based not on overheated passion but on the effects of urban rioting.

Even this distinction between literal and metaphorical word use is less important when we recognize the 'intertextual' nature of all language statements. For instance, while 'Born To Kill' is part of a paradigm of statements using 'Kill' in a dramatic way (e.g., sensational newspaper accounts of murder trials, film titles like *Dressed To Kill*), it also connects with a group of 'Born to . . .' statements, which emphasize ideas of heredity ('born to be king') or of predestination or fate: song titles in this mode include 'Born To Be Wild', 'Born To Run', 'Born To Be With You' and 'Born To Boogie'. And each of those instances involves using the predestination form of statement to emphasize the singer's total commitment to one or other of the staple roles of rock lyrics: the wild one, the outsider, the lover, the abandoned dancer. The weight of this aspect of The Damned's song title (an aspect which ties it to more 'standard' areas of musical and cultural meaning than one might expect from punk rock) can be further demonstrated by recourse to the commutation test. Here, to replace 'Born' by 'Baptised' or 'Trained' would certainly modify the meaning of the whole title.

The kind of analysis which traces networks of connotations for a phrase like 'Born To Kill', networks deriving from similar usages in other places in the culture, and most particularly in the texts of popular culture, is based on the principle of 'intertextuality'. This term is mainly used in literary criticism, and in that field Terry Eagleton has offered one of the most cogent definitions of the process of intertextuality. If 'music' or 'lyric' is substituted for 'literary' here, the applicability of the description to popular song can be grasped:

> All literary texts are woven out of other literary texts, not in the conventional sense that they bear the traces of 'influence', but in the more radical sense that every word, phrase or segment is a reworking of other writings which precede or surround the original work. There is no such thing as literary 'originality', no such thing as the 'first' literary work: all literature is 'intertextual'. A specific piece of writing thus has no clearly defined boundaries: it spills over constantly into the works clustered around it, generating a hundred different perspectives which dwindle to vanishing point.[23]

Eagleton rightly points out that any text (in our case, any punk rock lyric) has 'no clearly defined boundaries'. But there are several levels at which boundaries are imposed on that text, places where, for various motives, the 'reworking' of other texts is limited. The first is a legal and commercial one: a song has to be a clearly separate entity both to take the form of a commodity to be marketed and sold, and to become a piece of intellectual property, to have an 'author' who owns a copyright in that song. (This issue of property and intertextuality can be seen most starkly in the occasional lawsuit when one composer alleges plagiarism against another.)

Then, a text will always be presented in a context, within a discursive formation, which will attempt to impose a way of reading or listening on the consumer. For Eagleton's literary texts, the distinction between reading inside the educational formation or inside a leisure context will produce different effects. Within popular music, the dominant discursive formation is that associated with the major record companies, the charts and music radio. It emphasizes the values of what Simon Frith has called 'orderly consumption'[24] and what elsewhere I have called the 'leisure apparatus'.[25] Here, entertainment is emphasized and enlightenment excluded, leisure defined as a passive relaxation and recuperation and feeling is extolled at the expense of thought.

Further, the drive for the largest possible audience causes the narrowing down of positions to be occupied by the listener. This involves both the 'unique and vaguely defined' addressee of the énoncé already discussed and a certain homogenization of music which occurs within the Top 50 system. Here very different forms of music are presented in a context of comparison and competition which can delimit the audience's awareness of their potentially radical differences. When the Sex Pistols finally appeared on the BBC TV chart show *Top Of The Pops*, how far was it a victory for 'punk'—its chance to present itself to a mass audience—or for the dominant discursive formation, which had now presented 'punk' as just another musical trend?

The shift by the BBC from the exclusion of 'God Save The Queen' to the inclusion of 'Pretty Vacant' (the first Pistols' record to be shown on *Top Of The Pops*) typified a dilemma for the leisure apparatus. One crucial way in which the institutions of popular music try to maintain their dominance is through ignoring musics which contain elements of alien discourses (e.g., politics, obscenity, explicit sexuality), for if those elements are brought into popular music, they may have a disruptive effect. When they are brought in (and here, the popular music institution is caught in an ambivalent posture, since it also feels the need for a renewing of its own discursive practice in order to replenish its products), there are procedures for incorporating those external elements (be they rhythms, hairstyles or lyric statements) to minimize their disruption of orderly consumption.

As Chapter 1 indicated, at the level of song themes, punk rock was responsible for the importation of elements not from 'real life' so much as from other discourses into popular music. Its rhetoric of social and political comment echoed much of the news discourse of the period, sometimes inflected with that of left-wing ideology. To an extent, popular music had earlier, with protest song, had to handle such themes; though here, the emphasis on violent denunciation made punk rock more of a destabilizing factor.

Even more destabilizing was that area of punk language which drew on discourses which not only had been previously absent from popular song, but which had been excluded from the mainstream media discourse of society as a whole: the area of 'pornography' and 'obscenity'. The first rock recording to include the word 'fuck' had appeared in 1969, when *Love Chronicles* by the singer-songwriter Al Stewart had included the lines: 'It grew a little less like fucking, and more like making love.' Although dutifully banned by the BBC, this usage was clearly a conservative one, and no doubt justifiable as 'artistically appropriate'. John Lennon achieved greater publicity when he transferred the swearing usage into song with his reference to 'fucking peasants' on 'Working Class Hero'. A number of other 'progressive rock' performers committed the word to wax during the early 1970s, including Joni Mitchell, Dory Previn, Buffy Sainte-Marie and Nilsson.[26]

It was left to punk rock to introduce 'fuck' and the rest wholesale to popular music. Both the 'explicit' sexual and the expletive swearing versions were available. Clash and the Sex Pistols went in for the latter, for example in 'All The Young Punks', an answer to subcultural critics of The Clash for 'selling out', where Joe Strummer refers contemptuously to them as 'All the young cunts'. The explicitly sexual usage was left mainly to the literal-minded Stranglers on tracks including 'Bring On The Nubiles' and 'School Marm'. The latter, and the Buzzcocks' 'Orgasm Addict' provided a 'bonus' of wordless pantings, punk rock's answer to the soft-porn sounds of the 1969 hit 'Je T'Aime, Moi Non Plus' by Jane Birkin and Serge Gainsbourg.

The Stranglers' songs mentioned have scenarios of pornographic fantasies, with strongly sadistic overtones, and elsewhere that group and the early Adam and the Ants produced litanies of detailed violent acts: 'I'll sew up your mouth', 'You kicked my cheekbones in', 'Smack your face, treat you rough, beat you till you drop'. In so far as these songs disrupted the discourse of mainstream popular music, it was through their ability to 'shock' the listener. But which kind of listener (a 'mainstream' one?, a 'punk' one?) and what kind of shock?

SHOCK EFFECTS

The idea that music, or any other artistic form, should aim to shock is an established part of avant-garde aesthetics. Writing in the 1930s, the German critic Walter Benjamin described the effect of the Dadaists in terms of shock: 'Their poems are "word salad" containing obscenities and every imaginable waste product of language. . . . One requirement was foremost: to outrage the public'.[27] This attitude of épater le bourgeois is a time-honoured one, and a motive that is consciously present in punk rock. In interviews, a number of musicians spoke of 'shock' as an intention.[28] But what precisely was entailed in the shock; was it simply to traumatize the recipients, or in some way to enlighten them? In Benjamin's writings, there are several approaches to this issue. His essay on the nineteenth century poet Charles Baudelaire considers two kinds of response to shock. The context is Benjamin's discussion of the new conditions of everyday life in the metropoli of industrial capitalism where the sudden jolt or shock is a frequent occurrence. Using Freud, Benjamin distinguishes between 'shock defence' which neutralizes the power of shock and a different response which integrates the content of shock into experience by the recipient's exposing him or herself more directly to the shock-effect. For this to occur, the shock must be 'cushioned, parried by consciousness'. In effect, Benjamin argues that the 'shock defence', the inability to 'digest' shock content produces trauma.[29] For the audience of an artistic event, the trauma involves what Barthes calls 'a suspension of language, a blocking of meaning'.[30] The resistance of the audience to the music or other artwork makes it impossible for any meaning to be registered. The viewer or listener turns off when confronted with the film of torture or the 'tuneless' piece of avant-garde music.

Theodor Adorno, a contemporary of Benjamin and a stringent critic of his ideas, discussed this kind of response to what he called the 'radical music' of Schoenberg. There the listener was faced with 'the dissonances which frighten' and 'speak to the very condition of his existence: that is the only reason why they are unbearable'.[31] Adorno, then, imparts a direct epistemological significance to the 'shock defence' identified by Benjamin. The rejection of avant-garde music by the mass of the population means that they have refused to face up to the truth about their lives. The theme of truth-telling at all costs is a familiar one in punk rock too: 'The Clash tell the truth' said Mark P. in Sniffin' Glue. For Barthes, in contrast, the cause of 'shock defence' and its accompanying trauma has a semiotic explanation: the shock-photo is the one for which the reader can find no connotation, no symbolism. Once a picture of a wartime atrocity can connote 'horrors of war' or 'imperialism' it can be integrated into the reader's consciousness. If it remains a pure denotation of sadism, the 'blocking of meaning' occurs.

The distinction between the two responses to the shock-effect—the negative shock-defence and the positive response which integrates the shock-effect—recurs in Walter Benjamin's essay 'The Work Of Art In The Age Of Mechanical Reproduction'. But here, as the title indicates, the argument is placed in the context of the history of different media, rather than the general history of industrializing capitalist societies. Briefly, his thesis is that the avant-garde movements of one artistic form are the heralds of a future cultural medium, whose technologies and techniques will be quite different:

> Traditional art forms in certain phases of their development strenuously work towards effects which later are effortlessly attained by the new ones. Before the rise of the movie, the Dadaists' performances tried to create an audience reaction which Chaplin later evoked in a more natural way.[32]

Benjamin then contrasts the shock-effects of Dada and the cinema. The Dadaist work 'hit the spectator like a bullet, it happened to him, thus acquiring a tactile quality'. But it also kept the 'physical shock effect' wrapped in a 'moral shock effect' (épater le bourgeois?); 'By means of its technical structure', film has dispensed with the moral wrapping and presents a shock-effect which 'like all shocks, should be cushioned by heightened presence of mind'.[33]

The suggestion is that Dada and other avant-garde art-forms were consciously motivated by a desire to make a negative impact, perhaps to arouse a 'shock defence' or trauma in a section of its audience through the 'moral shock effect'. Indeed, part of its success depended on achieving that negative response. But the 'technical structure' of film allowed it to make a new impact without recourse to such deliberate traumatizing. Film's shock-effects were positive, transforming the outlook of the viewer.

If Benjamin's ideas are applied to the 1970s, where does punk rock stand in the contrast between Dada and film, and in that between the two responses to the shock-effect? It seems to have contained characteristics of both a frenzied critique of established art-forms (e.g., Dada) and of the effortless achieving by new technical means of effects or results striven hard for by earlier avant-gardes. Like Dada's 'word salad', much punk use of language involved both the shock of the new (importation of obscenity, politics, etc. into popular lyrics) and the shock of the real (justification of this importation by the assertion that this is what happens on the street). Additionally certain organizational effects of punk rock may turn out to be harbingers of a future, more widespread medium. In particular, the very small-scale 'do it yourself' world of small labels but especially of home-made taped music represented the virtual dissolution of the barrier between performer and audience that was part of the ethos of much punk activity (these points will be taken up at length in Chapters 6 and 4 respectively).

On the other hand, there is a perspective within which punk rock seems more like Benjamin's description of the cinema, which can evoke 'in a more natural way' things strained for by previous avant-gardes. The punk opening up of self-production and distribution represented a relatively painless achieving of something avant-garde rock bands of a few years earlier had to go through debilitating tussles with record companies to get. Punk found ways of access to audience for new music in a manner which had totally evaded the earlier bands.

The production of shock-effects involves confronting an audience with unexpected or unfamiliar material which invades and disturbs the discourse to which that audience is attuned. The nature of the material will therefore depend entirely on the specific context. Adorno and Benjamin provide examples of shock-effects in the particular conjunctures of fine art in the 1920s (Dada) and classical music at a similar period (Schoenberg's 'dissonances'). The material used to produce punk rock's shock-effects can equally only be understood by reference to the characteristics of the pre-existing popular music discourse. A number of examples of shock-effects have been discussed in this and the previous chapter: effects which operate at the level of lyric theme, of choice of words, of rhythm, vocal sound and so on.

Clearly, the shock-effect actually occurs only at the point of impact on the listener. Until that moment the production of shock by the specific formal organization of musical material remains potential rather than actual. But it is possible to distinguish among the formal organizations between those which are more likely to achieve the full shock-effect and those which are less likely to do so. The other active element in all this will of course be the position of the listener her or himself: there will be varying degrees of receptivity, depending on that individual's idiolect and on the context in which they hear the music.

In discussing the potential of different types of organization of musical material to produce shock-effects, it is necessary to return to Benjamin's notion of the two types of impact, the 'traumatizing' and the 'integrated'. I want to suggest that while the first type can be produced by any punk text, only some are capable of going further to achieve the second type of response, which implies the listener's increase in awareness in some form or other.

To explain this further means introducing a distinction between *local* and *structural* shock-effects. A local shock-effect occurs when just one aspect of a musical piece is composed of shock-material, leaving the overall structure intact. When the Stranglers introduce obscene or sadistic lyrics, but retain vocal stylings and musical forms acceptable to the mainstream, a 'traumatic' response to obscenity is quite possible. But for a listener who is able to 'absorb' that shock and integrate it into their consciousness, there is little likelihood of a further 'pay-off' in heightened awareness. In fact, the most likely response is that hearing the music as a whole will mean hearing it as conventionally pleasurable. The local shock-effect is neutralized by the compatibility of the structure of the whole piece with the discourse of dominant popular music.

A structural shock-effect should have a greater chance of reaching the second level of impact, since it can potentially change the whole 'shape' of a recording or performance. 'Love Like Anthrax' by the Gang of Four includes sequences in which two vocalists simultaneously deliver different sets of lyrics, joining together at certain chorus lines. Although it is still possible to hear this as a 'normal' record—by making one vocalist the centre of attention and ignoring the other, the most probable effect is that it will force the listener into a different way of listening, a way which involves considering the relation of the two lyrics to each other, and so on. Somewhere between that organization of the musical material and the obscenities of the Stranglers come the examples discussed earlier in this chapter: 'Holidays In The Sun' and 'Oh Bondage Up Yours!'. How far those shock-effects work on the listener is, to repeat, in part a function of how that listener hears the music, and in particular whether and how the process of *identification* operates in the listening experience.

Systematic discussion of modes of identification in listening is very sparse, so it seems appropriate to adapt the ideas developed about looking in film theory, especially as the Freudian discourse (to which those ideas belong) indicates that the 'invocatory' (listening) drive is a basic component of the human psyche alongside the 'scopic' (looking) drive.[34] A primary form of identification is with that which occupies the central point of a representation, the place of the *hero*, where that term applies not just to a character but to a function which moves the 'narrative' (story or song) along and in doing so establishes itself as something both invulnerable and more perfect than the listener him or herself.

In the song, this position is most frequently occupied by the lead vocal, which as has already been remarked is conventionally mixed 'to the front' of a recording. Sean Cubitt points out that the identificatory power of this positioning is apparent from the way dancers at a disco sing along with the lead vocal line: 'We can . . . through vocal identification become the singer and produce the song as our own.'[35]

Laura Mulvey has shown that the comparable form of identification in watching a film can *potentially* affect any listener, regardless of gender, social class or ideological position. But she adds that it is frequently problematic or in some tension with differences between a listener and the 'hero-figure' (actor or singer).[36] This latter case can be seen in the instance of Mick Jagger's voice and the ambivalent position of certain women listeners, drawn both to identification with Jagger as the source of musical power and control and repelled by Jagger as source of a sexist, sadistic ideology expressed in the lyric.

The importance attached to the issue of identification in radical culture criticism can be traced back to Bertolt Brecht. His dramatic characterization was deliberately designed to foil any empathy between spectator and character because, he argued, such identification precluded the spectator achieving any critical awareness of the character's situation. Hence the Brechtian notion of 'alienation' or 'distanciation' whereby the actor (like Randy Newman with his redneck and as Bowie failed to do with Ziggy) *presents* the character to the audience rather than *becoming* it for them. In this way the artwork could make the audience think rather than simply feel.

Within punk rock, this Brechtian mode of non-identification can possibly be found in three ways. The first, and most questionable, derives from Roland Barthes's distinction between geno-song and pheno-song. His exposition of this distinction contains distinct echoes of the Brechtian theme when he describes the pheno-song as being involved in 'the ideological alibis of a period', including the 'personality of the artist'.[37] It is the presentation of the singing voice as primarily this 'personality' (in the mechanism which identifies the subject of the énonciation with that of the énoncé—see p.81), which is equivalent to the Brechtian identification and empathy. For Barthes it produces only *plaisir*, a form of enjoyment which merely confirms the listener in his or her status quo, without changing it.

In Barthes's account, change comes through *jouissance*, the more radical form of pleasure which 'shatters—dissipates, loses—[the] cultural identity, [the] ego'.[38] *Jouissance* proves the truth of psychoanalytic theory, that the self is not a unified whole, but a shifting bundle of elements, constructed by the drives of the unconscious and by social forces. And it is the geno-song of the voice that produces *jouissance* in the listener. By hearing those elements of a singing voice which are surplus to the communication of a message, Rotten's embellishments or Buddy Holly's hiccuppings, the listener escapes identification with the voice as ideal ego.

Such, at least, is Barthes's argument. But the implication of Sean Cubitt's account of identification with the singing voice is that such a distinction as that between pheno- and geno-song is irrelevant. The voice needs only consistency to become a place for identification.

Punk rock's second way of frustrating the primary identification with the singing voice occurs when a reading is structured so that there is no clearly presented centre of power and control. This can take two forms. First there are various 'avant-gardist' strategies which involve mixing a record so that the lead voice is displaced from the aural focus: the Gang Of Four disc considered above is one example of a text with no single centre for identification. Cubitt mentions also the 'post-punk' all-woman group, The Raincoats, 'who mix their voices down to the same level as the instruments'.

Secondly, there is the case of the voice which repels the listener's hope for identification by its 'unpleasing' character. Historically, this is always one effect of innovation in popular music—the introduction of material from a discourse outside the mainstream is recognized by many as 'unlistenable'. But some punk rock seems to re-double this effect by presenting itself as a *challenge* to listeners, as an act, not of a new version of the popular vocal tradition, but of defiance of that tradition's broadly ingratiating stance towards its audience. There is then a distinction between, say, early Elvis Presley, where the 'traumatizing' shock-effect was an unintended by-product of the novelty of the vocal style, and the Sex Pistols, where the provocation of the 'boring old farts' among listeners was often built into the structure of the record and frequently signalled in the lyrics, as the second-person addressees, as well as in the tone of singing voice.

If, then, this interdiction of identification with the singing voice as such, affected, 'shocked', every listener, it was also the point at which a 'punk' and a 'non-punk' listener began to be constituted. While the latter suffered Benjamin's shock-defence and switched off from any attempt at comprehension, the 'punk' listener made a second-level identification—not with the sound of the voice but with the singer or band making that sound. There is an analogy here, perhaps, with Randy Newman's redneck song. The Newman fan associates not with the subject of the énoncé, but with Newman's aim and motive in creating that subject.

The 'punk listener', however, is involved with another aspect. For his or her alignment with the musician's strategy of provocation must include a pleasure in the awareness of how the other, 'traumatized' listener will be discomforted. That is, the identity of punk as something different depends in part on its achieving a disquieting impact on listeners whose expectations are framed by mainstream popular music and its values. Punk is not alone here. Much 'youth' music or music of outrage depends on its fans not so much being outraged or scandalized themselves, but on their awareness of the results of unpleasant listening in other people. And, finally, we may note that it is quite feasible for the same individual to both feel the effects of shock and to observe and enjoy the disturbance thus caused. That person could well be an example of Benjamin's ideal audience, possessed of 'heightened presence of mind.'

Four
Looking

THE IMPOSSIBLE DREAM

> The Clash had just launched into their first encore on the Tuesday night, 'London's Burning', when the security, which the band had promised would be 'low-key', spilled over into viciousness as a kid who was trying to get up on stage was smashed. The group stopped playing immediately, horrified, and Mick Jones pulled the fan up on stage. Then for both that song and for 'White Riot', they let the kid chip in on vocals. And I don't mean they just tolerated him—the dream-come-true bloke probably sang more of both numbers than Joe Strummer. How many other bands can you imagine allowing that to happen? But that's what Clash are all about, speaking for, with and from working-class youth, instead of talking down to them.[1]

The impossible dream was to first abolish the distance, and then the difference, between performer and audience, the activity of one and the passivity of the other. Punk was formed in opposition to rock music which ranged the superstars with their banks of technology on stage against the audience with nothing but expensively acquired ticket stubs. One effect of the earliest punk bands was to turn listeners into players. The first and most dramatic was former fan Siouxsie Sue's performance of the Lord's Prayer at the 100 Club Festival in July 1976,[2] but later performances and recordings by the Sex Pistols and Clash in particular acted as catalysts for the formation of new punk bands.

That kind of emulation had previously been found in both the skiffle and Merseybeat eras. So, to some degree, had the second impulse in punk rock, to close the gap between musician and listener, between producer and consumer. Dancing had been one way of being active for an audience, and punk fans surging to the front of an auditorium to pogo responded in the same way as teds jiving in the aisles in the 1950s. Another approach to the same point was the assertion in various ways at different times of the 'folk' nature of rock music. Writing in 1970, Jon Landau stated it by saying that 'Rock, the music of the Sixties, was a music of spontaneity. It was a folk music—it was listened to and made by the same group of people.'[3]

If one strand of punk ideology repeated that virtually word for word, the rituals of punk performance took it literally in an unprecedented way. They pushed hard at the dividing line between stage and auditorium.

GOADING AND GOBBING

I first saw the Sex Pistols in April 1976, at the Nashville in London when they supported Joe Strummer's 101'ers. John Rotten stumbled to the front of the stage, held together with safety pins and wild conceit, his blond hair spiky and greasy, his dark eyes alive with venom. 'I bet', he screamed at the bewildered audience, few of whom were at all familiar with the group or its nascent attitudes, 'that YOU don't hate US as much as WE hate YOU.'...

He hung onto the mikestand like a degenerate strain of spider monkey, his attitude expressive of grossly exaggerated infantile petulance—a petulance which came to a head after 'No Feelings' when he walked off stage, claiming, quite falsely, that someone kept turning the monitors off. He soon came back again, of course, sneering that 'Seein' as you're the worst audience we've ever played to, this is just a rehearsal from now on.' But even if it were, each song was still a minor masterpiece of uncompromising contemporary rock....

The course of rap Cornwell takes is not the safest to bawl at a crowd of, by now, well oiled Welshmen. 'Why are you all sitting there like dummies? Why don't you come up here on the floor' (pointing to the small dance area between him and the front line

of tables),'or ain't you got legs? I suppose you all got your passports
to come and work in England?' . . .

Burns tells the audience they're the worst he's ever played to,
Algy vociferously echoes these sentiments, the Rat strolls avuncu-
larly to the edge of the stage and discusses the British Legion with
no-one in particular.[4]

Provocation and goading were even more prominent in punk rock performances
than in the recordings described in the previous chapter. The four examples quoted
above are, of course, firstly examples of the music journalism discourse and not direct transcriptions of live performances. Nevertheless, they are written by 'friendly'
witnesses as reportage rather than commentary and can be accepted as an *attempt* to
recreate the character of the performing methods of the bands described.

The clearest common feature of the four is the rejection of the ingratiating excess of the show business performer's attitude towards the audience, deftly parodied
by David Bowie when he had Ziggy Stardust sing 'You're wonderful, gimme your
hands'. Punk replaced ingratiation with aggression.

In the first and third cases, the aggression is aimed at an audience perceived to
be indifferent or even hostile to punk rock. As such, they can be understood as a kind
of counterattack against such enemies of punk. But what of the other descriptions—
the second and fourth (Pistols at Doncaster in 1977, The Damned in London,
1979)? Here, the bands are among their own—audiences already enthusiastic about
punk rock. Two interpretations offer themselves. In the first, the tactics are those of a
novel kind of showmanship, part of a repertoire of tactics to arouse and enthuse the
audience. Rotten's storming off stage, only to return soon afterwards, has the same
shape as the way a rock band ends a conventional set, leaves the stage and comes back
for an encore. By the latter point, the audience's anxiety to hear more will ensure a
rapturous response to the encore itself.

A more radical reading of these performance techniques would emphasize the
alienation-effect or defamiliarization involved. By drawing attention to the disparity
of situation between himself and them, the musician may actively frustrate conventional types of identification between the audience and him or herself. In doing
so, the actual power relations between the performers and audience could become
transparent.

The goading from the stage had its response from the auditorium. Just as the
musicians launched a ritual assault, the audience responded appropriately. Unable

to reply verbally (the power structure which put bands 'on top' was literally based on *electrical* power) the fans responded physically, in three main ways: can throwing, invading the stage and 'gobbing'.

Like the verbal insult, can throwing was an action whose standard meaning was disapproval—it was sometimes used at rock festivals to drive a disliked performer from the stage—but which punk rock inverted. Fairly typical was this incident at a 1979 Stranglers concert: 'A barrage of cans aimed at Cornwell, and resulting in a random culprit being dragged on stage to mime along.'[5] Elsewhere, seats were used instead of cans. At The Damned gig described above the arrival on stage of the band was 'the signal for most of the audience who can still stand up to race down to the front and begin ritualistically dismantling the furniture and throwing it at their heroes'.

As a ritual of performance, this is again susceptible to the two kinds of interpretation. While fans of Manilow or Dylan may light matches or candles, Damned fans signify a comparable commitment to their heroes with different objects (cans and seats). But the aggressive aspect of the punk instance suggests the difference was more than one of style and taste. For the audience's perception of the band's performance contained contradictory elements. On the one hand it involved a conventional pleasure in listening to music which it found appealing, but in doing so it was reminded (through the taunts or mode of delivery of the band) of its own inferior position, and the imbalance of power and opportunity between itself and the musicians it followed. The audience response to this contradictory sensation was an equally ambivalent one. Affection and appreciation were expressed through aggression. The playful and ritualistic nature of can-throwing may well have contained and been fuelled by an unconscious or barely-articulated resentment.

The forms taken by stage invasions by punk fans seem also be related to the question of imbalance in power between the musicians and themselves. In other musical modes, it had been female fans who had jumped on stage to make contact with their idols, in a manner which transgressed the expected hero-fan relation, while paradoxically reinforcing the star's untouchability. Because of punk's mainly male membership and its downplaying of sexual motivation, invasions by punk fans were not about touching the musicians. Some, like the Clash and Stranglers cases, involved the acting-out of fantasies about joining the band in a stage-level (but not street-level) equality. On other occasions, it was enough to reach the same level as the band, pogo briefly alongside, but separate from them, and finally to dive back into the crowd. Is there, in this separation, another ambivalence or tension in the fan's relation to the performer? A recognition that even the most 'democratic' gesture by a band—the reverse move by Iggy Pop and later Jello Biafra of the Dead Kennedys among others, of the singer actually diving off the stage into the audience—was still a gesture? The power relations, the cash-nexus, still remained.

Gobbing is special in two ways. It was punk rock's very own contribution to the lexicon of performers interaction, and it was one ritual indulged in by both musician and audience: they spat at, and often on, each other. In December 1976, Hugh Cornwell of the Stranglers was reported to 'pump his throat and spit'.[6] But this mime of masturbation (another instance of the band's leering literalism) was not a meaning retained by gobbing in general. The same month, a Sex Pistols audience was described as "'gobbing" at the stage, devoid of menace, obviously believing that was the correct behaviour at a Grundy rock-gig. Mr Rotten's elegant (honest) belated red jerkin and soft mulberry shirt were covered with saliva by the end'.[7] The following year, Steve Jones was observed with an 'expression in deadly earnest . . . which he breaks only to spit on the audience every few minutes'.[8] Up to 1979, punk bands like The Damned and the Ruts were being gobbed at in greetings from their audiences.

As a boundary marker, something which separated the punk from the rest, gobbing was an inspired gesture. Conventionally, spitting is an activity outlawed in public—old buses contained notices expressly forbidding it. It archaically was only acceptable as a gesture of contempt—a sign of strong and formalized emotion, usually in a face-to-face situation. Johnny Rotten told journalist Caroline Coon that in 1975, 'I used to go up and down the King's Road gobbing at the posers.'

The mouth spits, but it also speaks and kisses. Punk's inversion of gobbing, making it a gesture of recognition of a common bond between band and audience, played on this organ's important place in communication and in intimate expression. Yet gobbing, like can-throwing, remained inherently ambivalent, mixing resentment with affection. For what was being intimately exchanged was not words or the touch of lips but excreta.

On Stage

Popular music lacks a history and typology of the choreography and physiognomy of performance. Prior to Elvis Presley and Bill Haley, white mainstream music relied mainly on histrionic gestures taken from opera and from gospel-based black singing plus the well-drilled movements of swing band instrumentalists and the 'intimate' microphone techniques of Sinatra and the crooners. Presley extended histrionics below the belt and made some contribution to the other essential of (male) rock stage performance, the manipulation of the guitar.

These two aspects—the body and the guitar-as-body dominated subsequent rock modes along with variations on the mouth-and-microphone style for slow ballads. Some progressive rock musicians in the 1960s tried to escape from established presentation styles either by adding elements from other media (film, theatre) or by adopting a neutral, unemphatic style of performing, evading the stress on rock as body music. Pink Floyd combined both stances in their elaborately staged shows.

With a few exceptions, the stage presence of punk musicians tended to fall into these established modes. The 'mixed-media' and 'neutral' styles were less common than those which harked back to the more venerable physical/histrionic and guitar-as-body approaches. Punk's borrowings from other media were very much in the style of Alice Cooper. Pig's heads with police helmets were flourished on stage by the Angelic Upstarts and Suburban Studs as visual aids for protest songs, while the Newcastle group Punishment of Luxury followed John Cale in the performance of outrage through mutilating and assaulting dummies and dolls. The Damned's version of theatre, in contrast, drew on the horror film Dracula image for singer Dave Vanian and simple absurdity for Captain Sensible, whose wacky outfits included a nurse's uniform and ballerina's tutu.

If the addition of dramatic devices was primarily meant to emphasize meanings *beyond* the music (protest at police harassment, violent shock-effects), the immobility of other stage performances in the 'neutral' mode suggested a hidden depth inside the music or the performer: 'He once moved over the stage, squirming and jiggering, rarely motionless. Lately, he doesn't move. He can be quite sickeningly still. He sets my skin crawling.'[9]

Subway Sect were among the more celebrated exponents of this type of stage presence, as this 1978 description indicated:

> Paul Myers and guitarist Rob Simmons flank singer Vic Godard, their faces never altering as they chop out angular rhythms. Simmons stares at a point on the ceiling, holding his guitar to his chin, all the time playing rhythm guitar as lead. . . . Godard hunches himself and contorts around the mike stand, his hand clenching his hair in a paroxysm of tortured introversion, seemingly oblivious to the audience a few feet away.[10]

Immobility of the vocalist allowed ideas of inner turmoil and invisible drama to be projected onto him (an element that would be important in the intensity of attention paid to a band like Joy Division). It could also work as a tactic in punk attempts to frustrate the conventional relationship of audience and performer. The Damned, never renowned for psychological mysteries, sometimes had singer Vanian stand totally still for several numbers before springing 'into life'.

Stage liveliness was in some bands an athletic one. Barrie Masters of Eddie and the Hot Rods was wont to climb the stack of PA speakers and sing from the top before somersaulting down, while 999 singer Nick Cash would 'caper around the stage like a mad preacher giving a sermon, pointing and shouting'.[11] That last gesture had precedents in black American music, most recently in the stage act of James Brown, and in both soul and punk rock it fitted the 'finger-pointing' character of many songs. Similarly, the restless use of the whole stage by prowling or charging guitarists and singers had been pioneered by black performers like T-Bone Walker and Chuck Berry, whose 'duck-walk' as revived by Dr Feelgood guitarist Wilko Johnson undoubtedly had a direct effect on some London punk musicians. For the latter, as for earlier rock bands, the energy and type of stage movements had a direct relation to the volume and speed of the music, just as dancing would have for their audiences.

But the almost ever-present mode of stage performance in punk, as in rock generally, is that of the guitar-as-body: 'The stage is set for the men to parade around acting out violence/sex fantasies, sometimes fucking their guitars and then smashing them . . .'[12] Susan Hiwatt's comment deals with the 'cock rock' of the 1960s, but most punk bands shared with earlier groups the guitar-based line-up and the 'spontaneous' adoption of a narrow range of guitar-playing and parading gestures. Despite recognition of the Sex Pistols' difference in other aspects, lead guitarist Steve Jones was hailed by an early champion of the band in July 1976 as 'rewriting the whole Guitar Hero's Stances textbook, pulling his axe up alongside his cheek (great expression of exquisite pain) firing off early Pete Townshend dive bombs'.[13] The language of 'axe', 'firing' and 'bombs' confirms the violence-fantasy diagnosis of the gestures of mainstream guitar playing.

It was not necessary for the guitarists to adopt the extravagances of a Jimi Hendrix or standard heavy metal soloist. The macho connotations of electric guitar playing in rock were also to do with the height at which the instrument was held and how it was held. The 'natural', 'right', 'powerful' way was at waist level with the neck pointing upwards at an angle of about 30 degrees. Machine gun or penis substitute, the impact was powerfully phallic, whether or not the players knew it, whether or not their songs were sexist.

It may be possible to see the excesses of tempo and the eccentric athleticism of some punk players as a puncturing of this machismo, but there is no doubt it was there, at the centre of punk performance. It was registered, but not commented on, by even the most sensitive of journalistic observers. Robert Christgau's immediate response to The Clash on stage was through a military metaphor: 'They occupied their far-flung locations on stage like a unit of partisans charged with some crucial beachhead—instead of roaming around to interact, the way most exciting rock groups do, they held to their posts.'[14]

At the fringe of punk, there was some awareness of the value of deconstructing the live performance as 'act'. Throbbing Gristle (a group formed by performance artists from the avant-garde of high art) and Mark Perry's Alternative TV experimented with the use of pre-recorded tapes and radio sets on stage, shifting the emphasis from one of 'creation' to construction and presentation of material. An early gig of the Mekons in 1978, as described by Mary Harron, suggested another tactic:

> What I saw on stage was not the hideous confusion you might expect, but an intoxicating kind of randomness. The line-up seemed in constant flux, as the Mekons swapped instruments or wandered around stage as if searching for something in a vague but interested way. . . . And for all their careless insouciance, they kept on playing at breakneck speed.[15]

This performance replaced the high tension focused on one central point of power ('the three front-liners form an indivisible body'—Christgau on The Clash), with something more diffuse offering several aspects for contemplation.

But that was the fringe. The central grid of punk performance was inherited from the rock tradition and solidly imbued with macho values, both on stage and in the positions of watching offered to the audience. Traditionally, women performers had to take their place within this grid, or to try to find a space beyond it. Punk had women instrumentalists in male-dominated bands (notably Gaye Advert of The Adverts) caught between becoming one of the boys or becoming a pin-up (Gaye was usually motionless on stage): 'I couldn't take my eyes off Gaye at first, but then I noticed she was playing great bass-lines.'[16]

'I couldn't take my eyes off . . .': a classic instance of the scopophilia (sexual pleasure in looking) which has recently been explored in relation to cinema.[17] The argument posits two types of scopophilic look, usually of male at female. The voyeuristic look is one where the spectator gains power over what is seen because that observed person is unaware of being watched. Clearly most cinema takes this form, while in live performance the fetishistic look comes more into play: 'Fetishistic looking implies the direct acknowledgement and participation of the object viewed.'[18]

This is the position of the mainstream female singer in performance. She performs directly to the audience and is on display to the male gaze. According to John Ellis, the fetishistic look is 'captivated by what it sees, does not wish to inquire further, to see more, to find out'.[19] Therefore, classical Hollywood film narrative so constructs its plots that scenes can be presented (of a nightclub performance for instance) where a tableau of the female can be presented without 'interrupting' the realist flow.

Actual live performance cannot be programmed so exactly, but the placing on stage of the solo singer, the lighting, the sound balance, her immobility contribute to a similar effect. But it is then possible for a tension to develop between this 'objectified' position and, say, the content of the her songs, if these go beyond the romantic themes which underline the fetishistic role. That tension can take various forms in which the singer becomes witty (Bette Midler), a narrator (Joan Baez) or 'poetically' enigmatic (Nico, Kate Bush). In some cases, the tension between the passivity demanded by the male gaze and the performer's own will to be active and self-defining may become unbearable (Janis Joplin).

Among punk's female singers there was no Bette Midler, but elements of the stances I have attributed to Baez and Nico could be found in Poly Styrene and Siouxsie's performances. To describe a singer as a 'narrator' is to emphasize her distance from the autobiographical assumptions about positions of énonciation discussed in the previous chapter. Baez's narration of traditional ballads and Poly Styrene's 'Oh Bondage Up Yours!' persona could not be misrecognized as the 'truth' of their own personal lives. Beyond that point of contact, the effect of performance was quite different for each singer. As far as solo singers of the folk revival like Baez were concerned, they could quite easily be recuperated for the fetishistic look. On stage they were generally immobile and presented a 'gentle' persona which could be assimilated to a certain male-defined ideal of femininity (this is true of Baez herself only in the earlier years of her career). But in Poly Styrene's performance, the tension between objectified physical position and the nature of her songs was a forceful one.

Burchill and Parsons describe her as 'pretty, personable but determinedly sexual on stage',[20] emphasizing her intention to evade the traditional role of being on display to the male gaze.

Siouxsie, for her part, adopted the pose of the 'chanteuse', a European stance of female singing which could bypass the one-dimensional image of women singers in the pop mainstream (emoting and romantic), while admitting a dimension of 'mystery' that might nevertheless prove acceptable to the fetishistic look. But here, Siouxsie's strategies towards stage presence might be seen as a way of frustrating or unsettling that look. Like all punk's women singers (excepting the New Yorker Cherry Vanilla), she eschewed the bump-and-grind routine of, say, Tina Turner. Instead, a 1978 review described her in this way: 'Siouxsie swings and pivots in 90 degree arcs, legs and arms scything. Stylised, angular, full of latent violence and emotion . . .'.[21] The angularity contradicts the 'natural' body movements expected of the mainstream female singer of whatever genre.

Off Stage

Punk rock conformed closely to the norms of mainstream popular music in providing its own dance. The pogo, from one viewpoint, was the latest in a line stretching back through headbanging, the shake, the twist to jiving.

But while all those dances had anonymous originators, the pogo was credited with an inventor. During an early Sex Pistols gig at the 100 Club and before he joined the band, 'Sid Vicious started jumping up and down on the spot with excitement, bashing into people. And this was the first recorded incident of pogoing in the U.K.'[22]

At one level, pogo was the ultimate in minimal dancing, suitable for (and apparently inspired by) one rhythmic tendency of the music—to annihilate distinctions and differences. It also remained true to another aspect of punk strategy—to import elements from outside the popular music structure. While earlier dance innovations could be traced to some existing step, usually in black culture (the twist's relation to limbo dancing, for instance), the pogo had no such pedigree. As its name suggests, it looked most like the action caused by jumping on a pogo stick, a craze in children's toys of some years prior to punk. It was also similar to the jumping movement made by someone at the back of a crowd trying to see momentarily over the heads of those in front. But the pogo was repeated until exhaustion set in.

Other aspects, however, suggested different connotations. The intrepid reporter sent by *Rolling Stone* to cover punk observed:

Most are pogoing alone. Those with partners (usually of the same sex) grasp each other at the neck or shoulders and act like they are strangling each other. Every four or five minutes someone gets an elbow in the nose and the ensuing punch-out lasts about thirty seconds amid a swirling mass of tripping bodies.[23]

As Robert Christgau adds, this is a situation of 'airborne playfight' and for him it 'did justice to something about rock and roll that all the fast steps and sexy grinds ignored—its exultant competitiveness, its aggressive fun'.[24]

But the 'aggressive fun', and in pogo dancing it was virtually always male fun, had links with a broader, more traditional culture than punk's own. *Learning To Labour* is a book by Paul Willis which describes the 'white, working-class male school counter-culture' of the mid-1970s in the English Midlands. In discussing the role of violence and fighting in this culture, Willis has this to say:

> In a more general way the ambience of violence with its connotations of masculinity spread through the whole culture. The physicality of all interactions, the mock pushing and fighting, the showing off in front of girls, the demonstrations of superiority and put-downs of the conformists, all borrow from the grammar of the real fight situation.[25]

The issue in punk rock is not one of genuinely violent actions at gigs. As Christgau points out, the incidence of actual injuries at punk rock concerts does not seem to have been great, and the media uproar over 'riots' concerned damage to property (broken seats etc.) which was hardly greater than the routine vandalism of soccer hooligans of the period.

Pogo dancing, however, was one point where the punk rock of 1976–8 became locked into the wider masculine manual working-class ethos with which the later strands of 'Oi' music would more clearly identify. On the other hand, one strand of punk which did not fit so neatly with that traditional macho culture was the way many musicians and fans looked.

APPEARANCES

Clothes and appearance is one place where a distance opens up between the activity of punk *rock* (the musicians) and another punk activity (the fans or the subculture).

While some innovations in visual style undoubtedly came from the early bands, later shifts came equally from off-stage and outside the auditorium. It was here that the do-it-yourself part of the punk ethos spread productively to the audience. It was only outside the performance context that the passive audience role could be fully transcended: at the point where the performer/audience relationship no longer dominated. The present discussion, however, concentrates on the look of the musicians, since its purpose is to explore the contribution of visual elements to the meanings of punk rock, not of punk subculture.

Pub rock and glam-rock, punk's main musical forerunners offered contrasting visual images. Pub rock involved jeans and T-shirt (informal, reaction against superstar dressing-up) while glam, through Bowie, Bolan, Gary Glitter and so on involved virtually the opposite. Each was a sartorial starting point for punk bands. The Stranglers and The Clash showed an early penchant for 'working man' gear of various kinds, while The Damned and Siouxsie Sue opted for exotica ranging from Dracula opera-cloaks to fishnet tights.

While both the Stranglers and Clash maintained their links with the jeans and T-shirt approach, they grafted onto it various novel or 'shock' elements at various times, notably the use of slogans. Clash initially adopted the technique of adorning their clothes with graffiti, while Hugh Cornwell spent part of early 1977 sporting a shirt which itself sported a clearly written obscenity. In keeping with the 'partisan' aura noted by Christgau in their performing style, Clash maintained a certain radical machismo in each shift of style, which included guerilla combat gear.

The merging of the various origins into a recognizable punk style occurred in the Sex Pistols milieu, which was already saturated in fashion consciousness through McLaren's shop which was run in partnership with Vivienne Westwood, a dress designer. The 1976 look of the Pistols added a number of new elements to a jeans and leather jacket base. Quite a few of these were short-lived and didn't survive to become part of the standard punk mode. They included lurid ties, waistcoats and red mohair sweaters and jerkins. The crucial innovations involved *torn* T-shirts, wet-look and then 'bondage' trousers and a range of ornamentation: studded bracelets and belts, chains, safety-pins, crucifixes and dog-collars (not the clerical kind). The ensemble was topped off with the spiky hair characteristic of Johnny Rotten, though the practice of dyeing hair in one or more lurid colours came later, from the fans.

Before considering the meanings attributed to the torn and bound aspects of punk look, it is worth analysing the visual elements of women performers, in the context of the male-dominated performance space already described. Leaving aside the American singer Cherry Vanilla (leotard and tights with 'Lick Me' inscribed on her body), there were three main modes of dress, each of which was to a degree unconventional in terms of orthodox rock practice.

Gaye Advert opted for the leather jacket, wet-look trousers and dog-collar style shared with male musicians. In the mainstream, Suzi Quatro was already known for a similar style. More unusual was the mode adopted by Poly Styrene, Fay Fife (of the Rezillos) and Pauline Murray (of Penetration). While their garments showed varying degrees of eccentricity (Poly's plastic tablecloth dress and curious headgear) and archaism (the mini-dresses of Fay and Pauline), the outstanding feature was their use of garish 'cartoon' colours. Poly Styrene and Fay Fife in particular used bright oranges, yellows and reds which cut against the colour coding for 'sexy' women performers. But the choice of such colours had other connotations, of the place where they are appropriate—childhood. Fife's gamine image, Poly Styrene's 'infant' voice on some of her recordings overlapped with a general trend in media representations of female sexuality during the 1970s, that of the 'little girl'. The 'childlike' voice had been there before, of course, notably as part of Hollywood's 'dumb blonde' syndrome, but it recurred in a range of places now, including Louis Malle's *Pretty Baby*, a controversial film about child prostitution, and in the voices of singers as far apart in other respects as Kate Bush and Lynsey de Paul.

While Fay Fife's image seemed to evade the connotations of an adult sex-object, only to take on those of an infant one, Poly Styrene's more thorough-going surrealism of dress enabled her to remain 'determinedly asexual' in relation to such connotations. Meanwhile, a third group of women performers, led by Siouxsie and by Ari Up (of The Slits) appeared to take a more confrontational attitude to issues of sexual representation in dress and appearance. By the 1980s, Siouxsie had opted for a more severe chanteuse look in black, but her 1976 style (and that of Ari Up) included what seemed like a whole pornographer's wardrobe of garments associated with sexual fetishism.

Press reviews described a range of outfits:

> **Siouxsie (1):** Black plastic non-existent bra, one mesh and one rubber stocking and suspender belts (various) covered by a polka dotted transparent plastic mac.
> **Siouxsie (2):** A home-made swastika flash was safety-pinned to a red armband, black strap stilettos, studs gleaming, bound her feet;

fishnet tights and black vinyl stockings her legs. Her short black hair was flecked with red flames.

Ari Up (1): Dirty mac over latex tights.

Ari Up (2): Jubilee knickers (printed with a design celebrating the Queen's Jubilee celebrations) over wet-look trousers.

Ari Up (3): Thigh-length mini-skirt exposing embroidered underwear.[26]

In his discussion of the meanings of punk dress, Dick Hebdige speaks of it as

what Vivienne Westwood called 'confrontation dressing' . . . (where) . . . the rupture between 'natural' and constructed context was clearly visible. . . . The perverse and the abnormal were valued intrinsically . . . and placed on the street where they retained their forbidden connotations.[27]

This offers a thesis to test the specific examples of Siouxsie and Ari Up against: how far was their ensemble a clearly 'constructed' one, distanced from the 'natural' one? And how much did the objects on display on their bodies retain or lose their 'forbidden connotations'? Finally, how different was the effect from that of the wearing of those garments in a 'showgirl' or pornographic context?

We need firstly to note briefly where the 'natural' contexts for these items were, and then to consider them as ensembles. The garments with sexual, fetishistic connotations can be divided into the 'glamorous' and the 'forbidden'. The glamorous are those accepted into a public discourse of show business sexuality—chorus lines, night club singers, etc. They include suspender belts, stiletto heels, fishnet tights, miniskirts, embroidered underwear. The 'forbidden' is the paraphernalia of 'rubberware', bondage, sadomasochism: garments of latex and plastic including bondage and wet-look trousers, plus the studded and chained items, including the dog-collar worn by a number of musicians and fans (including Gaye Advert).[28] Ari Up's 'dirty mac' can be regarded as a jokey comment on this category of materials. Beyond those garments comes the use of political motifs (Jubilee, swastika) and the 'mutilation' of the face and head. This is represented here only by Siouxsie's artificially coloured hair, but wider usage including face-painting and heavy make-up plus the application of safety-pins to ear or nose.

Prior to considering the specific sets of garments listed above, it must be recognized that the performance area is a different place to Hebdige's 'street', where punk fans wore similar ensembles. Put simply, there are closer links between the stage and the pornographer's studio or film club than between the stage and the street. On stage and film, the primary role of the female figure is to be on display; on the street it may not be. It is therefore perhaps more difficult to present an outfit on stage as 'constructed' rather than 'natural'—the nature being that of the displayed body.

The possibilities for thwarting the fetishistic gaze seem to rest on the displacement of the fetishized garment from its customary relationship with the body. For instance, the displaying of what should be hidden-in-order-to-be-revealed in the wearing of knickers over trousers instead of under or (as some *fans* did) the wearing of a bra *over* a blouse. These would seem to defuse the expected thrill by bracketing out the 'forbidden connotations'.

Other instances here might have more ambivalent results, especially those where specific garments retain their usual fetishistic space on the body: Siouxsie (2) and Ari Up (3) might on stage have been presented with ironic intent, but in (for instance) still photographs they might well have had little different effect from soft porn or glamour poses produced intentionally. Burchill and Parsons make a similar point when they contrast the 'alluringly lurid press hand-outs featuring fishnet stockings, spiked heels and bondage' with the punks on the street who 'looked nothing if not nastily neuter in the cold clammy flesh beneath their revulsion-conscious efforts'.[29]

Even in performance itself, the danger of the punk attempt to parody male-defined sexual images falling back into those very images was considerable. Ian Penman, a journalist aware of the band's intentions, described a show by The Slits and observed:

> The degree of control over the meaning of what they're doing and what they're coming up against is minimal. . . . On stage the images, the faces, the sexuality are provocative beyond any futile use of parody. But the lad in the audience who tells Ari to 'get 'em off' is intimidated by these three girls going on the rock stage.[30]

Penman's point is that an attempt to parody 'sexiness' may simply miss its mark and be read by the omnivorous male gaze as the 'real thing', leaving aggressive confrontation as the only way to cut the fetishistic connection.

Despite the influence of figures like David Bowie and Alice Cooper on punk rock's formation, male performers showed little interest in using appearance to challenge established gender images. Captain Sensible's tutu owed more to pantomime dames than glam-rock. But particularly on the street rather than on stage, punk's general disregard for romance and sexual relationships as lyric themes was reflected in the 'unisex' dimension of punk appearance as a whole. Hair styles, bondage trousers, safety-pins and studs were elements of the style of both male and female punks on stage and on the street. And perhaps the sharp break with conventional forms of 'dressing up' was more crucial for women than men: 'Conventional ideas of prettiness were jettisoned along with the traditional lore of cosmetics.'[31]

THE PUNK LOOK

At some stage the shifts and innovations congealed into a basic 'punk look', albeit with a range of possible variations. Its organizing principles were those of binding and tearing. Far away from the flowing, loose clothes of the hippie era, nearly everything male and literally everything female was tight, holding in the body. At one level punk was joining a trend of the 1970s to bring 'above ground' the imagery of the machinery of 'bondage' and sadomasochism.

From the Ohio Players (a black American disco group) to Kate Bush, album covers adapted such imagery, and it also graduated into 'art' through the controversial work of Allen Jones. In a familiar pop-art manoeuvre, Jones reproduced images from pornography of female figures in various fetishistic garments and postures of degradation. These developments would have been familiar to the significant number of punk musicians with experience of art education, a topic which is considered further in Chapter 7.

The punk look took such images away from pornographic magazines and Jones's chic decadence to incorporate them into a style of street dress, alongside more mundane objects like bin-liners and safety-pins. As the earlier discussion of performers' clothing suggested, the public parading of garments derived from 'forbidden' sexuality could have ambiguous effects. While it could be seen as a parody or critique of sexual obsession, linking with the curiously puritanical attitudes of some punk songs, they might also provide a perversely exciting twist to already perverse pleasures. Both these meanings were additional to those most emphasized by the theorists of punk style: the urge to shock by displaying what should be kept hidden and the key theme of Hebdige's analysis, the fact that punk garments refused to be pinned down, flaunting their provisional nature.

This 'free-floating' character of punk style was most evident in those aspects of the punk look where 'tearing' predominated. The torn or ripped T-shirts and other garments, the ear, nose or even mouth punctuated by pins took up a half-formed range of pre-punk associations. The torn garment might signify the poverty, the lack of concern for appearance or the involvement with violence of its wearer. Each or all of these possibilities might then be contradicted by the effect of the ensemble of clothing of which the ripped piece was a part.

Something similar was the case with the punk safety-pin. An agent of holding-together, its punk use was perversely seldom to connect the torn edges of a garment. Its extra-punk associations were with babies, a highly utilitarian and visible form of attaching. The punk use was perversely not to connect fabrics but to link or puncture parts of face and head. The result was two-fold. The process could be incorporated into the fashion world by recognizing the pin as a new kind of jewellery or decoration, or the shock effect could occur. This was a jolt to the conventional idea of facial appearance, and to the role of the face in interpersonal relations, where it is the first point of reference in making contact. Mutilation with pins, plus the 'unnatural' colours of hair and make-up, undermined the possibility of such contact being made.

Instead, though, another kind of contact could be made, through the necessary implications of *naming*. As the punk look established itself, so bondage trousers plus spiky hair, chains and pins came primarily to denote a punk identity, rather than any of the other meanings or indeed the refusal of meaning so central to Hebdige's claims for the style of punk.

SWASTIKAS AND SUBVERSION

Perhaps the key test of Hebdige's thesis about the radical nature of punk style is the use of the swastika. This appeared on an armband worn by Siouxsie, drawn on the faces of fans, on a T-shirt worn by Sid Vicious in an advertisement issued in 1979, after his death. Punks were not the first post-1945 group to use this particular symbol as part of their dress. The Hell's Angels of the 1950s and 1960s had consistently worn it as part of their regalia. One explanation for this was given in the autobiography of Frank Reynolds, a leading Californian Angel. In reply to the question, 'Why do you wear swastikas?', he said 'We feel that we are a superior race. The swastika signifies a superior race.' In his classic study of the Hells Angels, Hunter S. Thompson came to a similar conclusion: although 'they insist and seem to believe that the swastika fetish is no more than an anti-social joke, a guaranteed gimmick to bug the squares, the taxpayers', Thompson had no doubt that 'the Angels' collective viewpoint has always been fascistic.'[32]

The Hells Angels, then, wore the swastika at least in part because they identified with its connotations of fascism. *Sniffin' Glue* 4 (October 1976) indignantly reported an incident in which punks were assumed to have the same motivation: 'A member of the Wild Boys (a group currently rehearsing) got mouth-wacked by a Disco-kid 'cause he was wearing a Swastika armband and got branded as a "burner of Jews"'.

Sniffin' Glue made clear, and other evidence suggests, that punks who wore armbands were not doing so because they endorsed fascism. Their purpose was to shock, as Dick Hebdige explains:

> The signifier (swastika) had been wilfully detached from the concept (Nazism) which it conventionally signified . . . its primary value and appeal derived precisely from its lack of meaning: from its potential for deceit. It was exploited as an empty effect. We are forced to the conclusion that the central value 'held and reflected' in the swastika was the communicated absence of any such identifiable values. Ultimately, the symbol was as 'dumb' as the rage it provoked.[33]

This analysis suffers from a very basic fault: it assumes that the meaning of a symbol's use in a particular context is *single* and is determined by the intentions of the 'producer' of that symbol-in-context. The point can be made by applying this analysis to the incident quoted above. No doubt the Wild Boy with the arm band 'thought' he was exploiting the swastika as an 'empty effect', that he was 'communicating' absence of 'identifiable values'. Unfortunately, the Disco-kid received the communication differently. To him, the wearing of the swastika armband (common feature of modern fascist bodies as well as the Nazis) signified that the wearer supported the political views signified by that symbol in public discourse.

This signifier (the swastika), like all others, is always *multi-accentual*. That is, there is always within it a tension between different potential meanings, the result, it could be said, of the pull of different discourses (punk, public political, Indian mythology) to have it read as part of their own meaning-system. And in the case of a long-established political *symbol* like the swastika, the accent placed on it in public discourse cannot easily be obliterated by the practice of such a provisional discursive formation as that of punk.

There is an important distinction to be made here between those elements adopted by punk which were already symbolic, already used to *stand for* something else, and those which weren't: between swastika and safety-pin. The latter in conventional discourse had no role as motif or symbol and therefore was less resistant to its transformation in punk discourse. Since it did not already 'mean' anything, it could easily be made to appear meaningful in a new way: there were no existing meanings to confront or contest the punk one. The same was not the case with the swastika.

SIGHT AS SITES

The swastika example typifies in some ways the confused effects of the visual dimension of punk rock. If confrontation with existing norms of dress, appearance and performance was its strategic heart, the results were remarkably mixed. Relationships between audiences and performers were plunged by punk rock into turmoil, as both bands and fans discovered themselves to be in contradictory roles. In order to produce and to deliver a *musical* message, groups like The Clash and the Sex Pistols were forced to accept their specialized and separate position as musicians; yet the subversive ethos of punk itself pushed them towards the dissolution of boundaries between artist and audience. In a renowned statement, Malcolm McLaren had once declared the Sex Pistols to be 'into chaos, not music'. But the real picture seems to have been that the major punk bands found themselves caught between the two. The same was the case for audiences: to attend to the music was to place themselves in the traditional subordinate, passive position; but to revolt against that position was to risk the disappearance of the music. Gobbing, in particular, was an inspired response to this contradictory situation, combining positive and negative elements in a single gesture.

The sights of punk rock were also the sites of two other major confrontations with convention. Punk dress as visual shock-effect depended very much for its success on context. The punk manipulation of 'taboo' sexual material was open to recuperation by the very discourse of fetishism and fascination which it had set out to ridicule and to use as raw material for shock-effects. This was especially true for still photographs, partially true for stage performances and least the case when such material was worn in the street.

Secondly, the visual was the level at which punk rock's stances towards sexism and gender relations had to become explicit. Punk songs had sidestepped the issue by turning away from lyrics of romance or sentimentality, but the performance of male artists generally showed an uncritical adherence to standard styles which emphasized macho postures.

In complete contrast, most of the best-known female punk musicians set themselves to undo the conventional performing roles provided as models by mainstream popular music. The contrast was underlined by the fact that here the conservatism of male punk style was supported by one of its supposedly radical dimensions. For the image and ethos of working-classness adopted by punk as a 'realist' music was very much that of the aggressive male adolescent, an ethos which produced the pogo as well as the stage choreography of The Clash and The Stranglers.

Picture Section

INTRODUCTION

The pictures presented here mainly illustrate points made in the text. They offer examples of the look of both female and male artists which is discussed in detail in Chapter 4. The final section of these illustrations shows some of the graphic styles associated with punk rock.

But photographs are not passive reflectors of 'real' events. They contribute to the shaping of the meanings of the styles or performances they are witness to. In particular, the provenance of a visual image is important in determining its effectivity. In the popular music field, there is a predominance of two modes. The publicity shot commissioned by management or record company is typified here by the photographs of Fay Fife (127), Pauline Murray (129) and The Stranglers (135). Then there is the live concert shot, characteristically taken by the professional rock photographer crouching at the front of the auditorium, aiming up at the highly-lit stage. Examples here are Ari Up (124) and The Clash (130–1). Somewhat different in their effect are those photographs taken by people outside that metropolitan big arena world. Thus, the spectacle is reduced in the pictures of the Sex Pistols at Doncaster (132) and of Jimmy Pursey (137), whose proximity to his audience could be read as an emblem of the democratic punk myth itself.

Still photographs also bring to the fore an issue considered at the end of Chapter 4. This is the question of the extent to which the avowed punk aim of subverting the significance of 'taboo' sexual material is itself subverted in photographic modes which allow portraits of punk figures to themselves be consumed as pin-ups of sex-objects.

Ari Up (The Slits) How much did the objects on display on their bodies retain or lose their 'forbidden connotations'? (David Wainwright/ Photofeatures)

(Photo above: Rex Features)

Siouxsie
The confrontational attitude to issues of sexual representation in dress. (Chris Pawlette)

Gaye Advert A style shared with male musicians. (Anchor Records)

Fay Fife Her image evaded adult connotations, only to take on infant ones. (Sire Records)

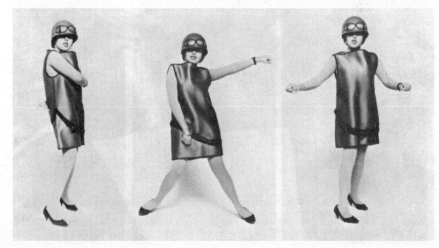

Poly Styrene A thoroughgoing surrealism of dress. (EMI Records)

Poly Styrene (Virgin Records)

Pauline Murray Garments with varying degrees of archaism. (Warner Bros Records)

The Clash (Max Browne)

The Clash Like a unit of partisans charged with some crucial beachhead.
(Chris Walter/Photofeatures)

Sex Pistols YOU don't hate US as much as WE hate YOU. (David Muscroft)

Sex Pistols—threatening (March 1977). (Peter Kodik)

Sex Pistols—playful.
(Bob Gruen)

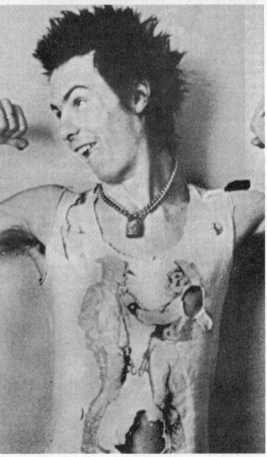

Sid Vicious and T-shirt
'Sex Pistols' foregrounds
the phallic symbolism of
the gun. (Virgin Records)

The Stranglers An early penchant for 'working man' gear of various kinds. (United Artists Records)

Jimmy Pursey 'It's a community, a gang, isn't it?' (Walt Davidson)

Dave Vanian The Damned's version of theatre drew on the horror film Dracula image. (Stiff Records)

Mark P. (Alternative TV) Shifting the emphasis from 'creation' to the construction and presentation of material. (Deptford Fun City Records)

Pop Press advertisements for the Sex Pistols' single 'Holidays In The Sun'. Influence of the Situationists' interest in the subversive potential of comic strips. (Virgin Records)

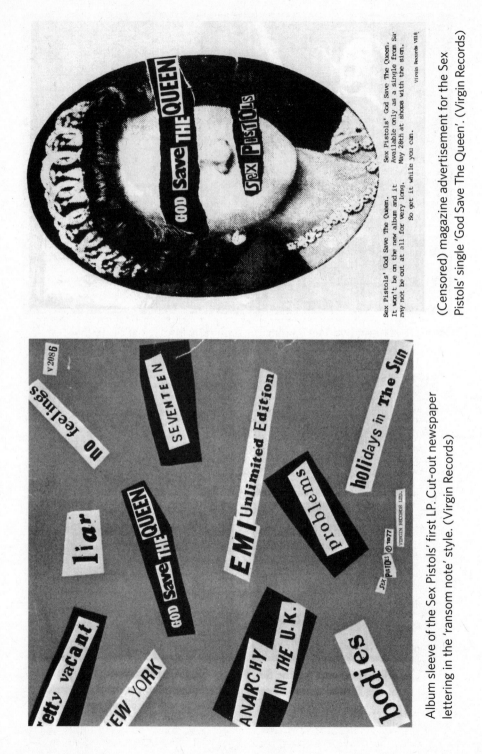

Sex Pistols' God Save The Queen.
It won't be on the new album and it
may not be out at all for very long.

Sex Pistols' God Save The Queen.
Available only as a single from Sat
May 28th at shops with the sign.
So get it while you can.

Virgin Records VS18

(Censored) magazine advertisement for the Sex
Pistols' single 'God Save The Queen'. (Virgin Records)

Album sleeve of the Sex Pistols' first LP. Cut-out newspaper
lettering in the 'ransom note' style. (Virgin Records)

Mark P.'s fanzine, *Sniffin' Glue*, 1977. (Mark Perry)

Lucy Toothpaste's fanzine, *Jolt*, showing notorious anti-pornography campaigner in unlikely pose. (Lucy Whitman)

Two punk fans. The shifts and innovations congealed into a basic 'punk look', with a range of possible variations. (Jenny Lens)

Five
Framing

A 'provisional discursive formation' was the description of punk rock offered on p.121. A discursive formation is a system which supplies for anyone entering it a series of positions to adopt, roles to play and rules to adhere to. The situation is clearest, perhaps, in the most formal of such formations, such as a law court. There, entry to the discursive formation is physically restricted and everyone inside has a role which dictates whether or not they may speak, how and to whom.

Such elements exist in more informal discursive formations, such as popular music, though it is possible sometimes to evade or modify some of the roles. Yet the context of, say, a Top 40 radio show or BBC television's *Top Of The Pops* does involve the listener in hearing music through the criteria of competition and comparison described on p.94. For punk rock to establish a different practice of musical communication it meant an attempt to disrupt or provide an alternative set of criteria and thus a different way of listening. The previous two chapters have considered the elements of the texts of punk (both aural and visual) which were intended to contribute to such a difference. But there is another, crucial, contribution to the process of establishing a discursive formation, which occurs even before a listener hears a note or sees a safety-pin: the set of expectations produced in the listener by the name of the formation itself. When a disc-jockey or journalist introduces a record or a new band as 'punk', a set of assumptions appears in the mind of the listener: she or he is now prepared to be shocked, exhilarated, made rebellious or whatever.

'Framing' is the process by which 'punk' as a description or definition came to be established. The process was a complex one, involving a range of institutions and individuals: both the established media (national and music press, broadcasting, political pundits, intellectuals and academics) and the newer voices from punk rock itself (musicians interviewed, fanzine editors, etc.). It involved both pro- and anti-punk elements, each striving to get its definition of punk publicly accepted.

The relationship between these two sides however was a complicated one. Far from being a position of pure confrontation, there were a number of points of overlap, where a kind of collusion in defining punk occurred between its most virulent opponents and its most impassioned champions.

The remainder of this chapter deals with the main themes in the power struggle to frame punk rock.

EXCLUSIONS AND CHOICES

One of the crucial ways a discursive formation establishes itself is by 'a play of prescriptions that designate its exclusions and choices'.[1] Boundaries are drawn according to certain criteria and a language is developed to distinguish between what it is to remain inside and what is to be banished. The first published review of the Sex Pistols (*New Musical Express*, February 21, 1976) managed both to include them in, and exclude them from, rock music. The band were described as playing '60s styled white punk rock', and thus defined as part of a genealogy of musical genres; then came the comment, 'That's how it is with The Pistols—a musical experience with the accent on Experience.'

The general trend of the language of exclusion was less subtle, however. A collection of descriptions of punk rock and punk primarily from daily and weekly newspapers shows a strong preponderance of words in these categories:

> **Mental illness:** demented, crazed, manic, pathological monster, degenerate, stupid, imbecilic, berserk.
> **Physical illness:** poisonous pus, puke rock, bad breath, outbreak of cholera, sick, scab.
> **Dirt:** filthy, spitting, shabby, rancid.
> **Unpleasant effects:** unpleasant, nasty, sinister, revolting, horror, shock, outrage, notoriety.
> **Violence:** aggressive, violent, savage.

At work here is a common ideological tactic, which aims to exclude something or someone from acceptable discourse by associating them with those things which the *doxa* (the corpus of taken-for-granted ideas in a society) has decreed to be undesirable or even to be feared. If punk and punks can be placed with dirt rather than cleanliness, sickness not health, the process of exclusion can be started. Particularly notable in this litany is the preponderance of terms from the lexicon of madness. Many authors concerned with new ideas in politics, art or morality, have commented on the fact that the first line of defence of the status quo is to confine the new with those deemed to be without reason.

Against the torrent of sickness associations, only a few enthusiasts for punk rock chose to describe it as 'healthy'. Two examples came from opposite ends of the political spectrum. The small marxist journal *Socialist Teacher* considered punk to be a 'strong and healthy style', while the paper of the fascist British National Party wrote that 'many sections of the young from Punk right through to the "teds" are of a definite racialist outlook and I think this is a good healthy sign'.[2]

Rather more pro-punk authors, in fact, accepted and reinforced its image as sick and dirty, following the classic shock-tactic of affirming values which were denied by the doxa. The punk specialists of the music press delighted in such tactics. Burchill and Parsons of the *New Musical Express* hailed Johnny Rotten for 'dancing like a rotten corpse', while in *Sounds* Garry Bushell turned the 'dirty' insult round by denouncing the (non-punk) organization Music For Socialism as 'well scrubbed politicians of rock'. The latter, in fact, belonged to a hallowed tradition whereby contact with dirt signified the genuineness and dignity of the common people. In the nineteenth century a political song of the Chartist movement had the refrain, 'We're low, we're low, we're so very, very low, we delve in the dirty clay', while American popular music offered phrases of praise like 'dirty lowdown blues'. The consensus that punk belonged with dirt was so well set by July 1977 that the *Sunday Times* could refer to 'good clean punk' and know readers would recognize the paradox.

The process of separating the true from the false, the acceptable from the unacceptable also took place 'inside' punk rock. After the first phase of punk's isolation from the cultural mainstream, the apparent monolith of punk could be presented as itself riven with fundamental divisions. This move had two sources. One was the growing number of music journalists whose earlier hostility to 'punk' shifted to a wary acceptance of some of the music. The acceptable was now given a new name, 'new wave'. This was then used to rescue such groups as The Jam, or The Stranglers from the negative associations of 'punk'. The Stranglers, wrote *Melody Maker*, are about 'music not sociology'. But this mode of internal differentiation was viewed with suspicion by the media which had worked hard to establish punk's pariah status.

'New Wave is Punk in Sheep's Clothing' warned the *Sunday People*, while the *Sunday Times* saw it as 'Punk deodorized and re-packaged'. This last quotation introduced the motif of the manipulation of hapless youth which was much beloved of the established media.

Another means of separating the good from the bad within 'punk' was to use the venerable criterion of 'individualism' by contrasting the true musician with the punk conformists. In *Melody Maker*, Ian Birch referred to the latter as the 'pogodrone', bemoaning how much punk rock had become a matter of repetition. This particular argument got a twist from performers like Joe Strummer and Mark P. whose view was that the essence of the punk spirit had been non-conformity and individuality. From this perspective, the 'true' punks were the individualists and the conformists were those excluded from the fold.[3]

RECUPERATION

In the 1950s, American sociologist David Riesman acutely diagnosed in popular music a process he called 'restriction by partial incorporation'.[4] This referred to the way in which the popular mainstream from time to time renewed itself by drawing in elements from musical genres (country music, rhythm and blues) which had previously remained separate from it. One strand of the process of defining punk can best be described as a variant on this type of 'partial incorporation'. This was a manner of discussing punk rock which 'domesticated' it not by re-admitting it directly into the discursive formation of the popular music mainstream, but by demonstrating how it shared many of the 'normal' features of discourses congruent with the cultural mainstream. This kind of recuperation of a milieu previously portrayed as threateningly alien turned punk into a kind of internal colony or Bantustan. This was done in three main ways: presenting individual punks as *family* members, metaphorically populating punk with familiar social types (Angry Young Men, a Queen, etc.) and, more specifically, placing punk rock within the 'family' of rock music, giving it a biography and a musical parentage.

Depiction of any extraordinary individual (film star, politician, sporting hero or heroine) as a member of a family is the standard manner of making them 'ordinary' for magazine and newspaper readers, making them 'just like us'. 'Johnny's top of the pops with me, says Mrs Rotten' proclaimed the *Islington Gazette*, while other journals interviewed parents of punks, featured punk weddings and described 'gymslip' punks.

Familiar figures from the social mainstream transposed into punk included Einstein (Hugh Cornwell was the 'Einstein of Punk' because of his university degree), hack sentimental poet Patience Strong (Patrick Fitzgerald), opinionated editor of *The Times* William Rees-Mogg (whose punk equivalent was said to be Mark P. of *Sniffin' Glue*) and a Queen (Deborah Harry). Another version of this trend to find in punk echoes of the cultural mainstream lay in its increasing use as an image, metaphor or theme within the established media. A random selection of such usage included an episode of the television comedy series *The Goodies* (complete with interviewer 'Bill Grumpy'); a character on the children's television show *Tiswas* called 'Spit The Punk Dog'; the hero of a children's story, Bully Bear, 'going punk' by having a mohican 'fur cut', buying a Walkman and going to a 'roller disco'; in politics, a Labour spokesman calling Chancellor of the Exchequer Geoffrey Howe a 'punk monetarist'; a letter from a self-styled 'punk vicar' in *Sounds* declaring that 'Jesus was a headbanger' and persecuted by the Establishment in much the same way as Johnny Rotten; and in France, *Le Monde* headlined an article about philosophy: *Schopenhauer: est-il 'punk'?*

In the music press, there were deep divisions over punk's relationship to rock. But what connected the for and against factions was their shared notion that punk's acceptability would rest on the possibility of incorporating it into rock music. 'Punk rock is the first genre to cut itself brutally away from the roots of rock' condemned John Collis in *Time Out*. The riposte came from Caroline Coon for whom punk was a 'new wave rock revolution', 'stripping rock to its bare essentials' ('bloated' and 'fat' were adjectives of condemnation often used by pro-punk writers to describe the music and performers they opposed). Elsewhere, punk was re-claimed by making it part of a tradition. The archivist Pete Frame brought it within the fold by drawing family trees of London and Liverpool punk bands, as he had for the musicians of the 1960s,[5] while A&M Records chief Derek Green recalled his youthful adulation of The Who and Stones: 'I get the same feeling from this band' he said of the Sex Pistols, a couple of days before cancelling their contract. Even the present author in 1978 was drawn to pin down punk as a combination of 'the rock 'n' roll musical ethos with subject-matter which is broadly sexual or political'.[6]

The only discourse by which punk rock could be defined as apart from the 'rock tradition' in a positive manner was that of the avant-garde, a discourse which emerged occasionally, in an intermittently coherent fashion, usually in connection with Siouxsie and the Banshees or Mark P.: 'The Banshees reject all rock 'n' roll as essentially reactionary because it never challenges the listener' explained one interviewer. In a negative recognition of the avant-garde project, *Sounds* condemned Mark

P.'s Alternative TV band for ignoring 'the cruel rock 'n' roll framework' (presumably its cruelty was suffered by those who decided to make music without it).

A final and resonant way of recuperating punk was to posit that it was prey to the sins of manipulation and commercialism, just as earlier youth musics had been. Punk, like rock 'n' roll and the rest, was the result of a plot by unscrupulous adults to mislead those who were too young to know better. Ironically, the newspapers which were the most enthusiastic exponents of this view were those which in other circumstances would have applauded the entrepreneurial spirit of the 'exploiters' they now rushed to condemn. 'The real four-letter word behind (the Grundy Affair) was CASH' said the *Daily Express*. *The Times* wrote of 'masses exploited to make a quick buck' and castigated EMI for forgetting its moral duty to uphold law and order in its haste to make profits from the Sex Pistols. 'Punk Rock Exploiters in record companies and concert promotion' were unmasked by the *Sunday People* and even the *New Musical Express* joined in by commenting that 'The Damned claim to be society's rejects, a very lucrative business'.

A curiously symmetrical argument came from 'within' punk rock itself. When Tony Parsons of the *New Musical Express* cried that 'The music business had pulled punk rock's teeth', he too had discovered commercial manipulators at work, outwitting the idealism of youth.

JUSTIFICATION

Precisely what was special about those extracted molars constituted another strand which contributed to defining 'punk'. This was a terrain belonging solely to the advocates of punk and one where justifications of punk centred on assertions of its sincerity and honesty. Whatever its excesses or its ugliness, these alibis were enough.

'Punk rock comes from the street, it's totally real' said Pete Townshend, while *Sniffin' Glue* told its readers that 'The Pistols reflect life as it is in the council flats, not some fantasy world that most rock artists create', and more succinctly, 'Clash tell the truth'. Defined by its opposite, punk rock was not about 'fantasy worlds' and also not made by 'posers': 'Rotten destroyed the pose and replaced it with the reality' (Tony Parsons); 'The bondage trousers I made meself, I'm not a poser' (interview in *Sounds*).

The defence of truth to life was the response of the punk discourse to the accusations of obscenity and horror directed at punk by the media. But while it worked to mark out a separate place for punk in a positive manner, it did so through a well-established discursive strategy, one that had served many forms of art in battles with censorship and defenders of 'public morals'. The celebrated trial in London in 1961 for obscenity of D.H. Lawrence's sexually explicit novel *Lady Chatterley's Lover* had made full use of such forms of argument, for instance.

They also fell within the broad aesthetic sphere of realism, the claim that an artwork's value lay in its ability to reveal aspects of 'real life'. Punk 'realism' belonged specifically to that part of the general aesthetic which emphasized the opening up by art of previously 'hidden' areas, notably of working-class life. From novelists like Zola or the Americans of the 1920s and 1930s (Upton Sinclair, John Dos Passos) to the film-makers of Italian neo-realism and the British 'angry young men' of theatre and cinema in the 1950s and 1960s, such an impulse had provided one main driving-force for the new and the critical in Western art.

The other driving-force had been the 'avant-garde', those artists who had contrived to shock established taste and morality not by revelations about life at the bottom of the heap, but by their rejection or transformation of the decorum and the conventions of art itself, including those of 'realism'. Within the discourse of punk rock, the notion of an avant-garde could coexist with that of realism because of this shared oppositional element: both represented a rejection of the cultural status quo. That there was also a deep contradiction between them was, for the present, less apparent and less important.

CONCLUSION

In the context of developing a more or less rigorous theory of punk rock's identity such a contradiction would have to be directly acknowledged and resolved. In the context of 'framing', of the construction of a discursive formation of punk rock, the existence of competing and inconsistent definitions and arguments had a different significance. Here, it acted as a strong confirmation of the necessary existence of punk, since so many things could be said about it. Indeed the volume of statements about punk rock (and the volume at which they were communicated) was a vital factor in the framing process.

That heterogeneity of statement is also apparent if an attempt is made to group together the statements from 'inside' punk rock (the fanzines, musicians, sympathetic journalists). These clearly do not compose some pure discourse of punk rock, markedly separate from other commentaries on punk rock. There are overlaps and echoes between pro- and anti-punk statements, as well as places where the arguments remain separate.

This is most striking at those places where punk definitions most clearly took up positions previously established in some other corner of the cultural sphere. Very little of this was conscious—though there is scope to speculate that the 'avant-gardists' within punk rock may have been presented with such ideas in the course of an art school education. In fact much of punk rock's energy came from its conviction that it was inventing such positions in a revolutionary manner, even when they had been invented over and over again before, even in popular music itself. The paradox was that at the moment when the framing of punk rock was contributing to its formation as a separate discursive area, with its own places for artist and listener, that area in its turn was traversed by themes and motifs originating in discourses and ideologies which punk had set its face against.[7]

Six
After

I n February 1978 the show business columnist of the London evening paper, *The Standard*, announced that 'Punk Is Dead' and was promptly reprimanded by *Sounds*, the most energetically pro−punk rock of the specialist music weeklies. For *The Standard*, the demise of punk was a vindication of its view that the music had been a passing fad, but by the end of 1978 even punk's staunchest defenders had begun to admit that its heroic age was over. The most embittered 'obituary of rock and roll' was Burchill and Parsons's *The Boy Looked At Johnny*, a short book by two *New Musical Express* journalists which claimed that punk's decline began as early as 1977. A more general view was that things began to fall apart in early 1978 when the Sex Pistols split as Johnny Rotten left the band to emerge six months later as the leader of Public Image Limited (PIL), an avant-garde outfit that was definitely 'post-punk'.

What 'killed' punk? The final section of Chapter 1 described the complex of factors involved in the disintegration of punk rock as a self-contained musical discourse, but here we are concerned more with the explanations provided by contemporary commentators. Here, as in the earlier phase of the 'framing' of punk, some curious alliances operated. Those for whom punk was simply the musical equivalent of the skateboard (and as short-lived) included not only the establishment media but 'mouldy fig'[1] rock critics like John Collis of *Time Out*, author of this picturesque formulation: 'When they said rock 'n' roll was a passing phase they were obviously short-sighted, but punk rock will have the lifespan of a scab.'[2]

More important, though, was the way in which the pro-punk obituarists, led by Burchill and Parsons, took the view that punk rock had been the subject of a deliberate assault by the forces of an uncaring music industry, a view that had been a commonplace of the 'underground' and hippie attitude towards record companies a decade earlier. For it was only in the 1960s that it was considered that music could have two stages, moving from purity to defilement or innocence to corruption. The initial context was that of the 'folk-rock' trend in America, when Old Left cultural ideologues condemned the results of the chart success of Bob Dylan and others: 'there is something slimy and powerful about the Top 40 industry that contaminates and controls most things that come into contact with it.'[3]

This model—of something to 'sell out' (a cause, a vision, a pact with the fans) and somewhere to sell-out to (the record industry, occupying a separate space from that of the original pure creation)—took hold of rock commentary in the later 1960s. So much so that even a writer who stood outside the radical political rhetoric of the rock criticism of the time was forced on occasion to acknowledge it. Lester Bangs wrote that 'Rock 'n' roll is in its core one of the most brilliantly conceived products by which a capitalist society ensures the diversion and pacification of its populace.'[4] In a characteristically provocative way, this statement challenged the basis of the radical position, by denying the moment of innocence or purity which the radicals argued had been 'sold out' to or swallowed up by 'capitalist society'.

The punk ideologues' version of this radical position drew on support from an unlikely source: academic sociology. In the mid-1970s, a group of marxist sociologists based at the Centre for Contemporary Cultural Studies at Birmingham University published studies of the various British youth groups of the previous two decades. By adapting the notions of 'subculture' developed in deviancy theory, these authors provided an image of the ted, mod and rocker not as delinquents or victims of capitalist society but as various sorts of unconscious working-class resisters to the system. The argument gave a special value to the *style* of these youth subcultures which then suffered from the effects of a 'commercial *defusing* . . . in order to make it widely marketable.'[5]

At other times the ivory tower source of such arguments would have ensured their lack of wide circulation, but the effects of changes in the recruitment and composition of music journalists in the late 1960s had provided an avenue for such a wide dissemination. These changes involved a break with the traditional pattern of staffing the weekly music press with young general reporters drawn from mainstream newspapers. Instead, journalists now often came direct from college or from London's burgeoning underground and alternative press. College background provided an access to academic discourse while the underground provided the notions of 'sell-out' and commercialism which were also implicit in the Birmingham academics' work.

The result, particularly in the *New Musical Express*, was a tone of hostility or disdain towards the music industry and a championing of musicians whose work appeared to go against the trends favoured by the industry. Papers like the *New Musical Express* and theories like that of 'youth subculture' were in this sense 'geared up' for punk rock, though each needed a new generation of personnel (Burchill and Parsons, Garry Bushell, Ian Birch among the journalists, Dick Hebdige the sociologist) to point it out to them.

Among the new journalists, the iconoclasm which recognized and championed punk rock could be turned to pronounce its end and to denounce those held to be responsible. But this was by no means the only view of what happened to punk in 1978. Other commentators were ready to contend that reports of its death were greatly exaggerated. Although an era had ended, it was felt a punk legacy remained to be taken up by new generations of performers or new forms of music. Broadly, the punk legacy was seen as either the *substance* of punk rock, or its *spirit*.

The idea of a punk substance persisting had three main aspects: genealogical, sociological and formal/stylistic. The punk family tree had The Clash, Pistols and Damned as the founders of a dynasty where the next generation included Sham 69, then the Angelic Upstarts and on down to the so-called 'Oi' bands like the 4-Skins and The Exploited. While that view was propagated mainly in the columns of *Sounds*, some writers in the *New Musical Express* found solace in a different family tree which was said to lead from the patriarchs via Siouxsie and the Banshees and Adam and the Ants to Southern Death Cult and a 'positive punk' in 1982–3.

The sociological element simply reiterated the position of the early *Sniffin' Glue*. Genuine punk music was rooted in a social group deprived by unemployment and oppression. When the Pistols split, bored inner-city youth still demanded self-expression. Hence punk couldn't die because it had to supply that demand. Thirdly, 'proper' punk music now had quite definite forms, just as the punk style of dress had assumed a fairly rigid formula in 1977–8. The model for self-proclaimed punk after 1978 derived from the Ramones via the eight-to-the-bar rhythm most characteristic of The Vibrators and Clash among the early British bands. It became essential to sound one particular way to be recognized as a 'punk band' now.

By way of contrast, the music which was held to retain the spirit of punk rock was not required to sound at all like the Sex Pistols or The Clash. This 'post-punk' music continued that aspect of punk itself whose ambition had been to subvert or undo the conventions of the popular music mainstream, rather than replacing them with a new set of conventions belonging to a punk genre. In direct contrast to the bands keeping alive the punk substance, post-punk performers 'sought to undermine the populist assumptions of transparency and subcultural identity, to mock the idea of a direct line from social experience to musical form'.[6] The sound of this music lost most of its links with the punk of 1976–8, and varied from the guitar-based Gang of Four and Banshees to jazz or electronic-influenced material, like that of Johnny Rotten's post-Pistols group, Public Image Limited (PIL).

The opposition between these two musics which developed after punk's demise can readily be seen to have been prefigured in the moment of punk rock itself. Substance versus Spirit corresponded to the tension between the realist and avant-garde stances. But the strands of the two positions had been tangled together in punk rock itself through the shock-effect. Both the dirty proletariat and the daring avant-garde had possessed the means to shock conventional values. What had made the Sex Pistols so central to punk rock had been the way in which these strands had been so closely interwoven in the group's work. It had retained connotations of a street-level aggression and expression while determinedly undermining musical forms and expectations.

One way of understanding the end of the period of punk rock's ascendency is to see it as the point where it was no longer viable to make music in which the two strands were still intertwined. While punk rock was still the embattled, shocking oppositional force of 1976–7, these contrasting musical stances found they had much in common. But this was essentially a 'negative unity', to take up the term from Chapter 1, brought about by the solid hostility towards all punk rock of established musical and social institutions. Once that solidity began to break down, through record company signings of punk bands, so did the unity of punk—as, for instance, some of its exponents were redefined as 'new wave'.

From 1978, musicians coming from a punk background went either the realist/populist or the avant-garde/experimental route. And the collapse of the old punk unity was increasingly underlined by a new pop music which proceeded from the premise that punk no longer mattered, or that pop exponents could thankfully ignore punk. Already in December 1977, something called 'Power Pop' was being touted as a fun-loving alternative, a view echoed rather later by Duran Duran: 'After punk, things are getting more glamorous'.[7] And despite their early connections, The Police were taking their distance as early as May 1978: 'We're too young to have been into Woodstock and too old to be punks.'[8] Nevertheless, the influence of punk rock was demonstrated even in that group's line-up through Sting's choice of name. The rest of this chapter is concerned with the more substantial consequences of punk rock, including its international effect and its impact on record industry economics. First, though, the musical development of both the 'substance' and 'spirit' strands needs to be traced.

REAL PUNK

Whether or not punk rock was dead after 1978, punks themselves weren't. In a survey of British youth in November 1981, the *Sunday Times* found 'Bobby, a girl in Newcastle upon Tyne, who colourfully sported spiky hair, tribal make-up, bondage trousers in tartan, spiked jacket and big boots,'[9] With only a few additions and variations (notably the mohican haircut), this punk look solidified into a uniform, suitable to join the ready-made clothing advertisements in the music press, alongside the 'Skinhead', 'Mod', 'Bowie', 'Ska' and 'Ted' outfits.

Just as the rockabilly or ska kids had their own bands, so did punks. By 1981 the performances of bands such as The Exploited had all the atmosphere of ritual, including lyrics which had now become self-referential: songs about punk itself—'Snarling and gobbing and falling around.'[10] Vice Squad's 'Resurrection' also celebrated the 'rebirth' of punk: 'The immortal faction/The unconquered contingent.' On the surface there was a continuity with the anthems to 'the kids' that Sham 69 had sung in 1978. But while Jimmy Pursey's songs had implied that the punk approach might embrace a wide constituency of youth—might become a mainstream—the music of the 1980s that claimed to be 'real punk' was a shrunken version, songs for the (self-) chosen few, the remaining genuine punks.

The stance and fate of Jimmy Pursey was crucial to the direction taken by this strand of music. In 1978, Sham 69 had three Top 30 hits and two hit albums. Jimmy Pursey seemed to represent the new (second) generation of punk rock and was poised between his mainstream record-buying audience and the intensely involved punk and skinhead following evident at his concerts.

'Punk to me was a platform and I was saying this is how I feel', said Pursey in a *Sounds* interview.[11] He embodied to breaking point all the latent contradictions involved in the 'realist' approach to punk. For Pursey, even more than the early Clash, presented himself as a mirror of street-level attitudes. Although in early interviews he had acknowledged the influence of the Sex Pistols, the irony, sarcasm and outrageousness of Johnny Rotten were absent from Sham 69's music. With them went most of the things which had separated punk from the philosophy of that earlier 'youth subculture', the skinheads. When the Birmingham sociologists quoted a skinhead's definition of his own peer-group, it could easily have been echoed by Pursey himself, describing his 'punk' milieu: 'It's community, a gang, isn't it, it's only another word for community, kids, thugs whatever.'[12]

'Kids' was a key word in Pursey's lyrics. One of his hits, 'When The Kids Are United', was adapted from a Chilean freedom song 'El Pueblo Unido, Jamás Será Vencido' ('The People United Will Never Be Defeated') and the substitution of 'kids' for the left-wing, anti-imperialist 'people' underlined the ambivalence of Sham 69 to the political commitment of both left and right that was occurring in their audience. And while Pursey himself intended 'Kids' to have its own political charge (that of 'street politics'), its ambiguity allowed some of his fans to adapt the song in their turn. 'To "If The Kids" we sing "If the Arsenal Kill United" and to "Borstal Breakdown" we sing "Chelsea Breakdown"', explained one skinhead,[13] 'Kids' were no longer the broad stream of working-class youth, but the male football gang.

The political ambivalence of Pursey's proletarian punk came to a head in his relations with the Rock Against Racism (RAR) organization. Inspired by a racist outburst by Eric Clapton and by reports of David Bowie's admiration for Hitler, RAR was set up in August 1976 with a letter to the music press from a group of supporters of the far-left Socialist Workers Party.

After attacking Clapton in terms redolent of the rhetoric used to 'frame' punk ('puke', 'brain damage'), the letter called on readers to:

> fight the racist poison, otherwise you degenerate into the sewer with the rats and all the money men who ripped off rock culture with their cheque book and plastic crap.
> Rock was and still can be a real progressive culture, not a packaged mail order stick-on nightmare of mediocre garbage. Keep the faith, black and white unite and fight.[14]

Although the ideology sustaining this initial statement owed much to the Old Leftism of the 1960s—motifs of commercialism and the 'progressive'—during 1977 RAR promoted many gigs around Britain, providing punk bands with much-needed platforms for performance, often in harness with reggae groups. Its work also reinforced that of the Anti-Nazi League, a broad political body dedicated to combating what in the mid-1970s threatened to be a revival of fascist politics in Britain through the growth of the National Front (NF) party. In particular, the NF attempted with some success to recruit disaffected working-class white male youths from inner-city areas, the same skinhead milieu from which some of Sham 69's following came.

In February 1978, Sham 69 played a RAR concert at the Central London Polytechnic. Afterwards, Pursey was criticized in RAR's journal for failing to 'refute' fascist slogans chanted there by some skinheads:

> by allowing them to get away with it, you are betraying your songs and yourself. . . . At the moment we have 'fuck all'. . . . Your songs show that well, but what do we do about it? Nothing? Attack those who because of their colour already have 'fuck even less than us'? Or those that create the poverty? Write us a song about it Jimmy. 'Tell us the truth'.[15]

('Tell us the truth' and 'fuck all' were catchphrases from Sham 69 songs.) RAR's own implicit position, like that of Pursey, was one of 'realism': the role of the artist was to tell the truth. But the RAR leadership's marxist politics also led them to the view that an honestly realistic description of the state of things would *necessarily* imply a leftist politics. Thus, for RAR all Pursey needed to do was to follow through his existing insight to its (socialist) conclusion.

This position, like Pursey's own, lacked an awareness of the creative and moulding power of ideology. A particular experience (of poverty or oppression) did not automatically lead to a certain political stance. Depending on how the experience was *interpreted* it might lead to a variety of political conclusions. The RAR critique of Jimmy Pursey recognizes this point by asking him who is to be attacked for the perceived social injustices. But the point remains couched in the language of realism, making it seem that Pursey was somehow deliberately avoiding an obvious 'truth'.

But was Pursey 'betraying' his songs by his political neutralism? As I have already suggested, the youth politics of his lyrics, while embodying a spirit of rebellion, offered little clear focus. They had no implicit political message, but offered a politically sensitive space for such a message to be added by either (or both) the Left and Right. Fascist parties saw no problem in claiming punk for their own, arguing that it was 'totally white in origin' and had a 'message of the frustration of the masses of white working class youth'.[16]

The musical politics of Sham 69 were not particularly new. The youth anthems of rock could be found in the 1950s and 1960s (Chuck Berry, The Who). But unlike those earlier bands, Jimmy Pursey was under intense pressure from orthodox political ideologies to translate his youth anthems into something else. That pressure (which sometimes was directly physical with skinheads fighting at Sham 69 gigs) did much to precipitate the band's demise in 1979.

One of Pursey's virtues was his keenness to use his success to provide opportunities for other 'real punk' bands. The most important of these were the Angelic Upstarts from the north-east of England. Like the London groups who emerged simultaneously, the Upstarts reflected in part the general working-class tradition of their locality (this development was a radical break with the iconoclasm towards *all* existing discourses of the earliest punk bands). Their broadly socialist standpoint fuelled anti-police and other protest songs.

Although many played concerts for radical causes like prisoners' rights campaigns, the 'Oi' bands which emerged in the wake of Sham 69 represented a form of musical ghettoization which Pursey had tried hard to avoid. Their collective name came from an aggressive shout ('Oi, you!') which neatly summed up the main feature of their music. But that music, and the names of the bands themselves had lost the positive, expansive energy signified by Sham 69 and Angelic Upstarts. Instead they seemed determined to reflect only the terms in which the mainstream social discourse rejected them: Infra-Riot, Exploited, Criminal Class, Vice Squad, Last Resort, Cockney Rejects, Cock Sparrer. The sexual innuendo was narcissistically male—the 4-Skins, and punk's exhibitionistic choice of individual names was almost totally replaced by gang-member nicknames. The Wattys and Hoxton Tom's far outnumbered Beki Bondage and Mark Docile.

Musically, 'Oi' was a sort of glum rock with vocal lines and choruses based on Pursey's anthems but inflected further towards the chants of football fans. Its main innovation was the holding of two Oi! Conferences in 1981, presided over by journalist Garry Bushell who had done much to champion the music. These discussed issues like which benefit campaigns to support and 'the bands' violent image which was felt to be unfair'.[17]

But Bushell for one seemed to have an unfortunately ambiguous attitude towards that 'violent image'. He compiled the first album of Oi! tracks but called it *Strength Through Oi!* (a reference to a famous Nazi slogan) and stuck a picture of a scowling, threatening youth on the sleeve. Not long afterwards, on 4 July 1981, came a provocatively-organized gig by the 4-Skins at the Hamborough Tavern in the mainly Asian district of Southall. Several coachloads of skinheads from the East End of London fought with Asian youths. Despite the band's disclaimer that it opposed 'Neo Nazi groups and the extreme left wing organizations' and that it 'simply tells

THE TRUTH about the British class system', Oi! had gained a national reputation as a music for racists, if not a music of racism.

A very few, short-lived punk bands were explicitly aligned with fascism and one 'Rock Against Communism' concert was held in London.[18] Far more significant was a self-proclaimed anarchist politics within 'real' punk rock. It was centred on the group Crass and other musicians associated with them, notably Poison Girls and Conflict. With their own record label, fanzine and even a commune to live in (which brought inevitable accusations of 'hippie' deviationism from proletarian purists like Garry Bushell), Crass attacked punk bands who had 'sold out'. One of their early songs included the lines, 'CBS promote the Clash/It ain't for revolution it's just for cash'.

Often castigated for the simplistic sloganizing of their lyrics, Crass neverthe-less had one of the best-selling punk records of 1983 with their anti-militaristic 'Sheep Farming In The Falklands'. Poison Girls were more challenging, offering a feminist-pacifist perspective in songs like 'Take The Toys From The Boys'. While remaining within the punk milieu, the group, led by an 'older' woman, Vi Subversa, were willing to confront both the machismo of rock performance and its implicit pro-youth prejudices.

Oi and the anarchists both drew on the spartan side of first generation punk rock, with their emphasis on the stark and the explicit. The inheritance of the 'dress-ing up' side of punk, exemplified by The Damned, Siouxsie and the Banshees and Adam Ant, was claimed by a *New Musical Express* article in February 1983 for a number of bands defined as 'positive punk'.[19] They included Brigandage, Southern Death Cult, Danse Society, Ritual, Rubella Ballet, Virgin Prunes, Specimen, Sex Gang Children and Blood and Roses. Musically, 'positive punk' retained the guitar focus of punk, but it was prepared to vary the tempo, the vocal approach and to use a greater range of recording techniques. Lyrically, however, these bands turned their backs on both the social realism and the shock tactics of their predecessors. Instead they dealt in 'mystery rather than history' and delved into mysticism and metaphys-ics, subject matter which has always provided a fascination for some of rock's autodi-dacts, whatever their musical genre—The Doors, Black Sabbath, Incredible String Band, Led Zeppelin. Where positive punk was most innovative was in visual style. It carried on the experimentation of early punk, producing such mixtures as 'a tasselled black haired mohawk with red pegs'. It was a look borrowed by Culture Club's Boy George, who harnessed it not to the Gothic echoings of punk but to a breezy main-stream rock sound.

PUNK EXPORTED

Ever since the arrival of rock 'n' roll in 1956, the issue of English-language dominance in the popular music of European countries has been a major one. Each new trend from America or Britain faced musicians with the choice of ignoring it, copying it or adapting it to existing national genres or concerns. Punk rock had a swift impact on music in Europe which in part involved imitation of the music of the Sex Pistols or Clash. And as had earlier been the case with conventional rock bands (Shocking Blue and Focus from Holland, Tangerine Dream from Germany and Burnin' Red Ivanhoe from Finland), many new punk groups chose English language names. Among them were The Cut, PVC (Norway), The Sods, Bad Semen (Denmark), The Rondos, Workmates (Holland), Stinky Toys (a French band who played at the 100 Club Festival in 1976), Big Balls and the Great White Idiot, Buttocks, Male, PVC, The Razors (West Germany), Tilt, Pershing (Poland), Flying Razors, Nasal Boys, Kleenex (Switzerland), Dirty Actions, X-Rated, Joe Squillo and Electrix (Italy), Watercloset Band (Czechoslovakia) and Sharp Ties (Greece).[20]

In addition, other aspects of British punk were imported into some European countries. In 1977 Switzerland had fanzines called *No Fun* and *Punk Rules* while the Austrian group Chuzpe had a big hit with their version of 'Love Will Tear Us Apart' by Joy Division. But as well as reproducing the stylistic aspects of Anglo-American musical hegemony in Europe (dominance of the English language and of genres originating in Britain or America), the example of British punk rock encouraged resistance to that hegemony. For its stance of opposition to the dominant institutions and styles of the music business was also taken up by punk's adherents in many countries. This involved both a determination to write about immediate and 'local' issues in song lyrics (as opposed to the 'transnational' approach of an Abba) and in some places the setting up of small-scale record labels in opposition to the multinationals. West Germany in particular saw the emergence for the first time ever of an alternative record distribution system, although this proved to be less durable than its British counterparts.[21]

In the countries of the Warsaw Pact, punk rock's relationship to the status quo had an ambivalence which in some ways paralleled that of Britain. The authorities in Poland, Hungary and East Germany to differing degrees unofficially tolerated the emergence of punk rock. In both Poland and Germany, punk bands were relegated to the edge of the music world, being denied access to radio or recording facilities. Occasionally, concerts were banned (as in Britain), notably when the band Deserter were forbidden to play in Krakow when that city was visited by Pope John Paul II. The level of repression was much lower in Hungary, though officially the growth of interest and participation in punk rock was seen as an intensification of the 'problem of youth'. In a valuable analysis of the pop and rock scene in Hungary, Anna Szemere argued that punk and the associated 'tramp' music followed by many teenagers arose from the interaction of three factors: the inflow of Western influences, the bureaucratic inadequacy of the existing Hungarian pop institutions to provide what the youth required, and the effect of economic recession on the strata of the population from which punk enthusiasts were drawn.[22]

Precisely those aspects which found a ready hearing for punk rock in Europe limited its appeal to the power structure of the American music industry—the radio stations and record companies. In relation to the dominant language of international pop music, punk was a dialect and one difficult to comprehend. Early tours by the Sex Pistols and The Clash made little impact, though later visits in which the latter were presented as a modern version of a mainstream rock band established The Clash within the United States.

As such, they were fulfilling the criteria for acceptance laid down in the first review of punk records in the influential magazine *Rolling Stone*. In October 1977, that journal's reviewer opined that the punk was unlikely to produce 'music that could stand the test of time' as had such figures as 'Presley, Berry, the Beatles, Dylan and many, many more'.[23] British punk rock appealed in 1977 only to the mavericks among American critics. These included both devotees of American punk, like Greg Shaw who devoted an issue of his journal *Who Put The Bomp* to chronicling the phenomenon, and those sophisticated writers concerned to explore the social and political implications of music without infringing music's autonomy in the process. These included Robert Christgau of the *Village Voice* and Greil Marcus in San Francisco.

But Christgau and Marcus had no influence over radio playlists or mainstream newspaper reviewers. Consequently, the most significant influence of British punk in America as in Europe was on those impressed by its cultural intransigence. Highly ghettoized punk scenes developed in Los Angeles and New York producing a kind of transatlantic 'Oi' milieu which set itself against 'art-damaged poseurs' and 'nostalgia-ridden popsters'.[24] New York punk rock called itself 'hardcore', borrowing the adjective from the sphere of pornographic films. Its exponents had names like Heart Attack, Even Worse, Undead, Nihilistics, Bad Brains, Pricks, Blister, Chaos and Damaged Goods.

POST-PUNK

In discussing visual style, Hebdige distinguishes between that which 'concentrates' attention on the *act of transformation* performed upon the object' and that which 'concentrates attention on the *objects-in-themselves*'.[25] He associates the first with punk dress and the second with that of the teds. But the evidence is that punk dress and punk music contained both elements: they contained 'objects-in-themselves' (uniform modes which conferred a punk *identity*) as well as 'acts of transformation' (those *avant-gardist* elements which foregrounded their critique of the 'natural' language of dominant clothing or musical styles). The punk rock strand including 'Oi' and positive punk was primarily concerned with confirming the punk identity through repetition of recognizable motifs. 'Post-punk' refers to that music which emphasized its commitment to 'reorganize the meaning of rock devices, to make self-consciousness, wit, detachment and thought the basis of musical emotion.'[26]

Post-punk involved various strategies. One was to draw on elements from musical styles outside rock—free jazz, electronics, even folk musics. It was this approach that brought together on independent labels musicians such as This Heat and Scritti Politti who had evolved within the punk moment and others (Robert Wyatt, Ted Milton of Blurt) who had a longer history of existence on the 'avant-garde' edge of the popular music scene. One important effect of punk was to construct an audience of some size capable of absorbing the work of a formerly isolated writer and singer like Robert Wyatt.

Perhaps the most publicized band drawing on extra-rock elements was Public Image Limited (PIL), the group formed by John Lydon (Johnny Rotten). In its recordings, the group used electronic keyboard sounds derived from a strand of German music associated with bands such as Can and Kraftwerk. But PIL also worked through a second post-punk strategy which might briefly be called deconstructionist. Exemplified in PIL's first record and in the group's 1983 hit 'This Is Not A Love Song', this approach involved playing with or undermining the basic, taken-for-granted elements of rock music. In the case of the 1983 hit, lyric conventions were transgressed as Lydon's words discussed their own generic status.

Additionally, Lydon carried forward from the Sex Pistols what could now be called his experiments with the singing voice. The attempt to evade the strong pressures to vocal conformity was particularly important for women performers in post-punk. While the declamatory imperative of punk rock itself had made it virtually *de rigueur* to reject the confidential and 'gentle' vocal tone of white rock women singers (which all too often carried connotations of submissiveness), the post-punk space offered the chance to explore wider vocal areas. Here, too, bands such as The Slits and The Raincoats came close to those, like the Feminist Improvising Group's Maggie Nichols, whose concern with vocal experimentation originated in the jazz avant-garde. The results were attempts to incorporate vocal sounds like cries, screams, laughter into the discourse of music.

One of post-punk's most ambitious attempts to deconstruct the conventions of rock lyrics was the first album by the Au Pairs, *Playing With A Different Sex*. This aimed to turn the love song genre against itself by presenting lyrics written from a feminist perspective within the established 'personal relationship' format. From a different angle, Scritti Politti's 'The Sweetest Girl' managed to integrate the discourse of politics with that of the love song, while the Human League, in its earliest, experimental form recorded a track ('Circus Of Death') which opened with a voice telling listeners the 'story' of the song they were about to hear.

INTO THE MAINSTREAM

Later, equipped with synthesizers and some traditionally well-crafted love songs, Human League were internationally successful in the mainstream of popular music. For while punk rock itself failed to become the Next Big Thing, many performers associated with punk found individual niches within the mainstream, usually because they were able to occupy an already established rock role. Foremost among these were two of punk original five bands, The Clash and the Stranglers.

Despite the considerable differences between them, both bands were close enough to the standard format of the all-male guitar-dominated rock group (classically personified by the Rolling Stones), to fit easily into the mainstream. Indeed, apart from a nostalgic element among their live audiences, the Stranglers merged almost totally into the standard rock milieu. Individual members made 'solo albums' of various degrees of pretension while the band turned in the early 1980s to sentimental hit singles whose underlying message was nevertheless as misogynistic as their earliest shocking punk material. 'Golden Brown' for instance preferred a boat to a woman, while 'Strange Little Girl' was about the 'simplicity' and 'mystery' of the female (compare 'Ruby Tuesday' by the Rolling Stones).

The Clash turned out differently. In some ways they fulfilled a wish expressed back in 1969 by the protest singer Phil Ochs who had euphorically stated that what was needed to bring about the revolution was for 'Elvis Presley to become Che

Guevara'. Certainly the element of topical political comment from a broadly leftist position remained in the work of The Clash after 1978, notably on the three-record set *Sandinista!*, named in honour of the revolutionaries of Nicaragua. In so doing, The Clash (like Tom Robinson and, in a slightly different way, Bruce Springsteen) gave a new lease of life to the idea of a 'rock tradition'. This one was differently based (in the Stones, Chuck Berry, the blues and rockabilly) than that 'three chord trick' which some commentators had made punk part of but it had a similar function; it fixed more firmly existing (and arguably limiting) musical values by 'proving' that they could be modernized.

Nevertheless, the example of The Clash in developing a dialect of political comment within the rock mainstream should not be underestimated. Without that example (as well as punk's general impact) it is unlikely that the songs of UB40 and of 'Two-Tone' groups like The Specials would have found the general popularity they enjoyed from 1979 onwards. Of course, their success was due also to two other factors which punk rock itself had turned away from. The music drew heavily on contemporary black styles (reggae) and it was strongly danceable.

The most popular of the other artists to shake off early punk associations and become stars of the mainstream were Blondie, the Boomtown Rats, The Police, The Jam and Adam Ant. Blondie's punk pedigree was derived from the band's origins in the same New York club scene that produced the New York Dolls and The Ramones, but the group's own appeal was a far more conventional combination of tuneful multinational pop songs and Debbie Harry's glamorous image. The Boomtown Rats and The Jam were among the groups most eager to reach for the 'new wave' label to replace 'punk', though they turned out to be intelligently updated equivalents of the Rolling Stones and The Who respectively. The Police's punk credentials were even slimmer; like Blondie, they happened to start out from the same milieu as some punk bands, although their musical credo was very different. Adam Ant, though, was a genuine ex-punk. From being a 'bad boy' of punk he transformed himself into the 'principal boy' of pop, retaining his penchant for dressing up in the process. Hardly changing his costume, he moved from playing the Marquis de Sade to Prince Charming. For a while, too, he even had his own subculture (the 'ant people'), in a pre-teen parody of punk itself.

A New Map of Production

Aside from the success of those individual artists, punk rock's major impact on the popular music mainstream lay in the unprecedented performance of small, punk inspired record labels in the years after 1978. There was seldom a week during which the Top 20 best-selling singles did not include at least one record on a label like Factory (New Order, Orchestral Manoeuvres In The Dark), Mute (Yazoo, Depeche Mode) or Graduate, UB40's own company. Additionally, there were a large number of artists whose early records had been in the small label system who then moved to one of the pre-existing major companies. Thus the Gang of Four and the Human League both left Fast Product, for EMI and Virgin respectively.

Despite that trend, the independent sector of the British record industry grew rapidly during and after the heyday of punk rock. One listing in 1980 showed nearly 400 labels, many of them existing to market the work of just one artist or group, but others, such as Factory and Rough Trade, with a considerable catalogue.[27] In turn, the majority of these labels were distributed to the shops by an independent company rather than by one of the multinational record companies.

Precise statistics as to the proportion of the overall record market occupied by the independents are difficult to determine, not least because the 'official' figures collected by the British Phonographic Industry (BPI) tend to a bias against the smaller independents in the way they are collected. However, Factory Records has claimed sales figures of over 100,000 for an album by the lugubrious Joy Division, while UB40's hit singles have sold over twice that number through independent distribution. One estimate of the independent share of the album market in 1982 held that it was over five million copies or nearly 10% of the total British sales. This was also said to mark a fall from the peak period for indies of the late 1970s.[28]

It may well be that the proportion of the market held by the indies will decrease during the 1980s as the big companies move to introduce new technologies such as the compact disc. But one irrevocable result of the punk era was a major change in what might be called the economic psychology of making records. Whereas the making of an album had previously been envisaged by most aspiring musicians as comparable in scale to the making of a cinema film (and therefore as far out of reach), punk showed that recording could be the musical equivalent of a magazine or paperback book. The punk example enabled the recording field to become as varied and as wide as that of print publishing, which stretches from the most expensive hard-cover book to the cheapest Xeroxed sheet.

Perhaps the logical conclusion of the punk idea in recording was reached in the sphere of 'do-it-yourself' cassette tapes. During 1980 the music press began to publish details of a system whereby for the price of a blank cassette, a reader would be sent a copy of a set of songs or piece of music directly from the performers themselves. Many of these recordings were themselves made at home with the aid only of a single track tape recorder. DIY tapes represented the punk idea of 'Xerox rock' in its purest form, by utilizing technology that was available to, and manipulable by, almost anyone.

PUNK CHIC

Newspaper descriptions of Belle and the Devotions, performers of the mediocre British entry for the 1984 Eurovision Song Contest, described their hairstyles as 'punk'. The word had now become an adjective in the discourse of mainstream fashion and style, denoting not a subculture or an attitude but simply certain, relatively unusual, variations in hair colour or decoration. The omnivorous industry of *haute couture*, eager for new sources of inspiration had seized on the punk look as early as September 1977, when dress designer Zandra Rhodes presented a collection containing jewelled safety-pins and 'wet look' satin.

Dick Hebdige sees this as a straightforward instance of an authentic innovation of a youth subculture being recuperated by the cultural mainstream and thereby losing its critical force.[29] But the early history of the punk milieu suggests a more complex picture than this decline from authenticity to commodity. The punk look itself emerged from a 'rag trade' context, McLaren and Westwood's Chelsea clothes shop, variously called Let It Rock and Sex, which operated on the interface of fashion and a politically-inspired desire to shock and outrage. After punk rock, Vivienne Westwood moved back into dress designing proper to become an *enfant terrible* of *haute couture*.

The punk look, then, came out of a milieu with an awareness of fashion, as well as the other factors which contributed to the formation of the sound and style in 1976–7. That this connection was not accidental was argued by Angela Carter, who suggested that the personnel of punk (both musicians and punks 'on the street') had strong similarities with the life-style of the older professions of rock music and fashion:

> those who cannot work because there is none to be had and so make their play, their dancing, their clothes into a kind of work, for reasons of self-respect, have a lot in common with those who either do not need to work or whose work is a kind of play, like pop musicians and fashion models.[30]

The implication of the narrative set out in Chapter 1 was that there was a strong sense in which the origins of punk and its final shape were moulded more by its character as a musical genre than as a youth subculture. Punk's close relations with fashion can be read in a similar way. There was an ambivalence at the heart of the punk look which was often not recognized by those keen to point out the subversive potential of punk.

For the punk look was also to some degree formed in relation to the existing discourse of fashion, the centre of whose power was its ability to reduce anything visual to a stylistic novelty.

This is not, however, to argue that the punk/fashion interface exhausted all meanings and values possessed by the punk look. That look survived its brief moment as the high fashion of 1977 to be preserved in the uniforms of followers of 'real' punk or as part of the fancy dress wardrobe of disco dancers. But perhaps its most potent survival was in its influence on a more widespread hairstyle. The close-cropped and spiky look was adopted by many women and took on a general association of a commitment to feminism and against traditionalist stereotypes of 'femininity'. The connotations retained punk's combativity but had shed its specifically exotic and outrageous aspects.

Seven
Conclusions

P unk rock has received a mass of definitions and explanations aimed at placing its origins and effects within the British class structure and political system. As a prelude to drawing together my own general ideas about punk rock, this chapter deals with a few of the more influential attempts at theorizing the music and its context.

CLASS

The most widespread view of punk's relationship to class is typified by this statement: 'British punk grew up in the late 1970s among young working-class people at a time when the country faced severe economic problems.'[1] As an assertion about the class *origins* of punk musicians this can be shown to be inaccurate. Table 5 compares the social background of 49 members of punk rock bands with slightly more personnel (58) of beat groups in the mid-1960s.[2] It suggests that a sizeable minority of both samples came from outside the working-class.

Table 5 Class origins of punk and beat group musicians

	Working class	Middle class	Ex-students (in whole sample)
Punk rock sample (1976–8)	57% (28)	43% (21)	29% (14)
Beat group sample (1963–7)	52% (30)	48% (28)	22% (13)

Figures in brackets indicate actual numbers of musicians.

This sample is limited both in numbers and by the *sort* of musicians it includes. Since published information is available only for those who were relatively successful, the sample excludes the 'rank and file' local bands of each musical genre. The distinction between social classes in Table 5 also needs explanation. The 'origins' of each musician are defined as that person's pre-musical job (if there was one) or by the occupation of the individual's parents. The basic criterion for dividing occupations between working- and middle-class strata lies in the latter performing some kind of 'professional', managerial or supervisory function. Thus an engineer, a teacher and a shopkeeper would be middle-class occupations, while those of clerk, labourer and shop assistant count as working-class jobs.

While the sample in fact shows that most punk rock performers had working-class backgrounds, that majority is not overwhelming enough to justify the claim that punk is fundamentally proletarian. Beyond that lies the effect of other influences on the class position of the musicians concerned. Two factors are important here: the role of further (post-school) education and the unusual position in the class structure of professional musicians themselves.

The final column of the table indicates that nearly a third of the punk rock musicians had been students of some kind. Most of these in fact had studied art, in a milieu (the British art college) which occupies a special place in the history of rock music in Britain. During the early 1960s such performers as John Lennon, Pete Townshend and Ray Davies had formed their styles in the art college context. And unlike the more formal academic institutions such as universities, art schools in Simon Frith's phrase were places where 'working class teenagers could go if they reject a working class future and don't have the ability or desire to tread a meritocratic path'.[3]

The art college, in fact, offered a training ground in a traditional way of life associated with artists and sculptors, the Bohemian one. This aspect of the punk background gives some credence to the suggestion by Robert Christgau, subsequently amplified by Simon Frith, that punk was a 'working class bohemia',[4] which set it apart from more mainstream modes of working class existence, notably those which were centrally defined by the specific occupation and skills of the individual: the Bohemian rejects the labour that Paul Willis's writing (discussed on p.113) argues is the main focus of the school education to which most working-class youths submit.

A different stress on educational background rather than class origin could be found in Cohn McCabe's contention that punk was 'one of the most encouraging first fruits of the comprehensive school'.[5] Although McCabe's remark was in some conflict with the reported views of Sid Vicious on the comprehensive school system—'They taught me nothing—except that I knew when I left there that there was nothing I wanted to learn from them'[6]—its suggestion that this shift in the British educational system was a vital influence on punk makes a useful contrast to the 'Bohemian' argument.

That both had some truth seems most likely. All the evidence is that the punk milieu was a heterogeneous and paradoxical one, something that might be expected to be reflected in class position and educational background also. But the one level at which there was something approaching a sociological homogeneity was the one which most often sunk from view for commentators and theorists. Whatever their class origins or experience of schooling, all the punk performers were professional musicians, a situation which gave them a place within the class structure as a whole.

That place was one which many popular musicians, particularly in the rock tradition, had occupied before them. It was a double-edged one. As live performers, punk groups were usually straightforward sellers of labour-power. They were employed to do a job under the direction of the promoter, with whom they negotiated a one-off fee for the job. But as recording artists, they were owners of intellectual property of potential economic value (their compositions) and contracted to receive a royalty on sales of their recordings. Thus while the live performer was in a position analogous to that of the standard working-class member, the recording artist's place had shifted towards a place more comparable to the self-employed (the classic petit-bourgeois with its equally classic ideology of self-reliant individualism or the skilled artisan less distant from the skilled employee). But the economic interest dictated by the royalty system then set the recording musician in an intimate relationship with the record company, since his or her income depended on the same factors as that of the company—the number of copies of a recording sold.

This is a complex area which deserves greater exploration in depth than is possible here:[7] the role of musicians' unions and the relationship between economic position and the stated political stances of various individual performers are important areas for discussion. But one initial conclusion can be advanced: the economic position of the recording artist is one which, in itself, offers little parallel with that of the proletarian who sells his or her labour-power. Further, the conditions of work are equally far removed from the collective situation of a factory or mill. If, then, punk musicians are 'working-class', that consciousness must derive primarily from outside their work situation.

There is in fact, a different way of linking punk and the proletariat, albeit one which by-passes the issues raised in a consideration of the musicians' economic class position. This is through the application of the concept of youth subculture, which was touched at on p.150. Dick Hebdige's *Subculture* provides a valuable summary of the basis themes of the subculture idea,[8] but a few further comments are necessary here. First, it is worth recalling the functions served by the theory when it was developed by a group of *marxist* sociologists in the early 1970s. It both tied the activities of youth to a specific social class (thus attacking the 'myth' of a classless youth life-style) and also validated the apparently aimless activities of mods, skinheads and others in terms of class struggle: even when they seemed to be mere consumers or delinquents, these kids were acting out a proletarian destiny, reacting against capitalism. Their culture was there, in effect, as a 'problem-solving' one, to 'express and resolve, albeit magically, the contradictions which remain hidden or unresolved in the parent (e.g., general working-class) culture.'[9]

The 'magical' way the youth could resolve these contradictions was through *style*, an arrangement of clothing, music, argot, means of transport, coiffure, etc., where there are 'homologies between the group's self-consciousness and the possible meanings of the available objects.'[10] Thus, teds gravitated to the speed and volume of rock 'n' roll, while hippies preferred the 'structurelessness' of progressive rock.

One significantly absent element from the youth subculture studies is any discussion of the relationship of members of those subcultures to other working-class kids who were not members. Perhaps this is because the only answer possible is an elitist one. Since mods, teds, skinheads and now punks had some kind of access to a *truth* of working-class existence (the 'contradictions which remain hidden or unresolved in the parent culture'), those who could not see that truth remained in thrall to the false consciousness of a 'mass' youth culture. This is certainly how subculture members themselves felt at times: true punks made their own outfits, the 'posers' merely bought theirs.

But this elitist position only had justification if it was really the case that its possessor had some superior insight into the nature of the system. Hebdige's careful reconsideration of the subculture thesis leads him to doubt that particular part of it: 'One should not expect the subcultural response to be either unfailingly correct about real relations under capitalism, or even necessarily in touch, in any immediate sense, with its material position in the capitalist system.'[11]

At this point, where both the class origin of punk personnel seems in doubt and punk's epistemological superiority is undermined, it is not clear what value is left in describing it as 'working-class'. And the concept of a distinct punk subculture is further vulnerable in two ways: in its incorporation of music as an element of its style and in its strongly masculine bias.

The 'style' of a subculture is closely bound up with its identity and its self-awareness: 'the group must be able to recognize itself in the more or less repressed potential meanings of particular symbolic objects'.[12] Among these objects is music, and it is clear that the 'repressed potential' meanings recognized by the ted or punk must be different from any unrepressed, already expressed meanings of a piece of music. The latter, presumably, would constitute the preferred meanings constructed by the discourse within which that music had originally appeared.

Now there are certain songs which have a kind of split-level meaning. Beyond the surface sense is another *secret* meaning or significance available to a privileged few. The so-called 'drug songs' of the 1960s provide one case. Thus 'Along Came Mary' by The Association was superficially a love song, but for those possessing the code it became an anthem to drug-taking (Mary = marijuana). A slightly different instance it provided by the mainstream popularity in the same decade of several reggae songs including Desmond Dekker's 'Israelites'. It is safe to assume that the mass white audience for that record did not recognize the detailed Rastafarian references in the lyrics. In the hit parade they remain 'more or less repressed potential meanings', to be picked up only by those already within Rasta. This is despite the fact that originally, in Jamaica, the preferred meaning had been the Rasta one!

But did the lyrics of punk songs work in this way? In general, they did not. For, as the analysis in Chapter 3 indicated, many were aimed at 'them', targets outside the subculture, in such a way that the shock-effect of the impact on 'them' was an essential part of a song's success. That is, it was vital that the import of the lyrics, their message, was communicated to the target, because the outrage and shock thus generated (and the awareness of it) was part of the punk discourse itself. Far from keeping back secret or 'repressed potential' meanings from the mainstream listener, punk rock needed to communicate its full message to that listener in order to enjoy the results of such a communication. Punk was not separate from mainstream morality and culture, but symbiotic with it.

Angela McRobbie has effectively pointed out how much women are invisible in the accounts given by subcultural theorists of mods, teds, punks and the rest.[13] 'Style' here is always male style, and where women are mentioned it is as 'the people who were dancing over there in the corner by the speakers'.[14] It is here that male subculture members can least be presented as rebellious or radical, in sexual or family relations.

Within punk rock as a musical genre, gender representations did not offer quite such a dismally reactionary picture. Punk's deliberate refusal of romance as a theme for songs meant that it could avoid one of the most potent sites of gender stereotyping, although punk lyrics did not follow this through generally by offering positively anti-sexist approaches. Similarly, punk's stance against the cult of instrumental virtuosity had the side-effect of undermining one of the main sources of male dominance in musical performance: the general rock assumption that women were not capable or competent to play 'properly'.

But, as shown in Chapter 4, such anti-elitism did not preclude the reproduction of macho styles in stage gestures and movement. Male punk musicians moved and manipulated their instruments in ways ultimately similar to the musicians of the rock 'n' roll tradition, from Elvis Presley to the Rolling Stones. In direct contrast, though, many female punk performers deliberately organized their acts to evade or escape the standard women's roles in rock music. It was as if the empty space left by punk's anti-romance and anti-expertise positions made it easier for women performers to themselves work in a radical manner. It wasn't, then, punk rock itself which was positively anti-sexist (indeed the refusal to deal with love themes at times had a misogynist tinge), but its negative operations opened up greater possibilities for such work within popular music.

POLITICS

If the 'class position' of punk rock proves to be elusive on close inspection, what about its *political* position? The music was widely recognized as unusually politically concerned for a rock genre, and both its lyric themes (see Chapter 1) and its song structures (see Chapter 3) incorporated into musical discourse terms and phrases from the political discourse of the wider British society, notably the 'crisis' rhetoric of 1974–5.

But in their political statements, many punk bands were eager to avoid anything that smacked of programmatic commitment. Thus, Billy Idol stated: 'We haven't a set political stance—we're not communists or fascists.' This did not, however, mean that the stance of punk lyrics could in some way be politically 'spontaneous' or original. Flavoured frequently by the general rhetoric of 'crisis' (see Chapter 1), punk lyrics tended to be either *populist* or *bored* in their orientation. Populism speaks on behalf of, or about, a named or implicit social group and their grievances. Beginning there, and not from a political belief, it can then take on a left- or right-wing colouring.

Punk populism, such as that of Jimmy Pursey, usually defined the 'people' in terms of 'the kids' rather than a wider working class although The Clash often opened out populism into an anti-imperialist dimension.

'Boredom' as politics was a novelty. Its theoretical source was the philosophy of Situationism, 'one of the most radical, revolutionary perspectives of the late 1960s'.[15] Acknowledging its roots in the anti-art of Surrealism and Dada, it proposed a 'revolution of everyday life', finding the genuine resistance to capitalism in wildcat strikes, industrial sabotage and the ghetto riots of the USA. The high point for Situationism had been the May Events of 1968 in Paris, when its slogans ('Be Reasonable, Demand The Impossible'; 'Take Your Desires For Reality') had been widely disseminated.

In Britain, the pro-Situationists were a small circle of drop-outs, art students and intellectuals who included Malcolm McLaren, Tony Wilson (later of Factory Records) and Richard Boon (later manager of The Buzzcocks). Their activities were intended to conform to true Situationist practice, which aimed imaginatively to disrupt the everyday life of capitalism in order to expose its oppressive nature. A group of American Yippies who invaded a live television show hosted by David Frost were hailed as carrying out exemplary Situationist actions, while McLaren took part in a bizarre supermarket caper aimed at deriding consumerism. The Bill Grundy/Sex Pistols confrontation had something of a Situationist flavour to it.

Even this, though, was not enough to satisfy the stern guardians of Situationist orthodoxy. The anonymous author of a 1982 tract, *The End Of Music* (clearly one of the 1960s activists), denounced McLaren for using Situationism to radicalize rock rather than to destroy it: 'Punk music, like all art, is the denial of the revolutionary becoming of the proletariat'. Here, all culture has become the opium of the masses, distracting them from realizing their political destiny.

Such a critique, like the critique of Jimmy Pursey by the activists of Rock Against Racism (see pp.154–5) indicates the, heterogeneity of the political views taken into punk rock and refracted to its listeners. But there is another sense in which an artistic form can have a political dimension: there is a specific politics *of* music as well as the reflection of political ideas *in* music. This other sense was best formulated by the theorist of the shock-effect, Walter Benjamin, when he intervened in the debate among left-wing European writers during the 1930s over the real character of politically valuable art. Benjamin wrote that the question was usually proposed of a work: 'what is its position *vis-à-vis* the productive relations of its time, does it underwrite these relations, is it reactionary, or does it aspire to overthrow them, is it revolutionary?'.[16]

Instead of that question, which concerned the message or content of a work of art, he suggested another:

> Before I ask: what is a work's position *vis-à-vis* the production re-
> lations of its term, I should like to ask: what is its position *within*
> them? This question concerns the function of a work within the
> literary production relations of its time.[17]

The adoption of the term 'production relations' shows that Benjamin is shifting the discussion from the issue of what artists can do for the workers (in portraying their struggles or the iniquities of capitalism) to what artists can do *as* workers. It becomes clear that he has in mind the methods and techniques of artistic production, the apparatus which the progressive artist should try to change 'within the limits of the possible'. To supply a revolutionary message by the same methods as others supply non-revolutionary messages risks negating the impact that is intended. Benjamin goes on to consider some artists who have undertaken this 'functional transformation' of technique, including the dramatist Brecht and the photo-montagist John Heartfield, whose work inspired some interest in punk circles, resulting in the Banshees' song 'Mittagerzen (Metal)' (see p.86).

Punk rock was unusually concerned with the 'production apparatus' too. Its earliest exponents saw that to make music against a system, meant naming music that was against the music of that system. Hence the hostility towards the forms and methods of progressive rock and mainstream pop described in Chapter 1. But how far was the resulting music and its techniques of production a 'functional transformation'? Greil Marcus pointed towards a certain paradox in the punk rock revolution when he wrote that it 'used rock and roll as a weapon against itself'.[18] This point has two aspects. First, if it is assumed that punk was, in McLaren's words about the Sex Pistols, 'into chaos, not music', then it was self-defeating to become, in effect, another musical genre, however radical. This is the perspective of the super-Situationist critic in *The End Of Music*. Yet, such an aim would have been naively overreaching in the context of the powerful and sophisticated institutions of the leisure apparatus, like expecting a single act of disruption to bring down the whole system.

But even as music, the paradox of punk's critique of existing forms was evident. Here, as in many places, there were two strands within punk, pulling in contrasting directions. The first did try to use rock against itself by 'stripping the music to essentials' (Marcus), rather like putting a bloated, decadent person on a diet to restore them to health. This was less a musical transformation than a return to an imagined uncompromised and genuine past. The second strand, however, implied going beyond the set of conventions which had made up the whole of the 'rock tradition', to oppose what for a brief period in the music press was called 'rockism' (in an analogy with those other -isms to be opposed, sexism and racism). Here, in the post-punk strand it was a case of deconstructing, not reconstructing rock and roll.

There was, however, another level at which the issue of punk's 'functional transformation' was resolved less equivocally. This involved its (limited but genuine) widening of access to the means of production and of distribution of recordings. The main features of this access have already been discussed: the recognition that effective recordings could be made cheaply outside the orbit of the large traditional record companies, and that it was no longer necessary to rely on those companies to get records to a sizeable and interested audience. By the early 1980s, the 'independent' sector was an established part of the recording industry in Britain, with its own charts in the music press listing only discs and tapes released by smaller labels. (The mainstream chart also listed the significant minority of independent records which sold enough copies to enter its Top 50.)

To be 'independent' did not automatically signify a different type of music from mainstream rock. But if the independent sector was less than an artistic revolution, it was also more than simply an economic one. For this was the place where punk rock's alternative discursive formation was to be found. A record signalled to a listener as 'independent' set up a different set of expectations, however faintly. Instead of the associations of leisure/relaxation/passivity characteristic of mainstream music, there were counter-associations of alternatives/seriousness/experimentation.

Of course, these were not absolute oppositions, any more than punk's 'subculture' was fully outside the wider cultures. When independent records 'crossed over' into the mainstream Top 50, they found themselves within the discourse of the leisure apparatus, into which the majority of them fitted neatly. Others, though, continued punk's work of troubling it. Despite its situation of coexistence with the dominant system and its priorities, the independent sector continued in the mid-1980s to provide a base for a range of radical music unimaginable a decade earlier.

MEANING AND PLEASURES

In the Introduction, 'meaning' was set out as the focal interest of this book, and notably how far punk's meaning differed from the sorts of meaning to be found in other popular music and popular culture. It should be clear by now that the answer is not simple or single. Punk rock was an extremely heterogeneous cultural movement, whose various impulses I have distributed into two types, through both of which punk sought to challenge the dominant discourse of popular music. On the one hand, it aimed to *undermine* the structure of that discourse (by threatening the stability of the performer/audience distinction, for instance), on the other it wished to set up an alternative discourse, with its own conventions and routines (the establishing of generic sounds and visual images recognizable as 'punk'). While at the beginning the two were unified in their situation of exclusion from the musical mainstream, the story of the 'decline' of punk rock is, at one level, the story of their separation: most dramatically and symbolically in the split in the Sex Pistols between Rotten/Lydon (underminer) and the rest ('punks').

With the proviso that this dichotomy indicates tendencies within punk rock rather than absolutely separate positions, so that both aspects are frequently found in the work of the same artist or even in the same recording, it can be further extended to show how it informs the essentially paradoxical character of the music. For the dichotomy is echoed in a number of other contrasts which appeared in punk at various levels.

First, there is the implicit aesthetic contrast between the 'realist' and 'avant-garde' impulses in punk. Whether or not these positions were consciously adopted, key figures and practices within punk found themselves slotted into these spaces which had been established artistic positions for more than 100 years. The nuances and the terrain of their argument had shifted over time, but not its essence: is new art properly to be that which gives a more direct and correct access to the truth of the world, or that which concentrates on replacing the outworn methods of the old art? However innovative its advocates felt it to be, punk rock could no more escape implication in this debate than could any new trend in any other art form. The situation was underlined in the aftermath of the punk moment, when the two main lines of punk-influenced music emerged, a 'real punk' clinging in part to subcultural realism and a 'post-punk' more concerned with unmaking and exploring musical languages and meanings.

There are also parallel contrasts to be found *within* the process of signification itself. The distinction between the two kinds of shock-effect discussed on p.98–9 is one instance. There, a difference was pointed out between the 'local' type which affected only a single aspect of a recording or performance (e.g., the use of obscene language) and the 'structural' shock-effect which put in disarray the very system of communication appropriate to popular song: the manner in which the lyric of 'Holidays In The Sun' or 'Oh Bondage Up Yours!' denied the listener an individual to identify with in the lyric, for instance.

The concept of shock-effect is a way of describing the relationship between punk rock and its listeners, and so, in a partly linked fashion, is the binary pair of terms, pheno-song and geno-song (see pp.71–3). In that contrast, the geno-song was what was left over when a song as message (in the broadest sense) had done its work. The representational work of the 'pheno-song' was not only in the verbal meaning of the lyric but in the signifieds of emotion provided by recognized musical elements. But the geno-song' is what, for a particular listener, remains as a signifier with an elusive signified, an obscure object of desire which cannot be pinned down as a feeling or a person.

Roland Barthes's account of the 'geno-song' tends towards defining it in almost physiological terms (he writes of its place in 'language and its very materiality' in the singing voice) and equally in individualistic terms: my 'geno-song' is an indicator of my unique construction as a psychological subject. But the latter needs to be qualified by stating that only certain elements of recorded music are likely to be candidates for 'geno-song'. The remainder has been so heavily colonized and coded by 'pheno-song' that it is difficult for it to escape its established signifying role, unless it is torn from that role and placed elsewhere, as Johnny Rotten's vocals did with the rolled 'r' in 'God Save The Queen'.

The phenomena described by the term geno-song' are presented in a less individualized context in the work of Julia Kristeva, the author who inspired Barthes's own comments (she is also one of the theoretical founders of the arguments in Dick Hebdige's *Subculture*). Kristeva applies different terms (the 'semiotic' and 'symbolic') in a picture which is both more dynamic and more socially determined:

> The semiotic area . . . is the site of those signifying or pre-signifying practices which do not take the form of signification in the linguistic sense and which language so to speak represses so that they can only emerge into the symbolic area in the form of interruptions of ordered discourse.[19]

While 'interruptions of ordered discourse' recalls the whole punk strategy and especially the shock-effect, it is necessary to look more closely at what Kristeva understands by her semiotic/symbolic distinction. First, the boundary between the two is very much the result of social pressures and the exertion of power in discourse. The semiotic is that outlawed as meaningless, irrelevant or obscene; that which cannot signify, or which shouldn't. For Kristeva as a feminist, this process is a crucial part of the way patriarchal society organizes its signification so that 'woman' can only be defined in terms of 'man' in the symbolic, with all elements which trouble that definition excluded into the 'semiotic'. There is something here which can apply to some of the work of women performers in the punk and post-punk context, performers concerned to elude precisely such definitions of the feminine.

More generally, though, the role of the avant-garde in Kristeva's theory is to be the site of the return of the repressed, the privileging of the semiotic so that the sedimented meanings of the symbolic are challenged or subverted. And this is a shifting process. Over time, elements such as vocal sounds or rhythms can pass from the semiotic to the symbolic as they take on anchored meanings within established discourses. This was in turn the fate of some aspects of punk rock, notably those which congealed into the 'real punk' style.

Perhaps the single term around which all these antinomies can be made to revolve is *identify*. Punk rock possessed an impulse to construct an identity that would be an alternative to the institutionalized or *passé* identities of the status quo, but would nevertheless be recognizable. The identity would be associated with all the features gathered together under the sign of 'subculture'. But punk rock also contained impulses which aimed to dissolve identities—of 'performer', 'audience', 'rock and roll'—without any concern to make new ones.

These two positions in relation to identity align with the two kinds of pleasure in 'texts' which Barthes has defined, that of *plaisir* (translated as 'pleasure') and of *jouissance* ('bliss'):

> Text of pleasure: the text that contents, fills, grants euphoria; the text that comes from culture and does not break with it, is linked to a *comfortable* practice of reading. Text of bliss: the text that imposes a state of loss, the text that discomforts (perhaps to a point of certain boredom), unsettles the reader's historical, cultural, psychological assumptions, the consistency of his tastes, values, memories, brings to a crisis his relation with language.[20]

Plaisir and *jouissance* provide the final poles around which the various elements of punk rock can cluster. The 'realist' song cannot break with 'culture' without risking the loss of its message. Thus many of the most politically effective statements in punk rock—those which directly linked the music with the political world outside it—invariably offered the first type of pleasure. In doing so they needed to limit the polysemic nature of their communication, to repress the influx of the semiotic, to provide little opportunity for the fascination of geno-song. So Clash's 'White Riot' and Tom Robinson's 'Power In The Darkness' need to provide a recognizable identity for their listeners so that their effect is optimum.

Those are songs of opposition, and their impact depends on something shared with what is being opposed: both the oppressor and the oppressed must be represented in the same discourse, both must be recognizable. But the kind of musical opposition which produces *jouissance* for the listener breaks rules of discursive practice, mingles elements from contrasting discourses and in the process denies the listener an easily recognizable position or identity. In punk rock *jouissance* came from the shock-effects which undermined structures of meaning as well as systems of ideology.

Punk rock was a genre shot through with paradox at every level. It contained elements of a subculture and of an avant-garde, the one building identity, the other subverting it. It provoked in the music industry a similarly ambivalent response: a recognition of a new musical style which might regenerate sales graphs, and a dangerous threat to the very values of the industry and its musical product. Fundamentally transversed by these conflicting pulls and pressures, punk rock's moment of triumph was brief, though its effects were, and remain, far-reaching.

Eight
Chronology

The purpose of this chapter is to provide a brief narrative of the events mentioned in this book, from 1975 to 1980. It should help situate both the development of punk rock itself and the parallel trends in the **mainstream of popular music**, to which punk so vigorously opposed itself.

1975

JANUARY: Naughty Rhythms Tour, with 'pub rock' bands Dr Feelgood, Chilli Willi and Kokomo. **Status Quo No.1 with 'Down Down'.**

SPRING: Managed by Malcolm McLaren, the New York Dolls perform in New York with 'Red China' visuals. **Bruce Springsteen hailed as 'the future of rock 'n' roll'.**

SUMMER: Sex Pistols form at McLaren's clothes shop, and play their first gig in November. ▪ A review of the 101ers describes Joe Strummer as a 'Chuck Berry/Eddie Cochran amalgam'. **Rod Stewart disbands the Faces.**

DECEMBER: Top pub rock R&B group Eddie and the Hot Rods signed by Island Records. The Stranglers play a support gig at London's Nashville, including Dionne Warwick's 'Walk On By' in their set. *Tubular Bells* by Mike Oldfield is the year's No.1 album.

1976

JANUARY: Gary Glitter announces his 'retirement'.

FEBRUARY: The Sex Pistols play at The Marquee Club and are banned from there. *New Musical Express* gives them their first review. ▪ The Damned are formed by Chris Miller and Ray Burns (later Rat Scabies and Captain Sensible). **Slik No.1 with 'Forever and Ever'.**

MARCH: Sex Pistols and Stranglers gigging in London, notably at the Nashville and the 100 Club. 101ers tour as support band to the Troggs. **EMI re-release 22 Beatles singles.**

APRIL: *Sounds* article on Sex Pistols. Rotten is quoted as saying 'I hate hippies, long hair and pub bands'. The group is reported as including 'Substitute' (Who), 'Whatcha Gonna Do About It' (Small Faces) and 'Stepping Stone' (Monkees) in their set. After a fight, they are banned from The Nashville. **Brotherhood of Man win Eurovision Song Contest with 'Save Your Kisses For Me'.**

MAY: Release of the first album by The Ramones. Sex Pistols appear at London's Screen On The Green. Music press describes American artists Blue Öyster Cult and Nils Lofgren as 'punk'. Pistols record three tracks with producer Dave Goodman. ▪ Patti Smith and The Stranglers in concert at The Roundhouse. **Princess Margaret attends Rolling Stones concert at Earls Court.**

JUNE: In *New Musical Express*, Mick Farren attacks Rod Stewart for spending £5,000 on a party when 'for less than half that you can get a bunch of poverty stricken punks on the road.' **In Seattle, Wings set world record for an indoor concert with 67,000 audience.**

JULY: 'After seeing the Pistols', Joe Strummer disbands the 101ers and forms The Clash. ▪ The Ramones and Stranglers play The Roundhouse. Sex Pistols, Slaughter & the Dogs and Buzzcocks play Manchester Free Trade Hall. Sid Vicious does the pogo. ▪ Pistols banned from Rock Garden Club and from the French punk rock festival. ▪ *Sounds* publishes an 'A–Z of Punk Rock'.

AUGUST: Sex Pistols appear on Granada TV's *So It Goes*, performing 'Anarchy In The UK'. ▪ Stiff Records release their first single. ▪ *Sniffin' Glue* 1 appears. ▪ The Vibrators are formed and Rock Against Racism founded. **The Knebworth open-air festival features Rolling Stones, 10cc and Lynyrd Skynyrd.**

SEPTEMBER: Notting Hill Carnival riots. Junior Murvin's 'Police and Thieves' released. ▪ 100 Club Festival (Pistols, Damned, Clash, etc.) receives wide publicity. **Stupidity by Dr Feelgood tops the album charts.** ▪ **Paul McCartney proclaims 'Buddy Holly Week'.**

OCTOBER: In a double-page spread on punk, *The Sun* quotes Sid Vicious: 'You just pick a chord, go twang and you've got music.' ▪ Pistols signed to recording contract by EMI. ▪ Stiff release 'New Rose' by The Damned. ▪ Fan has ear bitten at Clash gig at London's ICA. **David Soul No.1 with 'Silver Lady'.**

NOVEMBER: Record releases: 'Anarchy In The UK' by Sex Pistols, 'We Vibrate' by The Vibrators, 'Blank Generation' by Richard Hell (Stiff). ▪ Sham 69 play their first gig. ▪ 'Punk Takes Off' (*Sounds* headline). **Premiere of Led Zeppelin film, *The Song Remains The Same*.**

DECEMBER: On the 1st, Bill Grundy interviews the Sex Pistols on Thames TV's early evening *Today* show. On the 2nd,

1976

newspaper headlines include 'Foul Mouthed Yobs', 'Were The Pistols Loaded?', 'Sex Pistols Sent Packing'. From the 3rd, many projected gigs on the Pistols and Clash 'Anarchy In The UK' tour are cancelled. In Derby, councillors order Pistols to perform in front of them. The band refuse. 'Anarchy In The UK' enters Top 20 with sales of over 50,000. ● The Stranglers sign recording contract with United Artists. ● Roxy Club open with performances by Siouxsie and the Banshees and Generation X. ● New bands: The Slits, The Boys. ◆ Radio Luxembourg suspends a disc-jockey for doing a live interview with the Sex Pistols. **3.5 million applications are received for tickets for Abba concerts. ● Bob Marley shot in Jamaica. ● Gary Glitter does 'comeback concert'.**

1977

JANUARY: EMI finally cancel the Sex Pistols' contract. The band get £30,000 compensation. ● Buzzcocks release 'Spiral Scratch', an EP on their own New Hormones label. It sells 15,000 copies. ● New fanzines appear: *Bondage, White Stuff, Anarchy In The UK, London's Burning*.

FEBRUARY: The Clash sign with CBS Records. The Jam sign with Polydor Records. Release of The Damned's album on Stiff Records. ● Stranglers in controversy with Greater London Council over 'obscene' T-shirt worn by Hugh Cornwell on stage. ● Hot Rods headline at The Rainbow but are dismissed by the *New Musical Express* as 'young *passé* rock'. **Keith Richards of the Rolling Stones charged in Toronto with possessing heroin.**

MARCH: Sex Pistols replace Glen Matlock with Sid Vicious. They sign recording contract with A&M Records (10th). Three days later, A&M cancel the contract, following alleged pressure from their other rock artists. Pistols collect £75,000 compensation. ● The Stranglers' 'Grip' enters the Top 50. ▪ Dave Goodman's independent company The Label releases the first single by Eater. ▪ Iggy Pop tours Britain. ▪ The Damned tour with T. Rex. ▪ Release of 'White Riot' by The Clash. ▪ Groups formed: Alternative TV, Stiff Little Fingers. ▪ *Sniffin' Glue* 8 appears, with 'five figure' circulation. **Abba's 'Knowing Me Knowing You' is No.1.**

APRIL: The Damned play at CBGBs in New York. Their album enters the British charts. They abandon gig at Stirling University after bombardment with beer cans. ▪ Record releases: 'In The City' by The Jam. *Rattus Norvegicus IV* by The Stranglers. ▪ Warsaw (later Joy Division) formed in Manchester. ▪ McLaren issues Easter picture of Johnny Rotten 'crucified'. ▪ Mark P. announces the formation of his Step Forward Records. ▪ Lou Reed banned from the London Palladium. He blames the 'backlash against punk'. ▪ John Cale appears at Croydon and beheads a dead chicken on stage. **The Eagles appear at Wembley Pool.**

MAY: Rainbow Theatre 'wrecked' after Clash gig on the 7th. Subsequently, a wave of cancellations of punk gigs at Leeds, Nottingham, Stafford, Retford, Torquay, Bristol, Southend and Southampton University, where staff go on strike. ▪ Sex Pistols sign to Virgin Records. Release of 'God Save The Queen' (27th). Television advertising for the disc is banned. ▪ New Records: 'One Chord Wonders' by The Adverts, 'Remote Control' by The Clash—released by CBS against the group's wishes. ▪ New bands: XTC, 999, The Police, The Models. ▪ British tours by Blondie and Television. **Rod Stewart No.1 with 'I Don't Wanna Talk About It'.**

JUNE: Many more punk gigs cancelled, including seven on The Stranglers' national tour. Jam forced to cancel concert at

Chelsea Football Ground. A student is stabbed to death at a punk festival in Dublin. In Britain, punk musicians are assaulted, including Sex Pistols' Rotten and Cook, Bob Geldof (Boomtown Rats), Dave Vanian (Damned) and members of The Adverts. ■ Despite banning from all broadcasting and refusal of multiple stores to stock it, 'God Save The Queen' enters the charts. ■ Ensign Records sign Boomtown Rats. **Led Zeppelin play six concerts at Madison Square Gardens, New York. Net receipts are $1 million.**

JULY: Sex Pistols release 'Pretty Vacant' (with advance orders of 20,000) and perform it on BBC TV's *Top Of The Pops*. Councillor Bernard Brook-Partridge says he will ban all punk gigs in London. **Boney M No.1 with 'Ma Baker'.**

AUGUST: Sex Pistols undertake tour disguised as 'The Spots'. ■ EMI sign the Tom Robinson Band. John Cale produces the first Sham 69 record for Step Forward and releases his own record, 'Chicken Shit'. Street fighting as the fascist National Front tries to march through Lewisham, South London. ■ Ian Dury releases 'Sex & Drugs & Rock & Roll'. ■ 'I Can't Stand My Baby' by The Rezillos released on Sensible, Scotland's first punk label. **Elvis Presley dies.**

SEPTEMBER: Record releases: *No More Heroes* by The Stranglers, 'Complete Control' by Clash, their 'answer' to their record company. ■ **Marc Bolan dies.**

OCTOBER: Sham 69 sign with Polydor. ■ Rat Scabies leaves The Damned. ■ 'Holidays In The Sun' by the Sex Pistols enters the charts, as does Tom Robinson Band's '2–4–6–8 Motorway'. ■ *Never Mind the Bollocks, Here's the Sex Pistols* released on Virgin Records. **Godley and Creme unveil their electronic 'gizmo' and their 3-album set, *Consequences* (price £11).**

1977

NOVEMBER: Sex Pistols sign recording deal for the US with Warner Bros. ▪ *Never Mind the Bollocks* debuts at number one on the UK Album Charts. **Elton John announces his retirement from live concerts.**

DECEMBER: Sex Pistols undertake British tour. ▪ Roxy Club closed down. ▪ *Sounds* publishes article about 'Power Pop', in which New Hearts group member attacks punk for singing about 'boredom' and 'being on the dole'. **'Mull of Kintyre' by Wings is No.1 for eight weeks. Best-sellers of 1977 are Abba (albums) and David Soul (singles).**

1978

JANUARY: The Sex Pistols embark on a disastrous US tour. ▪ Johnny Rotten announces he has left the Sex Pistols. 'Fuming Finns Tell "Sick" Sex Pistols—"You Are Banned"' (headline in *The Sun*). ▪ Fast Records' first release—'Never Been In A Riot' by The Mekons. ▪ Rough Trade shop and distributor refuses to handle 'Pretty Paedophiles' by Raped. **Dire Straits signed by Phonogram. Steeleye Span split up.**

FEBRUARY: Sid Vicious and Nancy Spungen arrested on drugs charges in London. ▪ Riots at Sham 69 gigs, including one for Rock Against Racism at Central London Polytechnic. ***Rumours* by Fleetwood Mac is No.1 album.**

MARCH: Damned split up, Dave Vanian joining Doctors of Madness. **A 'Chart-hyping' scandal is exposed by the news media.**

APRIL: Clash, T.R.B., X-Ray Spex and Steel Pulse play at Anti-Nazi League Carnival in East London to 20,000 people. ▪ John Ellis leaves the Vibrators. **Kate Bush has No.1 album with *The Kick Inside*.**

1978

MAY: Johnny Rotten (now John Lydon) announces the formation of Public Image Limited. ▪ *Revolver* TV series begins, featuring some punk artists. **Saturday Night Fever is No.1 album.**

JUNE: Siouxsie and the Banshees sign recording contract with Polydor. ▪ 'Clash on Parole' tour of the UK. **Bob Dylan plays eight shows at Earls Court.**

JULY: Release of 'No One Is Innocent' by the Sex Pistols with Ronnie Biggs. The BBC, Capital Radio and *Revolver* ban it. ▪ Spartan set up national distribution for independent records. ▪ Vibrators split up.

AUGUST: Siouxsie and the Banshees' 'Hong Kong Garden' is a hit. ▪ EMI issue *The Roxy London WC2 Jan–April 1977* album. **Roxy Music re-form.**

SEPTEMBER: Elvis Costello headlines Anti-Nazi-League Carnival in Brockwell, South London. ▪ The Stranglers appear with strip-tease performers at an open-air concert in London. **Death of Keith Moon.**

OCTOBER: Sid Vicious charged in New York with Nancy Spungen's murder. ▪ Public Image Limited release their first single. ▪ Factory Records formed in Manchester.

NOVEMBER: Release of Clash's *Give 'Em Enough Rope.*

DECEMBER: Rezillos split up. ▪ Public Image Limited first album released. ▪ Stranglers are No.32, Buzzcocks 41 and Sex Pistols 46 in *Melody Maker*'s list of best-selling album artists of 1978.

1979

JANUARY: Release of Ruts' first single on People Unite label.

FEBRUARY: Sid Vicious dies of a drug overdose. Following John Lydon's lawsuit against McLaren, Glitterbest (Sex Pistols' management company) goes into receivership.

MARCH: Strangler Jean Jacques Burnel releases a solo album, *The Euroman Cometh*. The Specials release 'Gangsters' through Rough Trade. It goes on to sell 250,000 copies.

APRIL: 70 arrested in Chelsea after the banning of a free concert by The Clash. ● Damned re-form after 'Love Me' is a Top 20 hit. ● Virgin sign the Ruts, paying them £25,000 advance. **Mike Oldfield tours Europe at a cost of £250,000.**

MAY: Release of Undertones first album on Sire.

JUNE: Sham 69 play their 'farewell' gig. ● Jimmy Pursey joins up with ex-Pistols Cook and Jones. **Elton John tours the USSR.**

JULY: Tom Robinson Band splits up.

AUGUST: Fascist sympathizers announce the formation of 'Rock Against Communism'. **Led Zeppelin top the bill at Knebworth Festival.**

SEPTEMBER: Jimmy Pursey re-forms Sham 69. **Gary Numan has three albums in the Top 30.**

OCTOBER: American Express sue Virgin Records and the Sex Pistols over the advertising for the 'Rock Around The Clock' single. ● Both the Adverts and Penetration split up. **Richie Havens and Country Joe tour Europe as part of a 'Woodstock 10th Anniversary' package.**

1979

DECEMBER: Surrey University bans all punk gigs after trouble at a UK Subs performance. ▪ Virgin release *Sid Sings* by Sid Vicious. ▪ Clash release their *London Calling* album. **Eleven die in scramble at Who concert in Cincinnati.** ▪ **Blondie are top-selling group of 1979.**

1980

JANUARY: Hugh Cornwell jailed for two months on drug offences.

FEBRUARY: Paisley Rock Against Racism issue an EP on their Groucho Marxist label. ▪ 1,000 Sid Vicious fans march in London to mark the first anniversary of his death.

MARCH: 'Going Underground' by The Jam enters the chart at No.1.

APRIL: President of Hairdressers' Federation urges members not to deplore the punk style. **Gary Numan releases first rock video cassette to be retailed.**

MAY: Death of Ian Curtis of Joy Division. ▪ Chrysalis sign Stiff Little Fingers, paying an advance of £30,000. *McCartney II* **tops the album charts.**

JULY: Death of Malcolm Owen of The Ruts. ▪ A Scottish record dealer found not guilty of 'shameless and indecent conduct' in selling *Some Product* by the Sex Pistols to a 10-year-old. ▪ Phonogram sign Teardrop Explodes from independent Liverpool label Zoo.

AUGUST: Release of *Breaking Glass*, described as a 'post-punk' film. ▪ *Sounds* features the growth of the 'do-it-yourself' home-made tapes market. **Pink Floyd play a week of concerts at Earls Court.**

Appendix 1

Song Titles

(A) PUNK ROCK ALBUMS

The Damned: *Damned Damned Damned* (Stiff 1977), 'Neat Neat Neat', 'Fan Club', 'I Fall', 'Born To Kill', 'Stab Yor Back', 'Feel The Pain', 'New Rose', 'Fish', 'See Her Tonite', '1 Of The 2', 'So Messed Up', 'I Feel Alright'

The Clash: *The Clash* (CBS 1977), 'Janie Jones', 'Remote Control', 'I'm So Bored With The USA', 'White Riot', 'Hate & War', 'What's My Name', 'Deny', 'London's Burning', 'Career Opportunities', 'Cheat', 'Protex Blue', 'Police & Thieves', '48 Hours', 'Garageland'

The Stranglers: *Rattus Norvegicus IV* (United Artists 1977), 'Sometimes', 'Goodbye Toulouse', 'London Lady', 'Princess Of The Streets', 'Hanging Around', 'Peaches', '(Get A) Grip (On Yourself)', 'Ugly', 'Down In The Sewer'

The Sex Pistols: *Never Mind The Bollocks, Here's The Sex Pistols* (Virgin 1977), 'Holidays In The Sun', 'Bodies', 'No Feelings', 'Liar', 'God Save The Queen', 'Problems', 'Seventeen', 'Anarchy In The UK', 'Submission', 'Pretty Vacant', 'New York', 'EMI'

The Vibrators: *Pure Mania* (CBS 1977), 'Into The Future', 'Yeah Yeah Yeah', 'Sweet Sweet Heart', 'Keep It Clean', 'Baby Baby', 'No Heart', 'She's Bringing You Down', 'Petrol', 'London Girls', 'You Broke My Heart', 'Whips And Furs', 'Stiff Little Fingers', 'Wrecked On You', 'I Need A Slave', 'Bad Time'

(B) UK Top 50 best-selling singles of 1976

1. 'Save Your Kisses For Me' (Brotherhood of Man)
2. 'Don't Go Breaking My Heart' (Elton John and Kiki Dee)
3. 'Mississippi' (Pussycat)
4. 'Dancing Queen' (Abba)
5. 'A Little Bit More' (Dr Hook)
6. 'If You Leave Me Now' (Chicago)
7. 'Fernando' (Abba)
8. 'I Love To Love (But My Baby Just Loves To Dance)' (Tina Charles)
9. 'The Roussos Phenomenon' (EP) (Demis Roussos)
10. 'December 1963' (Oh What A Night)' (Four Seasons)
11. 'Under The Moon Of Love' (Showaddywaddy)
12. 'You To Me Are Everything' (Real Thing)
13. 'Forever And Ever' (Slik)
14. 'Sailing' (Rod Stewart)
15. 'Young Hearts Run Free' (Candi Staton)
16. 'The Combine Harvester (Brand New Key)' (Wurzels)
17. 'When Forever Has Gone' (Demis Roussos)
18. 'Jungle Rock' (Hank Mizell)
19. 'Can't Get By Without You' (Real Thing)
20. 'You Make Me Feel Like Dancing' (Leo Sayer)
21. 'Mamma Mia' (Abba)
22. 'Hurt' (Manhattans)
23. 'Silly Love Songs' (Wings)
24. 'Convoy' (C.W. McCall)
25. 'Kiss And Say Goodbye' (Manhattans)
26. 'You Just Might See Me Cry' (Our Kid)
27. 'Love Really Hurts Without You' (Billy Ocean)
28. 'You See The Trouble With Me' (Barry White)
29. 'Let 'Em In' (Wings)
30. 'No Charge' (J.J. Barrie)
31. 'Jeans On' (David Dundas)
32. 'Don't Take Away The Music' (Tavares)
33. 'Howzat' (Sherbet)
34. 'Rodrigo's Guitar Concierto de Aranjuez' (Manuel and The Music of the Mountains)
35. 'Bohemian Rhapsody' (Queen)
36. 'Misty Blue' (Dorothy Moore)
37. 'Heaven Must Be Missing An Angel' (Tavares)
38. 'Dance Little Lady Dance' (Tina Charles)
39. 'I Am A Cider Drinker (Paloma Blanca)' (Wurzels)
40. 'Music' (John Miles)
41. 'Love Machine' (Miracles)
42. 'Aria' (Acker Bilk)
43. 'Let's Stick Together' (Bryan Ferry)
44. 'In Zaire' (Johnny Wakelin)
45. 'The Killing Of Georgie' (Rod Stewart)
46. 'Girl Of My Best Friend' (Elvis Presley)
47. 'Play That Funky Music' (Wild Cherry)
48. 'You Don't Have To Go' (Chi-Lites)
49. 'I Only Wanna Be With You' (Bay City Rollers)
50. 'Arms Of Mary' (Sutherland Brothers and Quiver)

Appendix 2
Punk Singles in Top 30 Charts

1977

Adverts: 'Gary Gilmore's Eyes'
Boomtown Rats: 'Looking After No.1' and 'Mary Of The 4th Form'
Clash: 'Complete Control'
Tom Robinson Band: '2–4–6–8 Motorway'
The Rods: 'Do Anything You Wanna Do'
Jonathan Richman: 'Egyptian Reggae'
Sex Pistols: 'God Save The Queen', 'Pretty Vacant' and 'Holidays In The Sun'
Stranglers: 'Peaches', 'No More Heroes' and 'Something Better Change'

1978

Boomtown Rats: 'Rat Trap', 'Like Clockwork' and 'She's So Modern'
Buzzcocks: 'Promises' and 'Ever Fallen In Love'
Clash: 'Tommy Gun' and 'White Man In Hammersmith Palais'
City Boy: '5 7 0 5'
Ivor Biggun: 'Winkers' Song'
The Jam: 'David Watts' and 'Down In The Tube Station At Midnight'
Public Image Limited: 'Public Image'
Rezillos: 'Top Of The Pops'
Rich Kids: 'Rich Kids'
Tom Robinson Band: 'Glad To Be Gay'
Sex Pistols (and Ronnie Biggs): 'No One Is Innocent' / 'My Way'

Sham 69: 'Angels With Dirty Faces', 'If The Kids Are United' and 'Hurry Up Harry'
Siouxsie and the Banshees: 'Hong Kong Garden'
Stranglers: 'Nice And Sleazy', 'Five Minutes' and 'Walk On By'
X-Ray Spex: 'Identity' and 'Germ Free Adolescents'

Appendix 3
Select Discography

The records listed here are those mentioned in the text plus others which add up to a broadly typical coverage of British punk rock, its antecedents and its successors. The record labels and dates are those of the first United Kingdom release.

(A) AMERICAN PRECURSORS

Various Artists: *Nuggets* (Elektra 1972/Sire 1977), a double album of 'garage band' punk groups from the mid- and late 1960s

MC5: *Back In The USA* (Atlantic 1970)

Velvet Underground: *Velvet Underground And Nico* (Verve 1967)

Iggy and the Stooges: *Raw Power* (Elektra 1975)

New York Dolls: *New York Dolls* and *Too Much Too Soon* (Mercury 1973 and 1974, reissued as a double-album, 1977)

Alice Cooper: *Greatest Hits* (Warner Bros 1974)

Various Artists: *New York New Wave: Max's Kansas City* (CBS 1978), includes Cherry Vanilla, Wayne County, etc.

Richard Hell: 'Blank Generation' (Stiff 1976)

Patti Smith: *Horses* (Arista 1976)

Ramones: *Rocket To Russia* (Sire 1977)

(B) BRITISH PRECURSORS: PUB ROCK

Count Bishops: 'Speedball' (Chiswick 1976, EP)

Bees Make Honey: *Music Every Night* (EMI 1973)

Dr Feelgood: *Stupidity* (United Artists 1976)

Eddie and the Hot Rods: 'Teenage Depression' (Island 1976)

101'ers: 'Keys To Your Heart' (Chiswick 1976)

(C) British precursors: Mainstream

Plastic Ono Band: 'Give Peace A Chance' (Apple 1969)

Third World War: *Third World War* (Fly 1971)

Slade: *Sladest* (Polydor 1973)

T. Rex: *Electric Warrior* (Fly 1971)

Gary Glitter: *Greatest Hits* (Bell 1975)

David Bowie: *The Rise And Fall Of Ziggy Stardust And The Spiders From Mars* (RCA 1972)

(D) Punk rock: Singles

Sex Pistols: 'Anarchy In The UK' (EMI 1976), 'God Save The Queen' (Virgin 1977)

Damned: 'New Rose' (Stiff 1976)

Stranglers: '(Get A) Grip (On Yourself)' (United Artists 1977)

Adverts: 'Gary Gilmore's Eyes' (Anchor 1977)

X-Ray Spex: 'Oh Bondage Up Yours!' (Virgin 1977)

Buzzcocks: 'Spiral Scratch' (New Hormones 1977, EP)

Chelsea: 'Right To Work' (Step Forward 1977)

Generation X: 'Your Generation' (Chrysalis 1977)

The Fall: 'Bingo Master's Breakout' (Step Forward 1978, EP)

Alternative TV: 'How Much Longer' (Deptford Fun City 1978)

Jam: 'In The City' (Polydor 1977)

Stiff Little Fingers: 'Alternative Ulster' (Rigid Digits 1978)

Desperate Bicycles: 'The Medium Was Tedium' (Refill 1977)

Rezillos: 'Can't Stand My Baby' (Sensible 1977)

Dave Goodman and Friends: 'Justifiable Homicide' (The Label 1977)

Notsensibles: 'I'm In Love With Margaret Thatcher' (Redball 1979)

Ruts: 'In A Rut' (People Unite 1979)

Punk rock: Albums

Sex Pistols: *Never Mind The Bollocks . . .* (Virgin 1977)

Clash: *The Clash* (CBS 1977), *Give 'Em Enough Rope* (CBS 1978)

Damned: *Damned Damned Damned* (Stiff 1977)

Stranglers: *Rattus Norvegicus IV* (United Artists 1977), *No More Heroes* (United Artists 1978)

X-Ray Spex: *Germ Free Adolescents* (EMI 1978)

Slits: *Cut* (Island 1979)

Siouxsie and the Banshees: *The Scream* (Polydor 1978)

Alternative TV: *The Image Has Cracked* (Deptford Fun City 1978)

Tom Robinson Band: *Power In The Darkness* (EMI 1978)

Various Artists: *Fast Product: The First Year Plan* (EMI 1978), includes the first recordings of Human League and Gang of Four

Boomtown Rats: *A Tonic For The Troops* (Ensign 1978)

Buzzcocks: *Another Music In A Different Kitchen* (United Artists 1978)

John Cooper Clarke: *Disguise In Love* (CBS 1978)

Sham 69: *Tell Us The Truth* (Polydor 1977)

(F) After: 'Real punk'

Angelic Upstarts: *Teenage Warning* (Warner Bros 1979)

Sham 69: 'If The Kids Are United' (Polydor 1978)

Crass: *Penis Envy* (Crass 1980)

Dead Kennedy's: *Fresh Fruit For Rotting Vegetables* (Cherry Red 1980)

Various Artists: *Oi! The Album* (EMI 1980), includes 4-Skins, Cockney Rejects and Angelic Upstarts

Poison Girls: *Total Exposure* (XNTrix 1981)

Vice Squad: *No Cause For Concern* (Riot City 1981)

The Exploited: 'Dead Cities' (Secret 1981, EP)

(G) After: 'Post-punk'

Public Image Limited: *Public Image* (Virgin 1978)

Joy Division: *Unknown Pleasures* (Factory 1979)

Raincoats: *Odyshape* (Rough Trade 1981)

Gang Of Four: *Entertainment!* (EMI 1979)
Pop Group: *For How Much Longer* (Y 1980)
Au Pairs: *Playing With A Different Sex* (Human 1981)
Robert Wyatt: *Nothing To Stop Us Now* (Rough Trade 1982)
Scritti Politti: *Songs To Remember* (Rough Trade 1982)

Bibliography

Note: This is only a bibliography of the books cited in the text.

Ackroyd, C., et al. 1980, *The Technology Of Political Control*, London.

Adorno, T.W. 1973, *The Philosophy Of Modern Music*, New York.

Allsop, K. 1967, *Hard Travellin'*, London.

Anon. 1982, *The End Of Music*, Glasgow.

Barthes, R. 1973, *Mythologies*, London.

Barthes, R. 1975, *The Pleasure Of The Text*, London.

Barthes, R. 1977, *Image—Music—Text*, London.

Barthes, R. 1979, *The Eiffel Tower And Other Mythologies*, New York.

Benjamin, W. 1970, *Illuminations*, London.

Benjamin, W. 1973a, *Charles Baudelaire: A Lyric Poet In The Era Of High Capitalism*, London.

Benjamin, W. 1973b, *Understanding Brecht*, London.

Bennett, T., et al. (eds.) 1981, *Culture Ideology And Social Process*, London.

Burchill, J., and T. Parsons 1978, *'The Boy Looked At Johnny'*, London.

Cohen, S. 1973, *Folk Devils And Moral Panics*, London.

Collis, J. (ed.) 1980, *The Rock Primer*, Harmondsworth.

Coon, C. 1982, *1988: The New Wave Punk Rock Explosion*, 2nd edition, London.

Copper, B. 1975, *A Song For Every Season*, London.

De Turk, D., and A. Poulin (eds.) 1967, *The American Folk Scene*, New York.

Eagleton, T. 1983, *Literary Theory*, Oxford.

Eisen, J. (ed.) 1971, *Twenty-Minute Fandangos And Forever Changes*, New York.

Ellis, J. 1982, *Visible Fictions*, London.

Fiske, J. 1982, *Introduction To Communication Studies*, London.

Foucault, M. 1977, *Language, Counter-memory, Practice*, Oxford.

Frame, P. 1980, *Rock Family Trees*, London.

Frith, S. 1978, *The Sociology Of Rock*, London.

Frith, S. 1981, *Sound Effects*, New York.

Gillett, C. 1970, *The Sound Of The City*, New York.

Hardy, P., and D. Laing (eds.) 1976, *The Encyclopaedia Of Rock*, 3 vols., London.

Harrowen, J. 1977, *The Origin Of Rhymes, Songs And Sayings*, London.

Hartley, J. 1982, *Understanding News*, London.

Hebdige, D. 1979, *Subculture: The Meaning Of Style*, London.

Hoggart, R. 1957, *The Uses Of Literacy*, London.

Humann, K., and C.-L. Reichert. 1981, *EuroRock*, Frankfurt.

Jefferson, T., et al. (eds.) 1975, *Resistance Through Rituals*, Birmingham.

Laing, D. 1969, *The Sound Of Our Time*, London.

Landau, J. 1972, *It's Too Late To Stop Now*, San Francisco.

Leonard, N. 1962, *Jazz And The White Americans*, Chicago.

Marcus, G. (ed.) 1979, *Stranded: Rock And Roll For A Desert Island*, New York.

Middleton, R., and D. Horn (eds.) 1981–4, *Popular Music A Yearbook. Vol. 1: Folk And Popular*,

1981; *Vol. 2: Theory And Method*, 1982; *Vol. 3: Producers And Markets*, 1983; *Vol. 4: Performers And Audiences*, 1984. London.

Miller, J. (ed.) 1980, *The Rolling Stone History Of Rock And Roll*, San Francisco.

Nicholas, A.X. (ed.) 1971, *The Poetry Of Soul*, New York.

Oliver, P. 1963, *The Meaning Of The Blues*, New York.

P(erry), M. 1978, *The Bible*, London.

Reynolds, F. 1969, *Freewheelin' Frank*, London.

Rice-Davies, M. 1980, *Mandy*, London.

Rosenberg, B., and D.M. White (eds.) 1957, *Mass Culture*, Glencoe.

Scaping, P., and N. Hunter (eds.) 1978, *B.P.I. Yearbook*, London.

Soramaki, M., and J. Haarma 1981, *The International Music Industry*, Helsinki.

Stevenson, R. 1978, *The Sex Pistols File*, London.

Tagg, P. 1979, *Kojak: 50 Seconds Of Television Music*, Gothenberg.

Tagg, P. 1981, *Fernando The Flute*, Gothenberg.

Thompson, D. (ed.) 1973, *Discrimination And Popular Culture*, Harmondsworth.

Thompson, H.S. 1967, *Hell's Angels*, London.

Tremlett, G. 1976, *The David Bowie Story*, London.

Vermorel, F., and J. Vermorel 1978, *The Sex Pistols*, London.

Willis, P. 1981, *Learning To Labour*, London.

Young, R. (ed.) 1981, *Untying The Text*, London.

Notes

INTRODUCTION

1. Philip Tagg, 'Analysing Popular Music: Theory, Method And Practice', in R. Middleton and D. Horn (eds.) 1982: 49
2. P. Tagg 1979 and 1981.
3. J. Hartley 1982:6.
4. Michel Foucault, 'The Order Of Discourse', in R. Young (ed.) 1981:52.

1: FORMATION

1. M. Soramaki and J. Haarma 1981: Appendix 1.
2. P. Tagg 1981.
3. *Sheet*, 24 August 1976.
4. P. Scaping and N. Hunter (eds.) 1978:132.
5. *Melody Maker*, 17 July 1976.
6. *Melody Maker*, 28 June 1975.
7. P. Hardy and D. Laing (eds.), 1976:3, 222.
8. *Let It Rock*, November 1972.
9. See P. Hardy and D. Laing (eds.) 1976:3, 222.
10. There are other views of collecting, however in their 'obituary' of punk, Burchill and Parsons (1978) regard the mania to collect rare punk records as proof of the music's demise (p.96).
11. P. Hardy and D. Laing (eds.) 1976:2, 277.
12. Ian Birch, 'Punk Rock', in J. Collis (ed.) 1980:274–80.
13. G. Marcus (ed.) 1979: 72.
14. *Who Put The Bomp* 17, November 1977.
15. *Sniffin' Glue* 1, July 1976, Reprinted in Mark P. (ed.) 1978.
16. C. Coon 1982:11. Originally published in *Melody Maker*, 28 July 1976.
17. In an historical survey of punk rock, published in *Sounds* in June 1976, Giovanni Dadomo considered the issue of definition: 'Shall I stop, as most punk purists do, at the start of the psychedelic movement? But then how to deal with the artists labelled 'punk' recently, i.e. most of the New York bands and a number of young

London bands who feature a certain proportion of punk material in their acts?' In the same paper in October John Ingham took up that 'punk purist' position, arguing that since the Sex Pistols, Clash and Damned were 'viciously original', it was 'historically inaccurate' to use the same word as referred to 'American garage bands' of the mid-1960s. Ingham preferred '(?) Rock', but he had already been outflanked by his own sub-editors, who had announced his article as a survey of 'Punk Rock'.

18. Interview with Malcolm McLaren in *Melody Maker*, 23 June 1979.
19. Quoted in Richard Middleton, 'Introduction', in R. Middleton and D. Horn (eds.) 1981:1, 4.
20. Donald Hughes, 'Pop Music', in D. Thompson (ed.) 1973:141.
21. *Melody Maker*, 28 June 1975.
22. Nicholas Garnham, 'Concepts Of Culture, Public Policy And Cultural Industries.' Discussion Paper for Greater London Council Conference on Cultural Industries and Cultural Policy, December 1983.
23. *New Musical Express*, 21 February 1976.
24. *Daily Telegraph*, 18 September 1956.
25. Music critic Sigmund Spaeth in 1928, quoted in N. Leonard 1962:32.
26. *Sounds*, 3 February 1979.
27. *Cream*, December 1971.
28. F. and J. Vermorel 1978:13.
29. Ian Hoare, *Let It Rock*, October 1972.
30. Roland Barthes, 'Lesson In Writing', in R. Barthes 1977:170–8.
31. Jean Rook of the *Daily Express*, quoted in G. Tremlett 1976:115.
32. Susan Sontag, 'Notes On "Camp"', in S. Sontag 1966:277.
33. C. Coon 1982:63.
34. *Sounds*, 3 February 1979.
35. C. Ackroyd et al. 1980:110.
36. D. Hebdige 1979:86, 87.
37. Peter Jones, 'Pop, Undated And Posthumously Prospering', in P. Scaping and N. Hunter (eds.) 1978:19.
38. This term was coined by Stan Cohen—Cohen 1973. It describes the process by which the mass media and various 'opinion leaders' define a particular incident or social group as a 'threat to societal values and interests'.
39. R. Stevenson 1978.
40. *Daily Mirror*, 2 December 1976.

2: NAMING

1. *Sniffin' Glue* 4, October 1976. Reprinted in P., Mark (ed.) 1978.
2. J. Harrowen 1977:120.
3. K. Allsop 1967:196.

4. See R. Barthes 1973.

5. For a more detailed explanation of this idea see J. Fiske 1982:111–2.

3: LISTENING

1. See Sean Cubitt, 'Maybellene: Meaning And The Listening Subject', in R. Middleton and D. Horn (eds.) 1984:211.

2. P. Tagg 1981:14.

3. R. Barthes 1977:182.

4. For an explanation of these terms see above, p.3–4.

5. R. Hoggart 1957:102.

6. For comments on this concept see above, p.150 and 170–1.

7. P. Tagg 1981:13.

8. S. Frith 1981:161.

9. Tom Carson, 'Rocket To Russia', in G. Marcus (ed.) 1979:108.

10. Robert Christgau, 'New York Dolls', in G. Marcus (ed.) 1979:135.

11. C. Gillett 1970:30.

12. Robert Christgau, 'New York Dolls', in G. Marcus (ed.) 1979:139.

13. See the articles by Alan Beckett and Richard Merton in *New Left Review* 47, January–February 1968.

14. See, e.g., Richard Merton in *New Left Review* 47, January–February 1968, and D. Laing 1969:144.

15. See, e.g., Susan Hiwatt, 'Cock Rock', in J. Eisen (ed.) 1971:141–7.

16. R. Barthes 1979:119.

17. B. Copper 1975:275.

18. R. Barthes 1977:47.

19. For a stimulating and related analysis of this song, see Greil Marcus, 'Anarchy In The U.K.', in J. Miller (ed.) 1980:460–1.

20. See P. Oliver 1963:151–2.

21. Even in those few lyrics which do deal with work, the addressee is almost never defined as a 'worker' as such. These songs of work include 'Chain Gang' (Sam Cooke), 'Working Girl' (Merilee Rush), '9 to 5' (Dolly Parton), 'Part of the Union' (Hudson-Ford), 'Right Said Fred' (Bernard Cribbins) and 'Crushed by the Wheels of Industry' (Heaven 17).

22. The lyrics of these songs can be found in A.X. Nicholas (ed.) 1971:55 and 61.

23. T. Eagleton 1983:138.

24. S. Frith 1981:270.

25. Dave Laing, 'Interpreting Punk Rock', in *Marxism Today*, April 1978:126.

26. This detailed information comes from an unpublished manuscript by Spencer Leigh, 'Censorship in Popular Music'.

27. W. Benjamin 1970:239.

28. For example, Hugh Cornwell of the Stranglers, *News of the World*, 5 December 1976; Siouxsie and the Banshees, *Sounds*, 10 May 1977.

29. W. Benjamin 1973a:115–8.

30. R. Barthes 1977:30.

31. T.W. Adorno 1973:9.

32. W. Benjamin 1970:251–2.

33. Ibid., p. 240.

34. See Christian Metz, 'The Imaginary Signifier', in *Screen* 16, No. 2, Summer 1975:59–61.

35. Sean Cubitt, 'Maybellene: Meaning And The Listening Subject', in R. Middleton and D. Horn 1984:212.

36. Laura Mulvey, 'Afterthoughts On "Visual Pleasure And Narrative Cinema" Inspired by *Duel in the Sun*', in *Framework* 15.

37. R. Barthes 1977:182.

38. Stephen Heath, 'Translator's Note', in R. Barthes 1977:9.

4: LOOKING

1. *Melody Maker*, 24 December 1977.

2. See C. Coon 1982:38.

3. J. Landau 1972:40.

4. *Melody Maker*, 4 June 1977; *Sounds*, 20 September 1977 (on the Sex Pistols); *Sounds*, 7 May 1977 (on the Stranglers); *Melody Maker*, 8 December 1979 (on the Damned).

5. *Sounds*, 27 October 1979. Could it be significant that while the Clash fan actually sang with the band, the Stranglers' fan only mimed?

6. *New Rockstar*, 4 December 1976.

7. *Sounds*, 18 December 1977.

8. *Rolling Stone*, 20 December 1977.

9. *Melody Maker*, 2 October 1976 (on Johnny Rotten).

10. *Sounds*, 1 July 1978.

11. *Sounds*, 1 April 1978.

12. Susan Hiwatt, 'Cock Rock', in J. Eisen (ed.) 1971.

13. John Ingham in *Sounds*, 31 July 1976.

14. *Village Voice*, 9 January 1978.

15. *Melody Maker*, 3 February 1979.

16. *Sniffin' Glue* 7, February 1977.

17. See Laura Mulvey, 'Visual Pleasure and Narrative Cinema', in *Screen* 16, No. 3, Autumn 1975. J. Ellis 1982.

18. J. Ellis 1982:47.

19. Ibid.

20.   J. Burchill and T. Parsons 1978:80.

21.   In *Sounds*, 13 May 1978.

22.   Ron Watts, manager of London's 100 Club, quoted in F. Vermorel and J. Vermorel 1978.

23.   *Rolling Stone*, 20 October 1977.

24.   *Village Voice*, 9 January 1978.

25.   P. Willis 1977:136.

26.   *Melody Maker*, 2 October 1976; *Sounds*, 16 October 1976; C. Coon 1982:105, 110.

27.   D. Hebdige 1979:107–8.

28.   This item was already part of the 'kinky' milieu in the 1960s: 'When not mixing in high society, they enjoyed to go slumming, Christine (Keeler) wearing a dog collar around her neck and Stephen (Ward) leading her by a dog's lead. In this fashion they visited seedy London clubs to buy pot.' From M. Rice-Davies 1980:98.

29.   J. Burchill and T. Parsons 1978:46.

30.   *New Musical Express*, 13 January 1979.

31.   D. Hebdige 1979:107.

32.   F. Reynolds 1969:8; H.S. Thompson 1967:256.

33.   D. Hebdige 1979:117.

5: FRAMING

1.   M. Foucault 1977:199.

2.   *Socialist Teacher*, 1978; B.N.P. quoted in *Sounds*, 30 April 1977.

3.   See, for example, the interview with Joe Strummer in *Sounds*, 13 December 1980, and the interview with Mark Perry in *New Musical Express*, 29 June 1978.

4.   David Riesman, 'Listening To Popular Music', in B. Rosenberg and D.M. White (eds.) 1957:412.

5.   P. Frame 1980:29.

6.   Dave Laing, 'Interpreting Punk Rock', in *Marxism Today*, April 1978:126.

7.   Sources for unattributed quotations in this chapter include a very wide range of printed media, from fanzines to national daily papers. Few detailed references have been provided because part of my argument is that a variety of authors 'combined' to produce and reiterate the punk discourse.

6: AFTER

1.   A term used in jazz circles to denote a diehard adherent of an early style (usually New Orleans jazz) for whom all later jazz is a dilution or a betrayal.

2.   *Time Out*, 17 December 1976.

3.   Josh Dunson, 'Folk Rock: Thunder Without Rain', in D. De Turk and A. Poulin (eds.) 1967:293.

4. *Let It Rock*, August 1973.
5. John Clarke, 'Style', in T. Jefferson et al. (eds.) 1975:188.
6. S. Frith 1983:160.
7. *Sounds*, 13 December 1980.
8. *Sounds*, 13 May 1978.
9. *Sunday Times*, 1 November 1981.
10. *Melody Maker*, 14 November 1981.
11. *Sounds*, 28 October 1978.
12. See T. Jefferson et al. (eds.) 1975:101.
13. *Sounds*, 9 September 1978.
14. *Sounds*, 28 August 1976.
15. *Temporary Hoarding* 5, Spring 1978.
16. Eddy Morrison, 'Don't Condemn Pop', in *Spearhead*, April 1981, quoted in *Searchlight*, the anti-fascist monthly, May 1981:8.
17. Jerry Harris, 'Oi!—The Story', in *Punk Lives*, nos. 9 and 10, 1983. A very useful history of the genre.
18. See the courageous report from inside this event by Vivien Goldman, in *Melody Maker*, 25 August 1979.
19. *New Musical Express*, 19 February 1983.
20. See K. Humann and C.-L. Reichert (eds.) 1981.
21. Between 1980 and 1982, 40 new labels appeared in West Germany, plus some 300 'self-produced' albums. Information from Wolfgang Hamm, 'Phonographic Industry And The Mass Media: The Case Of West Germany', unpublished paper delivered at the International Conference on Music and Information Systems, Milan, December 1983.
22. Anna Szemere, 'Pop And Rock Music In Hungary', in R. Middleton and D. Horn (eds.) 1983:121–42.
23. *Rolling Stone*, 6 October 1977.
24. *Sounds*, 10 October 1981.
25. D. Hebdige 1979:124.
26. Simon Frith, *New Statesman*, 2 October 1981:24.
27. *Record Business* magazine, *Small Labels Catalogue* (London 1980).
28. Phil Hardy, 'The Record Industry, The Case For Public Intervention', Greater London Council Economic Policy Group strategy document no. 16, London 1983:23. In July 1980 *Music Week* estimated the indie market share as 12.6%.
29. D. Hebdige 1979:96.
30. Angela Carter, 'Year Of The Punk', in *New Society*, 22 December 1977.

7: CONCLUSIONS

1. John Shepherd, 'Sociomusicological Analysis Of Popular Musics', in R. Middleton and D. Horn (eds.) 1982:169.
2. The artists in each sample were: *Punk Rock:* Sex Pistols, Stranglers, Clash, Damned, Jam, Poly Styrene, Sham 69, Mekons, Gang of Four, Adverts, Ruts, UK Subs, Alternative TV, Angelic Upstarts, Wah!, Slits and Buzzcocks. *Beat Groups:* Beatles, Rolling Stones, Tyrannosaurus Rex, Bee Gees, Cliff Richard, Alvin Stardust (Shape Fenton), l0cc, Fourmost, Billy J. Kramer, Gary Glitter, Slade, The Who, Brian Poole & the Tremeloes, Gerry & the Pacemakers, Nashville Teens, The Hollies, Manfred Mann and Dave Berry.
3. S. Frith 1981:76.
4. Ibid., p.266.
5. *New Statesman*, 9 September 1983.
6. F. Vermorel and J. Vermorel 1978:154.
7. The best discussion so far is in S. Frith 1978. Unfortunately this is somewhat curtailed in the revised edition—S. Frith 1981.
8. D. Hebdige 1979:73–99.
9. Phil Cohen, quoted in D. Hebdige 1979:77.
10. John Clarke in T. Jefferson et al. (eds.) 1975:179.
11. D. Hebdige 1979:81.
12. John Clarke in T. Jefferson et al. (eds.) 1975:179.
13. Angela McRobbie, 'Settling Accounts With Sub-cultures: A Feminist Critique', in T. Bennett et al. (eds.) 1981:111–23.
14. Ibid., p.117.
15. *The End Of Music*, 1982:1. Anon.
16. W. Benjamin 1973b:87.
17. Ibid., p.87.
18. Greil Marcus in J. Miller (ed.) 1980:452.
19. G. Nowell-Smith, 'Introduction To Julia Kristeva's "Signifying Practice And Mode of Production"', in *Edinburgh Film Festival Magazine*, 1976:60.
20. R. Barthes 1975:14.

Index

About
PM Press

politics • culture • art • fiction • music • film

PM Press was founded at the end of 2007 by a small collection of folks with decades of publishing, media, and organizing experience. PM Press co-conspirators have published and distributed hundreds of books, pamphlets, CDs, and DVDs. Members of PM have founded enduring book fairs, spearheaded victorious tenant organizing campaigns, and worked closely with bookstores, academic conferences, and even rock bands to deliver political and challenging ideas to all walks of life. We're old enough to know what we're doing and young enough to know what's at stake.

We seek to create radical and stimulating fiction and nonfiction books, pamphlets, T-shirts, visual and audio materials to entertain, educate, and inspire you. We aim to distribute these through every available channel with every available technology, whether that means you are seeing anarchist classics at our bookfair stalls; reading our latest vegan cookbook at the café; downloading geeky fiction e-books; or digging new music and timely videos from our website.

Contact us for direct ordering and questions about all PM Press releases, as well as manuscript submissions, review copy requests, foreign rights sales, author interviews, to book an author for an event, and to have PM Press attend your bookfair:

PM Press • PO Box 23912 • Oakland, CA 94623
510-658-3906 • info@pmpress.org

Buy books and stay on top of what we are doing at:

www.pmpress.org

MONTHLY SUBSCRIPTION PROGRAM

These are indisputably momentous times—the financial system is melting down globally and the Empire is stumbling. Now more than ever there is a vital need for radical ideas.

In the seven years since its founding—and on a mere shoestring—PM Press has risen to the formidable challenge of publishing and distributing knowledge and entertainment for the struggles ahead. With over 300 releases to date, we have published an impressive and stimulating array of literature, art, music, politics, and culture. Using every available medium, we've succeeded in connecting those hungry for ideas and information to those putting them into practice.

Friends of PM allows you to directly help impact, amplify, and revitalize the discourse and actions of radical writers, filmmakers, and artists. It provides us with a stable foundation from which we can build upon our early successes and provides a much-needed subsidy for the materials that can't necessarily pay their own way. You can help make that happen—and receive every new title automatically delivered to your door once a month—by joining as a Friend of PM Press. And, we'll throw in a free T-Shirt when you sign up.

Here are your options:

- ◆ $30 a month: Get all books and pamphlets plus 50% discount on all webstore purchases
- ◆ $40 a month: Get all PM Press releases (including CDs and DVDs) plus 50% discount on all webstore purchases
- ◆ $100 a month: Superstar—Everything plus PM merchandise, free downloads, and 50% discount on all webstore purchases

For those who can't afford $30 or more a month, we're introducing *Sustainer Rates* at $15, $10, and $5. Sustainers get a free PM Press T-shirt and a 50% discount on all purchases from our website.

Your Visa or Mastercard will be billed once a month, until you tell us to stop. Or until our efforts succeed in bringing the revolution around. Or the financial meltdown of Capital makes plastic redundant. Whichever comes first.

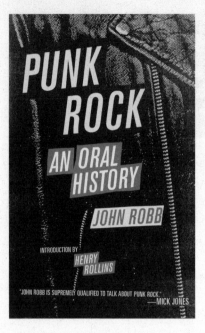

PUNK ROCK
An Oral History
John Robb
Introduction by Henry Rollins
$19.95 • 8.5x5.5 • 584 Pages
ISBN: 978-1-60486-005-4

With its own fashion, culture, and chaotic energy, punk rock boasted a do-it-yourself ethos that allowed anyone to take part. Vibrant and volatile, the punk scene left an extraordinary legacy of music and cultural change. John Robb talks to many of those who cultivated the movement, such as John Lydon, Lemmy, Siouxsie Sioux, Mick Jones, Chrissie Hynde, Malcolm McLaren, Henry Rollins, and Glen Matlock, weaving together their accounts to create a raw and unprecedented oral history of UK punk. All the main players are here: from The Clash to Crass, from The Sex Pistols to the Stranglers, from the UK Subs to Buzzcocks—over 150 interviews capture the excitement of the most thrilling wave of rock 'n' roll pop culture ever. Ranging from its widely debated roots in the late 1960s to its enduring influence on the bands, fashion, and culture of today, this history brings to life the energy and the anarchy as no other book has done.

BURNING BRITAIN
The History of UK Punk 1980—1984
Ian Glasper
$24.95 • 9x6 • 456 Pages
ISBN: 978-1-60486-748-0

As the Seventies drew to a close and the media declared punk dead and buried, a whole new breed of band was emerging from the gutter. Harder and faster than their '76–'77 predecessors, not to mention more aggressive and political, the likes of Discharge, the Exploited, and G.B.H. were to prove not only more relevant but arguably just as influential.

Several years in the making and featuring hundreds of new interviews and photographs, *Burning Britain* is the true story of the UK punk scene from 1980 to 1984 told for the first time by the bands and record labels that created it. Covering the country region by region, author Ian Glasper profiles legendary bands like Vice Squad, Angelic Upstarts, Blitz, Anti-Nowhere League, Cockney Rejects, and the UK Subs as well as the more obscure groups like Xtract, The Skroteez, and Soldier Dolls.